"The operation of our subconscious min  ally based with time, indicates how difficult ige in ones deeply held views, however mu ind the process involved is the reason w 'ish meaningful and positive change, as tl ent movements over the past fifty years cl

Annie Cap in her new book provides tools to explore and remove long-term obstacles to our growth, helping you to progress spiritually as well as physically. Annie believes we're constantly being guided by our repetitive words and thoughts to resolve our past and rectify any unsupportive or conflicting beliefs. The answers, what we need to do to help ourselves, are right there in our language if only we'd listen. This is a fascinating work offering valuable insight and methods for change from which you will derive great enjoyment and benefit."

Miceal Ledwith, L.Ph., L.D., D.D., LL.D., Author, lecturer and star in the hit movies *What the Bleep Do We Know* and its sequel *Down the Rabbit Hole*. He was Professor of Systematic Theology for sixteen years at Maynooth College in Ireland and is the author of *The Orb Project*.

"Annie Cap's new book 'It's Your Choice' not only gives us a great insight into how our language, thoughts and actions are an accurate indicator of our underlying beliefs about ourselves and our world, but also how you can change these beliefs to create a happier, more fulfilling life.

We all have bad habits and negative beliefs we want and have tried to change, many, if not hundreds of times. We've done our positive thinking, affirmations, try our best with the law of attraction, and even endured endless therapy - which may have uncovered where these limiting beliefs came from – but our lives remain the same – Why?

It is estimated by neuroscientists that up to 99% of our daily actions are governed by the powerful subconscious mind, which is a depository of learned behaviour accumulated over the course of our lives, once these behaviours are hardwired into the subconscious, the only way to change them is to access and alter these beliefs on that same subconscious level.

Our outer world mirrors our inner beliefs and much of our present life experience can be traced back to early traumatic memories where negative beliefs were formed, 'It's Your Choice' helps to locate these beliefs by the words and thoughts you use on a daily basis through a series of simple effective exercises.

'It's Your Choice' will help you access and change negative behaviours on a permanent level."

Karl Dawson, Author and creator of Matrix Reimprinting (author of *Matrix Reimprinting using EFT: Rewrite Your Past, Transform Your Future*)

"Annie Cap's 'iceberg' method has developed and evolved as a result of her many years of experience as a practitioner. She is lively in her approach and realistic about how people function. She has a human touch which is reflected in this easily applied method. There are close links with other energy modalities and the emerging science of biophysics. It has a refreshing simplicity that makes it accessible and immediately valuable in its application without the need to understand the cause and effect that may be at work within the body.

The Iceberg Process can be easily understood by the reader and successfully applied by practitioners and a wide-range of people who wish to change their lives in a positive, constructive way. Annie Cap gives a clear proforma that is very straight forward. Positive change can result from her step by step procedures or in one leap. It is an individual approach that can be used at any time depending on need and is a system that can readily become part of any person's positive and engaging life."

Jean Watson, BSc, Msc, Dip Ed - Scientist and educationalist teaching physics, chemistry and biology. She teaches at a leading independent school in England and is a qualified Trainer and Coach of Bioenergetic and Informational Health (IBIH)

"This book will enable people to see through the layers of illusion and to ultimately see a mirror of themselves. Upon reaching this point, if the reader is ready they will begin a journey of resolving the stories that no longer serve them, whereupon they can begin creating the life they are supposed to live. Why are we here? We are here to 'clean-up' our act and so embark upon the path of our 'true' destiny, the path that brings us joy and fulfilment. Annie's book is a valuable tool for all those seeking a way out from the minefield of attachment, to a place of freedom and light."

Peter Lee, spiritual teacher, healer and the founder of 'The Institute of Momentum' in Wellington, New Zealand. He has also worked with Dr Masaru Emoto who is famously known for his book 'Messages in Water'.

"My clients have nothing but the highest of praise for the excellent work Annie does. Each person has achieved the personal breakthrough they were seeking. There can be no higher accolade than that. However, in addition, Annie is an inspirational person to know and my life is constantly enriched through my relationship with her. I can't wait for her book to be published!"

Louise Cox Chester, Owner The Retreat at Witherdens Hall, Wingham, Kent

"The most wonderful thing has happened to me with the unadulterated guidance of Annie Cap...I have found me - the best of me...I was feeling very toxic, lost and fragile preceding Annie. Counsellors and books had helped over the years, but "toxicity" was still there. Now, I am excited about my future, my days are happy, my life successful and joyous...I shine."

Roberta Anderson, London

"Meeting Annie is one of the best things that ever happened to me. Annie has changed my life and made it possible for me to do things, I never imagined I could ever do again!"

Natascha Saul, London

"Exceptional. That is the best word I can use to describe Annie when I recently worked with her. In 2 hours we were able to accomplish more than I ever thought possible."

Caroline Jarvis, Private Banker, the City of London

"I gave the best performance of my life after working with Annie!"

Renee Salewski, Classical Soprano Singer, Actor, Voice-over Artist and Voice Coach

"Annie's strategies really work."

Christine Kendrick, mother, grandmother, daughter, non executive director

"Meeting Annie was an absolute godsend..."

Danny Stevens, Property Developer, London

"Annie Cap's gift is having an insightful nature that allows her to get to the crux of an issue."

Tess, Singer, Songwriter

Dedication

It is with gratitude and love that I dedicate this book to my mother and my father and to my best friend, partner and loving husband Simon who together encouraged me to become who I am today by pushing me further than I thought I could go.

Note from the author regarding client privacy, case studies and anecdotal content within this book:

In order to protect the identity and privacy of my valued and honoured clients, as well as my family members and friends, all names, cities and particular stories have been altered to maintain their anonymity. Anecdotal information has been sensitively adjusted to retain the over-all meaning and convey the significance, yet mask the identity of any person involved. Any similarities to particular persons, dead or alive therefore are purely by coincidence.

The comments regarding speech styles and behavioural patterns are based on hundreds of sessions with individuals exhibiting similar issues and are not based on any one individual. The examples offered as reference represent words and patterns of language used by numerous people and do not represent actual quotes of one particular individual; they represent characteristics of a way of thinking and living.

Acknowledgements

It is said that when the student is ready the teacher will appear. In the past, I found myself commonly thinking the same thought, "Why don't I have a mentor" as I looked around me for someone to tell me what to do! As I grew up I began to be more insightful and stopped regretting the lack of a visible leader. I started to listen to my own gut feelings and intuition. Then I came to realise the teachers were all around me and the most important one was within me. The mentors were always there but I hadn't been ready.

Now I know that we see what we are ready to see. We see what we want to see and we see what we expect to see. My lesson-givers, my teachers, my mentors were there in the form of family members, my friends, my enemies, the synchronistic events in my life and my problems as well as my successes.

I cannot say enough about the wisdom and life experiences offered to me by my mother, father and husband Simon, their curriculum so perfectly created to push my buttons! They forced me to look at things I might not have whilst somehow still maintaining love. These three were by no means the only influences in my life and the list would be as long as this book if I recounted them all. I wish to thank also all my siblings who unknowingly, dutifully and beautifully played key roles causing me to look within. I wish the best for each of them. I wish them clarity in their choices and happiness for eternity.

Very special thanks go to Sue Luff, Bridget Medhurst and Ayla Carpe for their many hours of listening to me, believing in me and helping me discover my inner knowing and to Barbara Dennard who helped me remember my value so long ago. Additionally I wish to thank my Aunt Marilyn and Uncle Fred and their family for entering my life after my mother's passing. They filled a void with love.

I am ever grateful for my good friends Kathy Sun and Diana Brito whom I met when I was in my early twenties just starting my career in telecommunications. I want to thank them for paving the way for my development and for being there when I needed them. Although they are many miles away they remain in my heart always. I also wish to thank Andy Maclean for volunteering to help me with my grammar in this book and both he and his wife Jan for being great friends. Lastly I cannot forget to thank Gary Craig, the founder of EFT, for his huge generosity of spirit.

I hope you benefit from the lessons I offer in this book. It's a long time coming and I am truly grateful that you have chosen to read it.   Annie Cap

It's Your Choice

Uncover Your Brilliance
Using The Iceberg Process

Annie Cap
www.anniecap.com

"See the final destination and not the problem, not every tiny thing that stubs your toe. Often we focus on the bit that tripped us up rather than what's in the distance. Start seeing 'the problems' as stepping stones on the path towards fulfilment and joy."

Annie Cap

Table of Contents

A Starting Foundation

Chapter 1:   It's Your Choice 1
               Introducing *Iceberg Words* and *Iceberg Programmes*
               How it Started

Chapter 2:   What You Choose and the Law of Attraction.......................7
               Your Personal Frequency (Vibration) and Conflicts

Chapter 3:   What You Choose to Say 19
               Troubled Words
               Watch Your Common Words and Phrases,
               So You Can Begin To 'Detox Your Language'

Chapter 4:   Language Limits in Business 39
               Success, Achievement and Productivity

Understanding Yourself

Chapter 5:   A Bit about NLP and Submodalities 45

Chapter 6:   What You Choose to Say about Yourself 49
               The Internal Critic

Chapter 7:   Thoughts and Emotions are Energy.................................61
               Vibration Matches Perception

Chapter 8:   What You Choose to Believe..71

Chapter 9:   Do We Choose our Symptoms?.......................................83

Chapter 10:   Do We Choose to be ill? 89

Chapter 11:   More Clues to Vibration: Expectation, Attitude and
               Responsibility 93

Secrets and Keys to Change

Chapter 12:   Making Conscious Choices for Transformation.................99

Chapter 13:   Uncovering Core Beliefs and Repeating Patterns...........109
               Discovering Why You Choose as You Do

Chapter 14:   Choosing for Yourself What You Want to Believe............123

Chapter 15:   What Other Choices Do You Make? 131

When Change is Difficult

Chapter 16: What Stops You from Improving Your Life?.....................137
Common Pitfalls, Reasons You Don't Succeed and
Self-Sabotage
Chapter 17: Breaking Those Tough Patterns.....................................147
Moving to Acceptance and Forgiveness
Chapter 18: How to Handle Your Controlling Subconscious...............153
Neural Networks

Using *The Iceberg Process* and EFT for Change

Chapter 19: Using *The Iceberg Process* (TIPs)...................................159
Summary of using *The Iceberg Process* (TIPs)
Your Words Can Reveal Your Positive Nature and Patterns
Using Words and *The Iceberg Process* to Speed Recovery
Chapter 20: How to Tap 171
Seven Quick Steps to Tapping
A Full Length Method of Tapping (EFT)
Basic Tapping Worksheet
Multi-aspect Tapping Information Worksheet
Chapter 21: Some of My Tapping Steps In-Depth 185
Taking a *SUDs* Level Rating
The Apex Effect
Chapter 22: 25 Suggestions for Tapping...197
My Greatest Advice is "Don't Give Up"!
Should You Do It Alone?
Signs You May be off Kilter
Chapter 23: In Closing 213
Reminder Tips
Epilogue 217

References

References and Recommended Reading 219
Index 223
About the Author...229

Foreword

"I heard this story told by a radio DJ late one night as I drove back from London after a long studio session. A friend of his had grown up in the former Soviet Union in the late Sixties and early Seventies at a time when access to Western pop music (Western anything) was extremely restricted. He recalled being in a park near the Moscow River on a hot summer's day and hearing The Beatles' music being played - something that was strictly forbidden - on a nearby portable record player. It was the first time he had ever heard them and his first thought was, "This is the truth and everything else is a lie".

The idea that language actually creates the world in which we live may seem counter-intuitive. We are used to thinking that the world exists "out there" and that we use language to describe it, but now psychology, philosophy and neuroscience are sharing similar perspectives - what we think, and particularly the language we use to think it, has a defining effect on our being, on our bodies and on everything and everybody around us.

Such ideas may seem remote, even irrelevant to everyday concerns, yet Annie Cap's 'It's Your Choice' combines her own experience as a life coach and therapist with the latest research in a variety of scientific and spiritual disciplines to produce a practical methodology to improve one's "mental hygiene", as she puts it. Drawing on first-hand experience from her work with various people she gives practical exercises and insights to improve our outlook on life using the sounding power of words and what we make them mean. Doing the exercises and choosing to accept the accumulating scientific evidence can only have a positive impact on our health and well-being and on the well-being of those around us.

As a musician, I have always been fascinated by the resonant power of words - not only what they mean, but how they sound. The combination of words and music in songs, the repetitions of words - this can be hypnotic, consciousness-altering. Perhaps we should not underestimate the power of the words "All You Need Is Love" being chanted incessantly over the airwaves of the Western world for that brief time."

Jack Hues, Wang Chung

Chapter 1
It's Your Choice

This is a book to encourage and empower you. It is intended to promote positive change in your life through the awareness and understanding of your choices because these choices form your life and opportunities.

Because much of what we do or think is done on a subconscious or unconscious level, becoming more aware of your choices and when you are making them is vital to creating the life you say you want. I will share with you the best techniques and information I know to help you do this. You will learn how you are making choices gaining an understanding of how they are driven by your beliefs and continually shape your future. You have choice at all times, whether you observe this privilege or not – *it's your choice*. Learning that you must choose and that you do choose, even if you deny it, can make a world of difference.

This book is filled with practical guidance as well as techniques and wisdom that you can immediately put into practise. It contains concepts and exercises using the evolving Meridian Tapping Techniques (MTT), also referred to as energy psychology or tapping. I offer you my most effective tools fine-tuned over the years as a coach and tapping practitioner. I combine my intuition, knowledge and experience with principles drawn from EFT (Emotional Freedom Techniques), TFT (Thought Field Therapy), Hypnosis, NLP (Neuro-linguistic Programming), Cognitive Behavioural Therapy (CBT), Transactional Analysis, kinesiology and the concept of the Law of Attraction.

My goal in presenting this book is to help as many individuals as I can improve their lives and my sincere hope is that I bring each of you a step closer to happiness. To do this I will illustrate how your choices affect you and reflect where you are right now and where you've been. Gaining this awareness will allow you to understand your patterns and most importantly eliminate those that are not productive or healthy for you. You'll not only learn to acknowledge you're limiting, sabotaging behaviour or internal conflicts, you will find out how to resolve them to allow you to create true change and abundance in your life.

"Limitless possibilities await you if you have the courage to challenge yourself."

Most everyone these days has heard the philosophy or theory that **'you create your own reality'** or heard the phrase 'like attracts like' – even if you haven't put much thought into it. This is the basic concept of what's been called the Law of Attraction. Believers in it attempt to use the power of their mind through conscious positive thought to bring good things into their lives. They accept, too, that concentrating or focusing on the negative can cause similar negative experiences to multiple and grow BUT it is often daunting and difficult to stop. That's where I come in and can help.

Understanding more about my own conscious and unconscious life-long preoccupations and that of my clients, I now firmly believe we hold the ultimate influential power over our experiences within us. I had to learn the hard way though; just like everyone else, I wasn't immune to difficulty. Perhaps the only difference between me and my clients (or you for that matter) is that I have a more clear perspective now and even appreciate the emotional or physical challenges that brought me to this point. Things are consistently much easier and joyful for me these days – because I've reached an understanding of *how it all works* and things can be easier for you too.

Now this isn't meant to be an exclusive Law of Attraction book per se, however it is about how to actively gain control and authority, *choice* over your life. I've dedicated the following one chapter to explaining my interpretation of the Law of Attraction because it relates to what I'm going to tell you in the rest of this book and sets a foundation for my personal theories and insight. I'm excited to share my findings, intuitive awareness and hindsight because you may be able to use my information and strategies to avoid unnecessary further struggle.

Even with my own rocky start, I actually still believe EVERYTHING you see in your life, in some way, you have chosen to allow into it. Once you've read this book you may feel just as I do. I'm going to show you how to easily spot what's going on inside of you, drawing experiences to you that you don't actually want! It can be so obvious where you are going wrong (or right) once you're aware of it.

In *It's Your Choice: Uncover Your Brilliance* I offer a new twist on explaining and clearing barriers to a healthy, happy and an abundant life. It's a book about increasing your awareness including how not being aware of what you are *choosing* impacts you. This book explains the choices you make every day and in every moment and how they affect you.

Although, it's your choice to say, think, feel and believe whatever you choose, it has an enormous and pervasive impact and force.

Learning to be observant and guide your choices can truly change your life. Expanding and improving your conscious awareness is the answer as it will bring your unconscious patterns to light, allowing you to start determining more successfully your future.

Introducing *Iceberg Words* and *Iceberg Programmes*

I've found that the words you *choose* to use represent the *tip of an iceberg* which is showing you where your mind is currently focused. Your language is pointing to the reasons why you perform as you do. It is showing you what you believe, what you think is possible AND ultimately what experiences you are likely to encounter or maintain. Your mind (or maybe your soul) is constantly attempting to guide you with your very words and thoughts to uncover the events and beliefs in your life that are holding you back. The actual words themselves are highlighting any unresolved issues within you and any fears that need to be addressed. They are telling you, almost screaming at you the answer to what has caused your non-constructive and self-sabotaging patterns. And until you pay attention to what's behind them and resolve whatever it is, they will keep announcing themselves in your language.

I call these your **'iceberg words'** and the patterns which were formed by your past experiences, your perceptions and subsequent beliefs **'the iceberg programmes'**. The words you are selecting in your everyday speech represent the **'tip of the iceberg'** which is connected to your underlying programming. Your language provides the vital clues to help you uncover these programmes which are being run over and over by your subconscious mind. On average only ten percent of the mass of an iceberg is presented above the water (the amount varies and can be anything from 50% to 99%). Your words represent this visible portion, the tip that is easily accessible to you. Whilst the programming below the surface represents what's operating underneath in your mind and once you become aware of it, you can do something about it.

Your actual words or thoughts are pointing to the events, emotions or particular elements (or *aspects)* of your life that influenced you, and continue to do so, the most. Your words are acting like sonar for your brain locating these decisive experiences and *the programming* they have generated. These programmed routines direct your central thoughts and under-pin your current choices and actions – until you uncover them and alter or replace those that are not beneficial to you. Soon you will begin to observe for yourself how your words are integral to your beliefs and based on your unique interpretation of your past.

As a therapist and coach my objectives are to help people feel better and to improve the quality of their lives and outlook, no matter what is going on with them. I see all types and I've found they all have something in common.

Their mind is preoccupied with something and that's why I've developed **The Iceberg Process** (or **TIPs** for short). Using it I have more rapid and greater success especially with those with long-term or very complex issues.

Often I've been the last resort for many of my clients who said they had "tried everything". I've assisted hundreds improve their careers, financial and personal abundance, relationships and health. My process and my collection of techniques continue to work across a broad spectrum of issues. It has helped elevate self-confidence and efficiency and provided my clients with relief from severe and chronic illnesses (including auto-immune diseases), complex phobias, anxiety and numerous other physical or mental limitations including Post Traumatic Stress Disorder, eyesight problems and mild to medium forms of depression. Because it works on the causes and contributing factors of any problem, it can be used universally.

Your choices (including your language) and what you choose to focus on are of the utmost importance but too often they are overlooked, ignored and forgotten. Most of them are not *knowingly* acknowledged by you because these *decisions* are being made automatically outside of your normal aware-ness, behind the scenes so to speak by your subconscious mind. So how can you effectively alter these? This book will answer this question and show you how with *The Iceberg Process*. To begin with, let me share with you how I became aware of this remarkable language connection and what your words may be trying to hint at, or yell out to you, about your internally orchestrated choices.

Once you get clarity and become more aware of the choices you are making, you will understand why things keep happening to you that you don't want (or that you do want for that matter). Then you can begin to have power and consistency over the outcome of events in your life. This is when the excitement begins. Becoming conscious of your true strength over your circumstances can change your world.

How it Started

It all started to become clear on February 14th, Valentine's Day 2006, when something fascinating and fantastic happened to me. I contacted a part of me, something deep inside, which was more intelligent and wiser than *'the me'* I was familiar with and used to. I had been taking a meditation class for relaxa-tion and on this particular night, whilst in quiet thought, I heard in my head a couple of repetitive words. They were persistent and I couldn't turn away from them. I opened the journal, I always kept in my hand-bag, and as quickly as I could I found the first blank page. I wrote down the words I was still hearing repeatedly in my head and then surprisingly more came. Startled by this, I just kept writing. Although everything seemed okay and fine, no great actually, I had a lot to write!

I didn't know where all the words were coming from or what exactly was happening. I wondered for a frozen moment if God or my deceased mother were trying to speak to me. Or perhaps this wisdom was coming from inside of me, from my deep subconscious or what I'd heard referred to as the super-conscious or my own higher self. Not wishing to doubt or alter whatever was transpiring, I reminded myself that this was a mediation class *and shouldn't I expect to receive some insight?* After all, wasn't that one of the major benefits? Although I was a newbie to meditating, I figured clarity and inspiration must be a common side-effect, a desire-able or even long-sought outcome for many. I'd only been meditating for a short time and part of me wondered what else might happen if I continued.

I'd felt undeniably different from that day forward as if I'd tapped into some-thing unknown and yet intimately known at some level. It was wonderful. I even thought I was actually sounding profound for a change! Whatever I was doing, accessing divine knowledge, my intuition or my super or subconscious mind – I liked it. I continued to meditate each week listening and waiting for my inner knowing. The others in the group got used to the sound of me scribbling as fast as I could in the dim candle light whilst they instead were swimming to Atlantis or hanging out on a cloud. It was this new *quiet and higher or wiser* perspective that paved the way for my discovery of how important our words are.

First I tested the ideas out on myself and my family, whilst at the same time witnessing and confirming the accuracy of my growing theory by listening to the language I heard in my client sessions. The more experience I gained with my concepts, the more I realised they were substantial and truly valuable as tools for change. Soon I couldn't help but acknowledge the amazing and powerful linguistic trend that had emerged. I was captivated, enthralled actually.

Still today I often sit in silence and write whatever comes to me as soon as I quiet my normally active mind. Sometimes the words I scrawl reflect an answer to a challenge I'm faced with, whether my own or that of a client, or they address aspects of life in general. Often the messages I find coming from within are so clear and appropriate I embrace them immediately, taking them on board and applying them to my life and later into my strategies for my clients' growth. Oddly enough, ever since I started writing in meditation and since my mum passed away I've never felt alone or lonely.

Throughout this book I will present some of these inspired ideas when they are supportive or add to the discussion at hand. I will present them in the follow-ing format and look: *"Surrounded by quote marks, bold and in italics in this particular font"*.

Some of the first 'higher perspective' words or phrases I heard when I initially began to access my internal wisdom were *"Shift your focus"*, *"Attend to your focus"* and *"Everything is our choice, we have nothing but choice"*. I now believe that if you accept these concepts as principles and consciously choose to be aware of your choices and particular point of focus you can actively take part in creating your dreams.

"Every thought, every action accumulates. Every thought, every action sets into place

a chain of events. You create your life, take it responsibly! Put the responsibility where it resides – within you. Not your God, your guide, your spouse or partner, YOU.

Even your doctor is not responsible for you, nor am I – I can lead you but you decide how you act and what you believe and what you believe you want and have right to.

Limitless possibilities await you if you have the courage to challenge yourself!"

Chapter 2
My Thoughts on the Law of Attraction

Let's begin exploring the reality we choose by first looking briefly at the concept of the Law of Attraction which tries to explain some natural workings of the universe. It has been around forever albeit hiding under different names or nameless. It has been with us since the beginning. Recently it may have been brought to your attention by the book or movie *The Secret* by Rhonda Byrne.

The Law of Attraction is considered a universal law or a law of nature, an unequivocal law that works whether you know about it or not. It is like gravity on earth; beneficial yet unavoidable (by most of us anyway). I can explain it quickly in just one sentence. **We get or attract what we focus on and what we think about expands or enlarges**. This is the basis of this law and this is the basis of *It's Your Choice: Uncover Your Brilliance*.

I feel it's important to consider the idea of the Law of Attraction because of the promise that through your own thoughts and actions you can attract or draw into your life what you want and eliminate what you don't want. It is all about your personal choices. In the 1980's in the USA and before, it was referred to as *manifesting* or *the power of positive thinking*. It is sometimes talked about as *magnetising*. Law of Attraction maxims have been written about forever by many a philosopher, prophet and guru. Whatever you wish to call it, I'll try to shed some new light on it, to help you have the happiest and healthiest experience you can.

One of the often less stressed or even ignored foundations of this universal law is the concept of taking personal responsibility. The main premise of the Law of Attraction is that you attract your entire reality, meaning **YOU create your life, ENTIRELY YOU, not anyone else**. But if you say you want one thing and the opposite thing, you dread, keeps showing up, it may be hard for you to believe or accept this.

Let's just say that you've been trying to change some things in your life for a long time and it feels no matter what you do, you are stuck in a repeating cycle. You heard about *The Secret* and the Law of Attraction or an abundance tool like a *vision board* and your life is still not what you want. You may *think* you are fully employing the techniques of the Law of Attraction but you are kept from fulfilling your dreams.

In *It's Your Choice*: Uncover Your Brilliance I'll show you that your life and mental or physical health is affected or even formulated or designed by your choices (current and past) whether it is clear to you or not. Whether you choose to believe this or not, that too is your choice. But just for fun, let's say I'm right. What risk is there to allow you this possibility? Granted, if you don't like what you see, it may be uncomfortable and difficult to consider that you may have been a party to the creation or development of your circumstances.

So for now, just set aside the idea that you participated in making your life as good or as challenging as it is today (we can tackle that later in the book). Don't blame yourself or reject my ideas. Although I believe we all participate in creating and perpetuating our situations, we usually have little or no idea that we are doing this or that we are continuing to do it. Our subconscious mind may be sabotaging our efforts due to fear and a sincere intention to protect us, for love and control or because of a simple misguided or outdated belief. Additionally I personally believe (although you don't have to) that our soul has taken a part in forming our curriculum.

In the following chapters we will discuss the basic steps to using the Law of Attraction along with the very important issue of frequency or vibration. You will see how to improve your success rate through understanding and monitoring your choices. You need to become aware of what you are actually choosing.

I'll show you that *The Secret* or the Law of Attraction really is simple, once you acknowledge you are choosing and begin exercising thoughtful positive choice. However the Law of Attraction and what you choose is very pervasive as well. You always have choice and you **are always attracting and creating**. You don't turn the Law of Attraction on and off like a light switch. These principles are always at work; a point that is not stressed enough in my opinion though it is so vitally important.

So why is it that some people appear to have a charmed life whilst others must work there butts off to get a scrap or keep a roof over their heads? **It's about predominate thoughts and beliefs.**

If your life is not meeting your conscious expectations, you may not believe that the Law of Attraction is working for you. If this is the case, it's time for you to consider what you really are expecting to happen to you.

What you believe about yourself and the world, whether right or wrong brings to you your experiences. What you carry with you *as luggage*, as one of my clients likes to say, and how heavy the bags are, will keep you from moving quickly towards your goals.

It sometimes takes detective skills to find out why your life isn't simply wonderful and that's what I'm going to teach you. I'll be giving you the tools to uncover your barriers. It is paramount that you become aware of the depth and subtle nature of your focus and choices because they are always attracting.

I'll help you not only discover your hidden limitations, but show you how you can clear them, allowing you to set your *luggage* down so you can move unencumbered, freely into your desired future.

The Law of Attraction or the perhaps more accurately named *consciousness revolution* that is building momentum all around the world is worth the hype it's receiving; because if you shift your focus you can move into the driver's seat.

The Simplified Steps to the Law of Attraction

The beauty of the natural Law of Attraction is that by using it you can have, do or be whatever you want, if you believe in the law or not. It's so easy to use and whether you recognise it or not it is in action behind the scenes.

Decide what you want to appear in your life and because of the Law of Attraction, you can (if you are clear) attract it to you. That which you desire is given to you.

The idea, the law if you will, goes further to say that the universe presents to you what you are asking for; everything you are asking for and nothing else. And it can give it to you instantaneously. There is no time delay needed.

So take notice of what is showing up in your life as this is a clue to your self-discovery. It will show you what you unknowingly or knowingly are choosing (or expecting).

The basic steps to the Law of Attraction as found in *The Secret* are simple, deceptively simple. Because they can be deceptive I am going to give you the three steps with my enhanced description of them.

Step One: Ask
Step Two: Believe
Step Three: Receive

Sounds easy, doesn't it? As if you simply ask for what you want and voi là it appears in your reality. Well, in principle it can be easy if you truly understand and are clear about what you want and here's the biggie – you do not have hidden obstacles or agendas within you. Let's look at the steps to attracting what you want now more in-depth.

A More In-Depth Look at the Law of Attraction

Step One: Ask
Ask for what you want!

Asking for what you want requires you to know what you want! This can be difficult which is why so many people attract things they don't want.

If you had never heard of the Law of Attraction before you picked up this book you may have been operating on auto-pilot. You may have been *asking* from a place of desperation or fear or from a place of happiness and abundance. Either way, you would be attracting more of the same sort of thing as you get more of what you are thinking about.

Now, *asking* can be simple if you know what you want but how many of us do? Ask yourself what you want in life. Making a list is one of the easiest ways to start asking. Write 'I want:' or 'What do I want?' at the top of a piece of paper and start brainstorming. Just write and write until you have filled the page if you can. Write all the things that you would like to see in the various areas of your life. Write even things you dismissed long ago because you thought you couldn't have them.

Be sure to list what you want physically, financially, career-wise, in your relationships with both partner and friends, in your social life, home, activities, spiritually, for education and growth, and for fun and entertainment including hobbies and holidays. There may be additional areas in which you want to see changes in your life; add them to the list too. If you want a pet, write that down as well.

If you are unable to write down what you want and you find yourself saying "I don't know what I want" don't be alarmed. This is very common. Often when I've given homework to my clients asking them to make a list of what they want, love or like to do, they come back with a blank list and a blank face saying "I don't know".

If this is where you are right now, don't worry just write down what you don't want instead. Write what you'd like **to not have** in your life. Write things that you currently hate or things that you worry about. Then from these lists you can determine what you do want by flipping them around or asking yourself what life would be like if you didn't have these concerns or problems any longer. For example maybe you don't want to be in poverty or debt and don't want to worry how to make your rent each month. Perhaps you want money in the bank to pay all your bills and have two lovely holidays a year without having to use a credit card or scrimp.

For each entry of what you don't want, figure out what it might indicate as far as a desire in you. Try to be specific. Perhaps you don't want to fight with your husband and you hate your job. You could write, "I want a loving supportive relationship with my partner" and "I want a fulfilling job that makes me want to get up in the morning".

Often I find that my clients say they are confused about what to write down as they have stopped hoping for things. Sometimes they have gone without what they wanted for so long that they have forgotten or decided it wasn't possible for them.

If you have been in survival mode or fighting mode long enough, you can become almost permanently engaged and focused on the things you don't want.

Another way to prompt an understanding of what you want is to decide or remember what makes you feel happy, laugh or smile. You could make a list of 'The things I want, love or like' as I mentioned I usually ask my clients to do. You might love cooking, gardening, reading, travelling, thunderstorms or taking a bath by candlelight. If you complete this list, you then can ask yourself, "What do I need to have or possess to do these things?" You may need time, money, a stronger body, a travel partner or something else. These things you need may then be added to your list of what you want in the form of "I want to have more time to garden each week" and "I want more than enough savings to allow me to travel to seminars on creative writing when it interests me".

Additionally, to help you determine perhaps an even grander desire you can day dream about what you would do if time, money, education or other circumstances were not a concern for you. If you could do anything and were assured of a positive outcome, what would you do? If you could add ten things to your life what would they be? Would it be deeper or stronger friendships, financial independence, a mentor, what would it be? Or if you were given £10,000,000 ($15,000,000) tax free with no strings attached what would you do with yourself? Would you buy a big house, travel, go back to school, become a doctor, an airline pilot, a teacher, an archaeologist, a chef, a mother, or a missionary? Would you spend your time taking photos, training animals, playing with children or going for long walks in the country?

Be creative and descriptive when you think about these things and decide what you really want. Remove the normal limitations or doubts that you may have and put what you personally and genuinely would like on your lists, don't worry about others for now, and just think about you. This is about expanding your current position and opening up to possibilities. This is not meant to be what you believe you can have right now but what you'd like to have. These are very different things as we'll be discussing in later chapters. So what would you welcome into your life if you could have anything? If no one would be jealous and you had all the resources and courage needed, what would you wish for or what would you change? These exercises and day dreams are about beginning to design your most desirable life. It's about putting thought into YOU.

Although I have asked you to list what you want, there are many that would jump up and down and shout that you must say it in the form of "I have x", "I am x" or "I'm grateful for x" in order to have it appear in your life. I don't believe the form of your request is so critical to your success. It's more about knowing what you want, knowing what you are asking for, and being aware of your focus and your choices (especially the hidden sabotaging choices). The Law of Attraction has been at work before you were exposed to the concept so it's been working on your recurring thoughts and feelings without any formulaic or fixed statements.

The form of your request can be individual. It's not important how you phrase it (in my opinion), but if you don't know what you want, if you don't set yourself some targets or ideals, you will waver and send out confused messages to the universe. You may end up asking for something that you thoroughly don't want purely by not clarifying your needs or desires or by not being specific or thorough.

When you decide what you want, I encourage you to cross through the word 'want' on your lists and replace it with 'have' if that is comfortable or appropriate for you. The point is that we want you to begin to feel as if you have or can have these items in your life and to feel like you expect them. Making your statements in the present tense helps to start training your mind to be positive and the universe to know what to offer to you. So you may change your list titles to 'I am grateful that I have these things in my life' if you choose to but it is not absolutely essential in my opinion.

Some examples of effective ways of asking in the present tense (once you have determined what you want to ask for) are to say to yourself or write:

"I'm so pleased that I earn easily and consistently _____ a week/month/year"

"I'm grateful for my loving, supportive husband"

"I cherish the expanding time I have to paint"

"I feel more and more secure and calm each day"

"I relish in the fact that I have close genuine friendships"

"I attract gentle kind and generous people to me each day"

"I'm surprised how easy it is to use the Law of Attraction and see my life improving".

"I have tons of energy and each day is a joy"

"I meet new exciting people and opportunities around every corner"

"My life is rich and abundant in all ways"

"I am inspired by all I do"

So Step One – Ask, is about defining your desires or developing desires and then stating those desires as if you already have them.

Remember, if you are one of those that think you don't know what you want, or only know of a few things you want, that's okay because knowing what you don't want will help you identify more. Once you reverse it, you can see things that you do want. Just probe a bit deeper by questioning yourself and you'll find the answers. You can even be thankful for those things you wish to eliminate from your life as they are telling you more in reverse what you do want to achieve or aspire to. Just think of them as necessary for formulating your sincere and strong desires.

If you've never thought about what you want before because you didn't feel you deserved to ask for anything, it's time you question that belief, set it aside for now and dream big.

The universe or divine is always listening and trying to give you what you seek. Your repetitive and dominating thoughts, feelings and images that you replay in your mind are doing the *asking* for you. So it's vital that you choose what you want and not to focus on what you don't want. Step One is to get clear about what you want. Now the next step of the process is to believe.

Step Two: Believe

This second step is often described as believing that what you long for or seek is already yours. In my view it's not so much believing that it's already yours but **believing it can be yours**. Some of us feel ridiculous saying we have a fabulous life when we currently do not, at least by our first-world economy high standards. So think of Step Two as believing it's possible, believing it's on its way to you and believing in a wonderful force, a divine energy that wants all the best for you.

Notice that this step is only saying 'believe', it's not telling you to start planning how. You believe and have faith and the universe or divine energy handles the how part. You do not control how it may happen; this is the magic that will appear. The universe will do everything it can to give you what you want once you clarify what that is.

Believing is acting as if you have what you asked for. It is about having faith. It's about knowing it will be there even if you can't see it yet. It might be there already if you look for it around you (you may not have noticed it). Or it will be coming to you as soon as you set your mind on it.

Your dominant thoughts will be reflected to you in the world around you, so you should do everything you can to convince yourself and *believe*.

So how do you *believe*? Well that's up to you but the easiest way is to imagine what it'd be like when you have it. Imagine yourself and your life once the things you have asked for have arrived. Just day dream, or draw or write what it will be like. There are numerous ways to do this. Some people visualise opening up their bank account statement and seeing a huge balance in the account. Some may tip-ex out the real balance and write in its place what they want to see and others may start looking at houses in real estate agents' windows acting like they have enough money for a down payment. Whilst others simply keep repeating their chosen *ask statement*, stating what they are grateful for now.

However you practise *believing*, I know that by just completing Step One you are already closer to receiving your desires. So have faith that it's coming. Throughout this book, I will teach you how to clarify what you want, stop asking for things you don't, and how to believe that you deserve a great life.

Leave the way it will happen to God, the divine or the universe. You decide and ask for what you want and believe it's coming or it is possible. Which leads us now to the third and final step: Step Three – Receive.

Step Three: Receive

This step is said to be all about feeling it. Feeling the way you will feel when you receive what it is that you are asking for.

This involves changing your current feelings to a place that is comparable to the receiving feelings. Your feelings need to match your desires.

Your vibration must be that of the vibration of a person who has what it is **you say you want.** You need to reach a state of happiness, thankfulness, contentment or excitement depending on your desire. This is another of the tricky bits which is why I said the three steps in *The Secret* are deceptively simple.

This step with a name like *receive* might make you think you just go to your front door and accept your package. Whilst it may be that you receive what you are asking for in exactly that way, being ready to *receive* means much more than that. <u>You need to break any habitual emotional states that separate you from the state that is equivalent to the *receiving feeling*</u>. The majority of your emotional day needs to be positive. Not every moment must match the *receiving feeling* but the greater part of your day must.

"During your average moment, how do you choose? This is what you should analyse. What are you going to choose right now? What are you going to choose tomorrow? What are you going to choose to perceive when the man on the road cuts you off? What feeling are you going to select from the many feelings you have at your offering? You have choices at every...millisecond, nanosecond. You have a choice to make and remember not choosing is a choice as well. The day to day activity is important for long term growth because the hours are many..."

I'm sure you've noticed that happy people seem to have more happy experiences, whilst those who are down in the dumps tend to attract or encounter more reasons to be blue and desperate. Consequently they maintain the feeling of worry and anxiousness; feeling they must have what they are asking for in the attraction process. But with these denser feelings what they are asking for won't come as a higher feeling is required to receive it. So you must try and find those happier feelings first.

I have also witnessed people giving away exactly what they said they wanted once they received it because they thought there was a mistake or they thought someone else was more worthy than them. It's common for people to spend their time trying to manifest a particular thing and then in essence reject it when it arrives. Everyone has seen someone reject a compliment. This pattern of rejection can be extended to other areas, as the principle is the same.

Step Three, *Receiving* then is about feelings (emotions) or about your vibration. It's about reaching *the feeling of receiving*, accepting the gifts that are offered to you and taking inspired action is often involved.

As you feel good or encouraged, you will be nudged to do things. Sometimes these nudges come through changing circumstances. Your diary may be rearranged unexpectedly by a cancelled engagement and then you may get asked to attend a function where you meet someone who tells you about something that helps you. Or you may be compelled to start reading a particular author you notice people talking about. You'll get prodded along.

Sometimes the inspired prompt comes like a bolt of lightning or a jolt out of nowhere. Other times it comes as an obvious alternative or an unavoidable obstacle or shift in your direction. Whilst it may be a simple or easy alteration, it may require that you act quickly. Inspired action is not normally difficult but you may need to trust your intuition and be willing to do something. You'll be pushed to take steps. Sometimes these steps appear to have nothing to do with what you want to accomplish and only in retrospect will it become apparent.

Your Personal Frequency (Vibration) and Conflicts

In this chapter, I've touched on the point that your vibration needs to be the vibration of a person who has what you want already because you attract things into your life that match your frequency of vibration. Science has confirmed to us that everything in the world vibrates. Even if it looks solid it is not, it is actually moving, vibrating molecules. Things just appear to be solid whilst they are wiggling, shaking or oscillating at a predictable and measurable frequency rate.

Like a radio station, you too have a frequency and this frequency is drawing people, events and situations into your life.

So if you are thinking that the Law of Attraction doesn't work for you even though you've followed all the steps, you may have to question what you are really asking for or what your intention really is. It may appear that you haven't received what you were asking for, or did you? Let me explain this a bit more.

Fundamentally your intention or objective must be in agreement consciously and subconsciously. If you have conflicts between your beliefs and values and what you are asking for, you will be sending a mixed message or inconsistent frequency. You may be blocked from receiving your **expressed desires**.

What you've been dreaming of and asking for might not show up because your request is confusing. Or it might show up in your world but you miss it. You choose something else or push it away due to some internal conflict. The conflicts may be in your values, beliefs or past experiences. **You cannot have controversy inside yourself if you want consistent results.**

"How you choose to think controls your experience. It nurtures your experience. It nudges your direction and intention is formed. Intention is the power house of change and growth or stagnation."

Just stop and think for a moment. What are you attracting if you hate yourself or think you are not capable? What are you attracting if you think you are unlovable? Clearing away self-doubt, improving self-worth, reducing fear and altering your beliefs of what you can have and what you deserve is what prepares you to *receive*.

Joe Vitale, in his audio book *The Missing Secret* discusses what he refers to as counter intentions. And it is these counter intentions which block the universe from granting our wishes. Counter intentions, **blocking or rejecting intentions** if I can call them that, might be a belief like 'rich people are greedy' so you find if you earn money it's just enough to get by but never enough to reach a level of wealth that would truly satiate your sincere need for security.

Or you may have a feeling that 'I don't deserve to be loved' because you are carrying some deep shame or feelings of abandonment because your father walked out on you and your mother when you were two. These feelings would keep a wonderful loving partner from entering your life and fulfilling your wish list because you have a counter strategy or contrary (rejecting) belief. You may be destroying your chances for love by never allowing anyone to get close to you because you're trying to avoid getting hurt. There may be multiple blocking albeit protecting counter intentions going on causing you to choose to miss out on a dinner party where your future mate was waiting.

You may have developed beliefs because of your experiences that 'it's too risky to try new things', 'I'm not good enough', 'it's dangerous to be thin and attractive', 'no one will ever love me' and the list goes on. These corrupted, distorted and limiting beliefs about ourselves are often deeply hidden and are referred to as *core issues*.

Unfortunately I believe, your frequency by default usually matches that of your counter intentions (blocking, rejecting intentions), your core issues or your core beliefs, which may be polar opposites of your stated goals or desires, but they are forming your frequency and thereby attracting your circumstances. This frequency is what is used to create your reality and experience. What shows up in your awareness or proximity matches it. So if you want to be healthy or successful how can it come to you if you are vibrating at the frequency of illness, depression, debt or guilt or the worst emotion, shame? If you feel, even unknowingly, fearful or shameful you won't draw wonderful things to you **with consistency**.

When internally you are in discord with wonderful things you won't be a frequency match for them.

So even if you are setting your stated intention or aim clearly (*asking* for it) and strongly visualising it coming to you, it might not come. Your vibration may push it away. I repeat: <u>your vibration or how you feel must be close to that of what you say you want and your actions need to be in line with your desire as well.</u>

"Be active. Don't wait for it to come to you. Seek it out. Idleness is the pattern and coping mechanism, even strategy of those who really are insecure...Idleness, waiting for someone to give you the gift does not happen. If you want to acquire the gift, go out and get it. You can wish for it but taking the step after this wish is the next lesson. Fix your net. Fix your damage. Work on yourself. Decide what you want and then act. Make yourself healthy and strong. Analyse yourself. Exercise your mind and body. Practise love and self-love."

Our underlying intentions keep us in our old ways. They keep us experiencing the same sort of things over and over until we uncover them and release them. We can be totally unaware that it's our own self that is causing our problems. Unconsciously we may perceive an internal benefit to not rocking the boat and we choose the old way of life or habit.

In the coming chapters I will help you become aware of what is keeping you from your dreams. The energy or vibration of happiness, health and success are closely linked to feelings of self-love and appreciation as well as those feelings of eager expectation and gratitude.

Chapter 3
What You Choose to Say

Now that I've explained some primary points regarding our ability to create what we say we want in our life, let me help you discover how to become more aware of your own underlying beliefs and intentions which might be stopping you. Your speech can be exceptionally revealing. I expect you probably have never really considered how important what you actually say is and how the words you use differentiate and make a tangible difference.

Language and words themselves can convey so much beauty and they've been cherished and analysed by many over the centuries. Words can convey intense feelings and can elicit strong emotional responses. You don't have to be a poet or philosopher to be touched by someone's expression.

But why do some people use particular ways of speaking? I now believe it is not just about our exposure to language, our communities, our education or social levels and privileges but *it's about us*. It's about our life, our history, our experiences, our fears and our expectations. It's also about our vibration and the patterns we have chosen or have not been able to release.

I'd like to bring to your attention the words you select to use each day. Think about your common statements. As a therapist and coach I have begun to piece together my own view on how important our choice of words is to us.

Observing Their Words
A few years ago, as I mentioned in Chapter 1, I began to see a trend. It happened innocently enough and coincided with my meditating. I didn't know anything about linguistics and even had trouble reading as a child. Other than basic American-English I can barely speak a few words of French and when I

read I recite each word to myself in my head.

When I began to make the connection, I had heard only a little about Neuro-linguistic Programming (NLP) a therapy that works directly with language to promote positive change in people. It was only briefly mentioned in my initial training in Emotional Freedom Techniques (EFT), one of the Meridian Tapping Techniques (MTT) but I hadn't trained in it myself or read about it then. So I wasn't looking at language as a way to categorise people or match their language to build rapport as NLP therapists might. However I was a good listener and a copious note-taker and soon my sincere attention and observation began to pay off.

At the same time as my *tapping* clients (often seeking relief from emotional and physical issues including anxiety, pain and phobias) and my coaching clientele (primarily seeking improvements in their business ventures or confidence) began to increase, my intuition was building as a result of my meditation practise. I was learning to be actively conscious of my own words and theirs. Then I started to notice a pronounced link between the phrases and words of my clients and their particular problems or limitations. The way they spoke seemed to reflect their actual illness and symptoms, or it showed their current state of mind, outlook on life or belief. This was true with business entrepreneurs, board directors as well as those unable to work due to severe anxiety or chronic illness. Although at first I didn't fully recognise the importance, their phrases and words proved to be invaluable to helping them recover or achieve success.

Their words, I discovered, mirrored the original and sometimes traumatic events that had influenced or impacted them so greatly. They often pinpointed the turning point in their lives which eventually brought them to me. Sometimes the crucial event was not known to them and even at first glance did not seem consequential or foundational to the current symptoms or issue displaying in their life.

At the start of all this, I found it a bit odd, coincidental and even wondered if I was putting too much stress on my findings. It was surprising to me. The sheer honesty with which people spoke of their history was remarkable, **if only they knew it.** Slowly, the enormity of what I was observing and becoming conscious of hit me. This was important.

As my practice grew my insightful thoughts continued to highlight the importance of each and every word used. I told myself to watch every single word as I now believed each had an impact or possible foundation or tale.

As I really listened to the exact words of my clients and observed my own repetitious and common statements or choice expletives, I became aware of the emotionally painful history that I still harboured within me. I found I had some of my own work to do.

Your words may be describing your state of mind, current beliefs, core issues and outlook or expectation.

Perhaps my first recognition that there was a connection between the words selected in normal conversations and one's life experiences came from listening to one of my early tapping clients a woman named Patricia.

Patricia had driven down from Essex to see me. She was a very dramatic person and had a life that was continually presenting challenges to her. During our initial discussion and consultation, Patricia selected to use the word 'nightmare' frequently to describe her life. She said it so many times I really should thank her because I could not avoid noticing it. This word alone told me so much about her.

Patricia continued to use the word 'nightmare' as she spoke. It appeared to be her favourite description, adjective and pronoun. Because of my cognitive therapy experience and what I was now beginning to realise about our choices, I knew that this was not healthy for her.

Her life was very frightening to her warranting the description of nightmarish. After the loss of her brother and father in a freak accident in her late teens, her life continued to be like a bad dream, surreal and in perpetual fear. Her feelings about her future matched those of her past experiences.

Patricia would say things like, "the traffic on the ring road was a nightmare today", "the class was nightmarish" and sadly she would often say "my life's a nightmare". Her current reality was like living a nightmare 24 hours a day.

Another client, Sally who saw me to help her get over her habit of procrastination preferred to say the word 'hopeless', she used it to describe herself and her life. Everything was 'hopeless' to her.

Sally wanted to uncover what was keeping her from reaching her goals. Although I had this word as a clue before we even started, we discovered relatively quickly that deep down she felt she had little chance of ever accomplishing anything meaningful. Sally did not exhibit signs of fear of failure but of resignation. Her belief that she would always fail was so strong that she didn't bother trying most things.

This belief explained the procrastination and meant her poor results were all but guaranteed. Believing her life to be truly hopeless, she felt she lacked the power and ability to change. Identifying that she felt this way helped us understand her struggle and helped me understand what I needed to do to begin to help her. I needed to find out how this belief was formed.

As we worked together, her use or non-use of the word 'hopeless' became an indicator of her progression and release of her self-imposed restraints. Using tapping (EFT and MTT), we uncovered ancient regret and long-held grief. No matter what she did as a child she was not able to receive the love of her parents.

As we worked together, I decided I would share my observation of her degree of using of the word 'hopeless'. We discussed the concepts of affirmations. The use of a positive statement to reinforce healthy self-esteem or encourage change and how in cognitive behavioural therapy (CBT) counter-statements are used to stop destructive self-talk. Affirmations and counter-statements consist of more supportive, encouraging and rational self-talk rather than deprecating or fear-based thoughts or statements that one may be in the habit of repeating.

I gained Sally's agreement that it would be a good idea to attempt to eliminate using the word 'hopeless' as much as possible. That word just couldn't be helping her feel productive in her life or feel that there would be any reason to believe things might improve. She agreed to try to replace the word 'hopeless' with other words when she caught herself thinking or saying it. Every time she said "It's hopeless" or "I'm hopeless" she would actively choose to correct this by saying or thinking "No, I'm okay", "No, it'll be fine, all will work out" or "I'm capable". She, too, saw immediately that this would be beneficial and would encourage a shift in her attitude in between our sessions together.

We also designed a tapping exercise of "Even though I feel hopeless, I choose to believe this can change for me". Tapping phrases can differ greatly from affirmations as they are used in combination with tapping on the body's energy system. Unlike affirmations, when creating tapping phrases, we focus directly and very specifically on the problem or issue. We purposely draw attention to the negative aspect which is not helpful in a stand-alone affirmation or US-style Cognitive Behavioural Therapy (CBT) counter-statement done without tapping or applying pressure to specific acupressure points. The EFT tapping process and principles are explained in Chapters 19-21, where you will also find tapping exercise templates for your personal use.

When Sally made the effort to catch herself saying "Hopeless" and replace it with the new statements, she was shocked how often she was saying it. It was almost the only word she used descriptively. She used 'hopeless' to describe all forms of displeasure and discomfort. In cases in which she felt irritated or frustrated, she would say "Hopeless". If she felt overwhelmed, she said "Hopeless". If she was sad or lonely, she or her life was "Hopeless". When she criticised herself, of course, she was 'Hopeless'. She was stuck in this hopeless state.

Although her extreme use of this one word was not startling to me, what was amazing was the response from a friend. Sally shared with a close friend who was some sort of complementary therapist that I had suggested she try to stop saying "hopeless". She spoke too of her new-found awareness of the frequency with which she said it. To her surprise, her friend took great offence and even expressed anger at me for suggesting such a strategy. She said *"That was just Sally"*, *"That it was part of her"* and that I shouldn't try to *"Change who Sally was"*. How dare I do that!

It was intriguing, because whilst Sally felt pleased to stop feeling and expressing hopelessness and clearly saw the connection as being associated with her problem of dragging her feet on her career, she never expected resistance from this friend. Sally wanted to break this destructive pattern. It was an alert to her to be aware that often people like to keep us where we are and expect us to stay the same.

Our friends and family can be uncomfortable with our changes. They may prefer us predictably disempowered for their own reasons or benefit. Our change elicits other adjustments that may affect them or alter how we interact with them.

Most people avoid change like the plague preferring to persevere in even the most uncomfortable situations because they fear the unknown even more. I've learned to embrace change, seeing it as the means to transformation. I try to see it as a welcome friend as I know we are dynamic in nature.

Sally rarely uses the word 'hopeless' to describe events in her life now and I often wonder if she still sees her therapist friend. Sally no longer needs my services and is the opposite of hopeless. She is optimistic and pioneering. Once the experiences of trying to gain the love of a parent were addressed effectively with tapping, Sally's core issues of feeling hopeless and unlovable were modified to more appropriate feelings and self-respect. Her life and prospects opened up.

Sally also was able to release feelings of unworthiness that came up. She at last could accept herself and could even accept her parents. She felt compassion for their position and realised that they were incapable of providing the display of love she desired. Sally forgave her parents and realised it was their own fears that kept them from offering her love and accepting it from her as well.

Uncovering or understanding your core issues or feelings is often a key to unlocking and releasing your self-imposed limitations. Core issues are, as the term implies, what is really at the core or centre of you. It is the root or cause of your problems, illness, symptoms, fears or behaviour. Core issues may also be the reason for the words you choose!

Sometimes it can be difficult to discover what your core issues are as they may be covered up by other things which act to distract you. In Chapter 13 I have included exercises to help you uncover your core issues or core beliefs *however* simply listening to your selection of words can be an extremely useful and productive exercise. It may save you a lot of time.

The words you say, as I've shown in these two examples, are expressing your current feeling (belief) about your life or yourself. Think about the impact on you if you say things are "difficult", "a problem" or "scary" versus if you say things are "brilliant", "gorgeous" or "easy". What are you telling yourself? What belief is being revealed?

Your Words May Keep You Focused on The Past

Additionally, the words you select to use may keep you focused on an event in your life that harmed, frightened or traumatised you in some way. Certain experiences in our lives, whether we remember them or not may be highlighted and even relived through our words.

In my practice, I have had the honour and responsibility to listen and observe people intimately for many hours. Often I'm the only person who has sat and listened to them in such an uninterrupted fashion in their entire lives, so it has been tremendously useful to find this connection in the words they choose as it provides a shortcut to the healing process.

When dealing with severe anxiety cases finding a means to accelerate the release of fear and a way to demystify the unraveling of often clouded complexities benefit us both.

Noting the words the client selects, not just the story, gives me directional signposts. They're telling me where to navigate to or what to look out for there, and the words indicate or confirm we are making inroads (and progress).

Using this valuable information is delicate business. Although in the case of my ex-hopeless client we weren't dealing with terrifying or life threatening events, it was very emotionally painful. To clear her problem we had to dig up memories when she felt unloved and impotent. Sometimes however the words used are highlighting more disturbing or abusive events in one's life.

When I see a possible word connection, I don't come out and say where I think our work may take us or what I have observed them say repeatedly. It's very important never to insert false memories into a client's mind. This is why I simply make note of my suspicions and the tell-tail words. I keep them to myself and watch things unfold more prepared than I would have been without them. Being prepared for what's to come in my sessions, I believe, allows me to be a better coach as I am ready to guide them to a more positive outcome.

Their words can offer me insight into more than their state of mind or internal feelings. They can often even tell me what has happened to make them feel as they do or at the very least, how they perceived what happened to them.

Think about something as simple as what you say when someone cancels an engagement with you or needs to postpone a lunch date. What would you say in response? Would you reply: "That's okay", "No problem", "No worries", "Oh, bother" or would you say "No trauma"?

Your Words May Describe Your Experiences, Illness or Problem

What do you think of the phrase or comment "No trauma"? One of my most lovely clients, Susan used to say "No trauma" over and over again to describe normal day to day events. Just as Patricia used 'nightmare' as her favourite adjective and Sally used 'hopeless', Susan must have had a lot of difficulty and trauma in her life to use the word 'trauma'.

When I started concentrating on the actual words used to describe a story rather than the story itself, everything became clear. I then began to realise the truth of their words and how they matched their history, illness and future for that matter. The choice of their words was actually very shocking at times. Some of the discoveries that were made were difficult to hear even though I had begun to anticipate what was likely to come out in the sessions. Sometimes I would know long before the client did that they'd been abused or witnessed or experienced something so awful that they had suppressed it, simply by listening to their words.

What's more, I knew when they were hiding something from me, for example if they had an addiction problem or eating disorder that they were too embarrassed to share in our first sessions together.

There were times I could even predict (to myself) the way they were harmed or abused or how these traumatic events were played out by picking up the advance clues. To illustrate this a bit more, I'll describe for you a few examples which I have altered significantly to maintain the anonymity of my clients.

One client who came to me because she was having uncontrollable panic attacks fifteen years after witnessing the stabbing of her brother by her step-father used many phrases with the word 'blood'. Although we both knew she'd come to see me because of her panic which was directly caused by this terrible experience, like all my anxiety or phobia clients I didn't know what part of it was keeping her stuck in the past experiencing life altering, limiting flashbacks. I first noticed her use of 'blood' as I asked her some fairly generic questions whilst filling in my consultation form. When I asked Marta (not her real name) what she did for a living (a standard question on my form) she commented that she was a *bricky* (a slang term for a bricklayer in England). I was intrigued as she was the first woman I'd ever met that did this for a living, so I probed and asked why she decided to become a bricky. Instead of saying "I love working with my hands" or "I wanted to follow in my father's foot-steps" she replied **"It's in the blood"**.

I was a bit amazed at this, as by this time I'd been noting a variety of colourful and descriptive words used by my clients and had even observed patterns of my own. But 'in the blood', I hadn't anticipated this literal use. I was now stunned at how trauma was so accurately being repeatedly played out in our words.

Marta sought my help because she was being triggered into extreme panic frequently. She was unknowingly panicked by the sight of anything red as it reminded her subconscious of the scene of the stabbing. It was a terrifying and surreal incident. There was blood everywhere. It was on the floor, the knife, on her brother, on the step-father, on her shirt, on her face and hands and even on the walls, the door, the door handle and the outdoor steps where her step-father had passed as he fled once Marta intervened to save her brother.

Marta only saw me for two, two hour sessions and we broke the cycle of panic which she had lived with for more than a decade. Traditional counselling and Cognitive Behavioural Therapy, Marta said had done nothing but re-traumatise her. Her panic was worse when she spoke to these types of counsellors about the stabbing of her brother without using the tapping techniques I offered her.

Another evocative case was that of Stephanie, a woman in her mid-fifties who had difficulty finding what she called 'nice men'. All her relationships were with unsuitable men who put her down constantly and whom she admitted were not good for her. Her relationships often were in some way degrading.

As we started our tapping sessions, I immediately picked up on her comments and knew she must have had a series of shameful experiences with men, potentially involving rape or consensual sexual exposure but at a very young age. As the session progressed even the details of the location came out in her words before her mind allowed the memories to surface. She talked about having difficulty "Letting her feelings out of the attic" throughout our sessions, a deviation on the English phrase "To let your feelings out of the cupboard".

As we worked together I decided to focus in on both the emotion of shame and the word 'attic'. To my surprise she quickly recalled and made a connection of repeated sexual abuse she'd experienced when she was very little. She told me she remembered, as we were touching the tapping points, that her first shame and confusion came from when she had been 'fiddled with' in the attic before she was five years old. Her home lacked storage cupboards so her parents had no option but to use their attic for storing excess duvets, blankets and linens when not in use. The attic was also filled to the roof with boxes of the family's seasonal clothes and memorabilia both theirs and that of their deceased grandparents.

In one of the corners of the attic, just next to the brick chimney, shelves had been fitted. They kept all the family's winter weight duvets on these shelves in the summer along with their extra bed linen. It was a tight squeeze but it was nice and warm on the shelves next to the chimney all year round. Stephanie told me that she had sex repeatedly with an older neighbour boy there amongst the linens as a child of four till she was ten. Her abuse took place literally in the attic, where she'd said she couldn't let her feelings out and where she used to hide away from her fighting parents.

Stephanie described herself also as a hoarder and claimed she had difficulty throwing things away. She had stacks and stacks of boxes of clothes that she no longer wore, papers and linens scattered around her lounge. There were boxes always around her. After we uncovered her past sexual abuse and cleared the shame she felt in the attic, something interesting happened.

The same week we released 'the attic shame' she found herself filling up bin liners (garbage bags) with stuff she hadn't been able to get rid of for ages. She'd previously tried and failed to clear away her clutter which had cramped her home. Unknowingly, the clutter was in some way keeping the abuse so many years ago on the shelves in the corner of her parents' attic fresh in her mind. To my surprise her home must have visually looked similar to living in that attic and felt as tight and confined as well.

Odd as it may seem, frightening, shameful or traumatic memories seemed to be replayed in my clients' everyday lives in many ways.

In some, on the surface, it appeared they were avoiding re-traumatisation by limiting their lives. However, whilst they might choose never to walk in the woods again in the case of someone who had been raped in the forest, they would be repeating the emotions or scene of the event in other ways. They might choose a dangerous and aggressive boyfriend, have a house at the edge of a wood, or use words or phrases describing the feelings of fear, shame and embarrassment or anticipating danger. Their words showed they hadn't resolved the event that took place in the wood even though they wouldn't walk in the forest any longer.

I've assisted many adults who had extraordinarily difficult and abusive childhoods who were social workers spending their days helping other young victims of violence, negligence and abuse. As well as abused women who as adults became wardens in prisons or counsellors specialising in crimes of abuse and volunteers working for the National Society for Prevention of Cruelty to Children (NSPCC), Victims Support hotline, Women's Crisis Centres and Good Samaritans.

Whether it is the job they select, the way they keep house, the car they drive or the type of men they choose, they stay focused on the perceived threat or past incidents. The patterns and cycles apparently continue until we eliminate or reduce the mind's preoccupation with the original emotions and experiences. I have worked with many people who change career once they free themselves from their fixation on their history.

Some of the examples I've given are easy to understand and you can make the correlation when I simply point out the words they used to you. But often people have had numerous and varied events that shock or bewilder them. These events shape and create their beliefs; beliefs perhaps of being unworthy, unlovable or unsafe. Their complex life history causes distortions and perceptions that are not always accurate. I often describe it as peeling the layers of an onion to get down to the various causes.

I believe most complex phobias like agoraphobia, panic or anxiety attacks, Post Traumatic Stress Disorder (PTSD) and chronic illnesses, like ME (Myalgic Encephalopathy) and depression and even the symptom of tachycardia (rapid heartbeat) are affected or even created by our beliefs and perception of the world around us.

The very real physical symptoms that are being presented come from within; they come from our beliefs, expectations and fears.

I've found that the words people use in casual conversation not only relate to their past experiences or trauma but they astonishingly seem to match or link into their physical illness as well.

This is when it seems logical to question, is it *the chicken or the egg*? Do they continually draw attention to their illness or their negative emotions and beliefs, or do they develop an illness or problem because of them? Is their illness due to continual negative conditioning or does their focus on their physical problems or condition show in their language? We may never know the answer to this question but I have found that as my clients become more aware and clear the debris from their past their language changes almost immediately. They no longer concentrate on those issues.

Troubled Words

Display Physical, Emotional and Mental Issues

To illustrate my findings let me reveal to you how I've heard people speak about their lives. It's not about hearing them say something once or twice; it's about repetition – saying a particular word or phrase frequently, almost all the time (almost compulsively). My clients repeated these sorts of phrases over and over. Remember they were not said as singular one-offs. Also it's prudent to mention now that when you are around certain people you may adapt to their frame of reference and enter into their mindset and language patterns.

Clients with eye problems tended to say things like:

"My memory is a bit foggy",

"I have a problem looking at that",

"I just couldn't see the point",

"I closed my eyes to it",

"I can't look at it",

"I'm a bit fuzzy about the details",

"I'm not clear on that part of the story",

"I could see his opinion was clouded",

"It was all a blur what happened next" or

"I didn't want to focus on it".

Clients with hearing problems or congestion said:

"I'm not going to listen to him any longer",

"I don't want to hear it",

"The volume of problems in my life is unbelievable",

"I was so upset, I couldn't hear myself think",

"I just wanted to shut off the fighting" and

"The silence was deafening".

Clients with heart problems like tachycardia, inflamed heart or atrial fibulation said things like:

"…in my heart of hearts I knew something was wrong",

"I put my heart and soul into that child",

"It was so heartfelt",

"I knew in my heart he'd leave me",

"With a heavy heart I resigned my post" and

"My heart hurts every time she goes away".

Clients with issues around alcohol have been known to say:

"Every time I try to speak in public I bottle out",

"I lost my bottle" or "I bottled" (meaning in England to have given up or lost your nerve),

"When times are tough, I go to spirit" (referring to God),

"I want to drink in the warmth of the sun",

"I pop out of my head when shocked" (referring to a feeling of being disconnected and this client preferred alco-pops)

"I've been keeping myself bottled up",

"She pissed me off" (to be pissed can mean to be drunk),

"We were at loggerheads over this" (logger sounds like lager, a name for a type of beer) and

"I'll drink to him for achieving so much" or

"I felt I'd hit the bottom of the barrel" (as in a cask of real beer or whiskey).

Sometimes it's ever so humorous to spot the phrases as clients with IBS (Irritable Bowel Syndrome) or diarrhoea problems tend to use the word 'shit' or 'ass' a lot. For example I've heard, "The queues were really shitty today" or "The teacher was a right ass". They literally have potty mouth! I even heard one client with diverticulitis who experienced bouts of constipation offset with bouts of the opposite say "Things were poopy at work"! Saying "I was gutted" is another of the favourites of those with IBS, stomach or digestive issues. They literally feel their emotions in their gut.

Sexual abuse, rape and incest victims tend to use words that relate to how they felt about what happened to them in the words of their age at the time of the incident/s. They also tend to use words that relate to the particular deed itself, the surroundings or location, including the view, their appearance or the perpetrators or the props that may have been used as well as their physical position during the abuse. Their subconscious mind must be trying to bring the event out of hiding so it can be adequately addressed.

I've heard words like 'gross', 'yucky', 'sticky', 'gooey', 'back passage' or 'bottom' used an inordinate amount of times by those who had been abused as children or youths. Also they repeatedly tend to use words like 'disgusting' and 'shameful' to describe how they feel about themselves and the past events.

The way the act was performed on them or what they were encouraged or made to do is sometimes also apparent in their words. Additionally, I've commonly seen in the cases of my adult clients who as children were forced to perform oral sex gagging or trouble speaking as a precursor to repressed memories surfacing, This often occurs just before the memory is released to their conscious mind.

Sometimes I've found that their physical response during the session with me can mirror the original events which were hidden deep in their mind, just as their words do. When this happens in my experience the body's remembered reaction is thankfully much more subtle, greatly reduced and very brief and it normally signifies the subconscious mind's clearing and release of the trauma for good.

Tapping helps resolve the suppressed, hidden or sketchy memories and can address how they felt about what happened. Whether their mind allows them to remember some of the circumstances or the whole affair is irrelevant. With these techniques the feelings which have stayed with them, anchoring into their beliefs and eroding their self-acceptance and worth can be alleviated. We can change how it left them feeling about themselves and how they feel now about the abuser.

Not surprisingly most victims of abuse feel high levels of shame, disgust, guilt, worthlessness and embarrassment. They often have a sense of self-reproach, feelings of being bad, naughty, dirty, damaged or cheapened. These can be connected with feelings of being out of control, to blame, frightened, confused, sad, and excited and a whole range of emotions which are all valid.

In many cases the victims of abuse are not able to share their experiences with anyone after they took place. Thus the memories were forced to sit quietly, yet not dormant, in their minds. I've heard people say they could never tell their story to anyone but me, as a family member or close friend was involved. So the dark nasty secret had been left to fester inside for a long time. It needed to be resolved and reviewed which is why I believe it was appearing in their language. The memory and emotions don't want to stay hidden and if you listen to their language it keeps repeating the memory remnant in some way. Even if they've tried to forget or have even convinced themselves that they had, their subconscious hasn't forgotten. Take a look at the following phrases and see if you can tell what might have happened to these people or how they feel about themselves.

"I got sucked into it",

"I'm always forced into things",

"My life is fucked",

"His gaze was penetrating",

"I'm bound by my morals",

"Talking about this makes me want to gag",

"This is disgusting",

"No matter what I do, I'm screwed",

"I feel there's no room to breathe",

"I want to put it to bed" or

"It was more than I could swallow".

Self-harmers who sometimes refer to themselves as 'cutters' used phrases like:

"I had to cut her out of my will",

"I severed all relationships with my family",

"The smoke was so thick you could have cut it with a knife",

"I cut my connections to him after the break-up",

"We've only scratched the surface",

"She stabbed me with her words,

"I sliced right through the queues today" and

"I was edgy about it".

Constipation sufferers said things like "I'm stuck in my ways" or "I just can't let go of my grief".

ME sufferers said they were "sick and tired" and of course they are, and in pain.

I noted the people who came to me to stop fainting had a very interesting way of speaking too. They said they wanted 'to switch off the world' or simply 'shut down' when they were afraid. Switching off or turning themselves off was exactly what they did. When they felt they couldn't handle anymore they'd turn off their own switch and promptly faint!

Those who suffer with panic attacks or anxiety may actually say "Don't panic" to others when indicating everything is okay. "Don't panic" is a well used statement by people prone to panic.

People challenged with fear, anxiety or worry, however perhaps not to the level of having panic attacks, often use words like 'afraid' or with the equivalent meaning in their everyday speech. It's common to hear them begin their sentences with the words 'I fear', 'it's worrying' or 'I'm afraid'. They also have a strong tendency to caution others about possible risk or hazards around them. For example: "Watch out, it might be slippery on the pavement (sidewalk)", "Be sure to drive safely" or "Ring when you get there to let us know you're alright'. They are perpetuating and passing on their fear innocently to others as well as reinforcing the feelings within them.

Take the phrase 'take care' which appears to be innocuous or harmless. In our society saying 'take care' when someone leaves our home or gets into their car appears very normal and courteous. But is this a euphemism for 'be careful' and are we implying that there is potential danger out there? It's worth considering what you think about these phrases. What do they insinuate or mean to you? Does 'take care' indicate that you are worried they are going to get into a car crash essentially and die? It may be just a habit in your family or our society but it may highlight an underlying feeling of being unsafe that has been instilled.

Examples of choice words by those who have safety issues:

"I'm afraid I won't be able to join you",

"There's nothing to be afraid of dear",

"Take care of yourself won't you",

"Be sure you have everything you need",

"You will call me when you arrive safely won't you?",

"Be in before dark",

"Be careful on the motorway",

"Her makeup was truly scary",

"I fear we won't be able to handle it" and "I'm scared I won't be able to cope" or "It's worrying how much he drinks".

Wouldn't it be nice to adopt more cheerful phrases when people leave our company as other cultures do? Why not replace 'take care' with 'see you soon' or 'until the next time' or even 'good bye' which is derived from 'go with God' or 'God be with you'.

Over-eaters or those with digestive problems including food intolerances or hypersensitivities tended to say "I'm fed up" or "I'm just never satisfied".

I was entertained by comments I've heard like "My grandson is so adorable I could just eat him up" or "The man at the desk was tasty". I've listened to many a food-related adjective like 'delicious', 'scrummy' and 'simply delectable' again focusing on the act of eating and the pleasure or disgust of it. I've had people commonly refer to themselves as pigs or porkers too, or chastise themselves by calling themselves lard-asses, fatsos, and chubby cheeks or by saying they made a pig's ear of something or were so large they looked like a circus tent or a blimp. Not the best comments to help with self-esteem, eh?

I've heard binge-ers or bulimics who purge themselves after eating massive quantities of food say "He vomited up his excuse", "I'd be sick if they left me", "Just the sight of her makes me want to heave" or "I want to shove it down his mouth when he says that". Once more the words selected are reminders of the eating or the purging act. Or they'd use digestive phrases or verbs in other sentences like "It's a gut feeling", "I felt I was being swallowed up by life" or "I couldn't stomach it any longer". With their attention on eating they too may describe something as 'feeling deliciously wrong' or being 'delicious looking' even though it wasn't something to eat.

Under-eaters, controlled eaters or people with a fear of choking or gagging also say they are "fed up"! I had one client say "I've had it up to here" indicating the top of her gullet at her jaw line; her father had always forced her to eat everything on her plate.

One lady who came to me because of problems with severe gagging, I later discovered had actually had a court imposed *gag order* as part of her terrible ordeal in a legal battle. She was restrained by law and could not discuss her case with anyone. Another person who gagged as I worked on them was reminded of the time they were forced to eat rubbish from a trough like a pig by an abusive partner.

A 55 year old client came to me for tapping last year wanting to improve her confidence. She said on the telephone that she thought since I had helped her with another issue earlier in the year that I'd be able to "Knock it on the head" quite quickly. Let's call her Wendy.

As Wendy and I worked through the reasons for her lack of confidence, she related that she had suffered a fierce and shocking blow to her head at the age of six when her older brother disapproved of something she had done.

Interestingly, not only was Wendy's speech hinting at this problematic memory, but she kept re-experiencing head injuries in various forms. When talking about her life, we discovered that she seemed to bang her head a lot, bumping into things all the time and that even her kids had *problems* with their heads. Extraordinarily her daughter had undergone surgery to remove a brain tumour. It seemed Wendy was always being draw back to the upsetting blow when she was six by her words, actions and those of her family. Some might say this is just coincidence but I'm getting a pretty good understanding that there are no coincidences. Also, I've seen this sort of thing with other people who have had head injuries. I hope I get a chance to work with Wendy again for another issue someday as I'm confident the blows to her head, which were so common, will have stopped now.

Those who experienced or witnessed violence, aggression or physical intimidation said things like "People are always attacking me" when they could say that someone is criticising them. I've heard them say "There's no safe topic", "I feel battered and bruised by her comments", "I was shattered" or just "I feel beaten again".

Other examples of things said by clients who experienced physical violence or have difficulty with conflict or confrontation are:

"I won't be backed into a corner or I'll come out fighting",

"I hope it doesn't cause too much pain to …",

"I'm fighting mad",

"I don't give up, I'm a survivor",

"They attacked me at work again",

"I took it on the chin",

"I'm so tired, I'm beat",

"I felt beaten to a pulp by her words",

"I have to fight for everything I get",

"Life's a struggle",

"I'm battling with this illness",

"It hasn't beaten me yet" and

"Everything has been an uphill battle for me".

A client who had a repressed traumatic experience involving a gun said "Shoot'" over and over as I asked if I could proceed with the questions during our initial consultation. I prepared myself for another tough and potentially emotional session that day.

Other comments made by people whose history involved guns in some way, either from battle in war or military conflicts (which I have learned are euphemistically called 'tours') or other incidents with guns have said the following to me:

"I was well armed for the meeting",

"I'm fully armed and ready",

"I need more ammo to battle this problem",

"He's known to shoot from the hip",

"He's a straight shooter",

"I'm glad I got shot of him",

"I'm aiming to get this done for next week",

"He's always on the attack" or "I feel everyone is attacking me" and

"That was a loaded question".

The emphasis on guns or gunfire is pronounced in their terminology, for example, I've heard "The noise was deadening" or "Shoot, I really wanted to do that" in the case when someone expressed regret because of a missed opportunity when someone else might have elected to say "Dang".

Although all of these words and phrases may be in most people's vocabulary so we can all understand the meaning or deduce what is being said, <u>why</u> they are chosen is what I feel is important. The why is significant and it is worth examining the words you choose.

Watch Your Common Words and Phrases,

So You Can Begin to 'Detox Your Language'

Find out what your common phrases or choice words are. Listen to yourself. Listen to what you say when you are really upset, irritated or sad. Also get an idea of what you say when you are very happy. Are you reserved when giving praise or words of elation? Do you reject kindness or compliments, dismissing them and discounting yourself? Do you expect that good things will always end or feel you should not brag, or can you say "Life is brilliant"?

In England I've found there are many cultural and class related phrases (representing their social group values and beliefs) that limit potential like "Pride before a fall". As an American living 11 years now in England, I am still surprised by the way some people hold themselves back, hindering themselves. No one is suppose to brag or say that they are pleased with themselves or tell another that they are great at something. It's not considered the right or polite thing to do and can be viewed as arrogance. In general they do not draw attention to their talents but down-play them or even deny them. I encourage just the opposite and work to break down these barriers to healthy, successful productivity and pride.

Once you begin to listen to what you say in different circumstances and you really hear yourself, you may be surprised. I thought about calling this book *Detox Your Language* (the title of one of my speeches) because that's part of what I'm going to be asking you to do in the coming chapters but that title wasn't grand enough. *It's Your Choice: Uncover Your Brilliance using The Iceberg Process* is about more than just eliminating some words from your mental diet, it's about the many choices you have and how you can make the most of them once you understand what your language is telling you.

Nowadays there is so much attention and excitement surrounding what we eat, with people attempting to buy free-ranged, organically grown and locally sourced sustainable food if they can fit it into their budget. Most everyone I know is concerned to some degree about what they are putting into their mouth, even my husband! You may have even read Gillian McKeith's excellent book *Your Are What You Eat* but what about what comes out of your mouth every day, lingering in your mind and thoughts? What damage could your language and internal dialogue be causing you? In my opinion and experience, what you say and think is even more important to how you feel than what you eat. It may well be the most important and decisive thing in your life as it represents the state of your powerful mind.

All the chemical free, nutritious *rabbit food* in the world won't be enough if your mind is filled with damaging memories and rubbish self-depreciating thought patterns. You will find that you automatically **detox your language** as you discover and upgrade your *iceberg programmes.*

What Do You Say When You Are Upset?

Here are some statements I've heard people say when they were describing being upset about something. Before you read my clients' statements think about what you are comfortable saying when you are mad or irritated.

"I was so irritated"…said by a person with skin irritation and chronic inflammation

"It was a real pain"………………………………...…said by a person with back pain

"I want to put it out of my mind"…………said by someone with a brain tumour

"I'm fed up"………..……………..……..said by a person struggling with weight issues

"I'm so cross"……………………...……………said by a religious church-going woman

"I'm pissed off"………………………………………....…..said by a recovering alcoholic

"I'm sick and tired of it"…………………………………………….said by an ME sufferer

"This sucks....................said by someone forced to satisfy her abuser orally

"This is overwhelming"...said by a workaholic

"It's fucking not fair............said by someone who was raped and who had frequent casual sex

"I saw red".......................................said by someone who was stabbed

"It was crazy busy"............said by an epileptic fearing he was losing his mind

"I was so mad I couldn't see straight"............said by a partially sighted person

Other poignant statements I've heard:

"I wouldn't like to rock the boat".......said by a person who lost her father in a boat accident

"It sickens me just thinking about it"...................said by an ME/CFS* Sufferer

*Myalgic Encephalopathy/Chronic Fatigue Syndrome

Now think about this, if you came upon a road closure with diversions which you knew would add twenty minutes to your journey and you were going to be late for your appointment, what would you say? "Oh, well, it'll be okay, "I'll just stop and ring", "Shit", "How irritating", "Not again! I'm so unlucky", "What a pain" or "This is madness"?

Every word you utter is a choice you have made. You frame a feeling with your selection or an unresolved issue inside you (on which you are focused) frames the phrase for you. You have an abundance of words, an array of them that you could use, so observing what you have chosen is informative and telling. Be conscious of these choices.

Even my husband, Simon was not free of my language scrutiny once I recognised the connection. His common phrases used to be "Don't worry, I'll be dead by the morning" which he said when he coughed. He also liked to say "Just what the doctor ordered" when he ate something he fancied. I heard him say "I had to sign my life away" numerous times over the years when negotiating various business agreements.

Simon's mother worked as a radiographer when he was growing up and he was used as a guinea pig whenever she or her colleagues needed to practise x-raying. He also worked as a porter in a hospital whilst putting himself through University. One of his responsibilities there was to take the dead bodies to the morgue each night (during the *graveyard shift*). During that same time his father, who was only in his late forties, was dying of Alzheimer's. Simon too had seen a lot of people die when he worked on the oil rigs in his twenties and had survived several helicopter crashes when others with him did not. My husband's words were illuminating his focus on death and dying and we had to change that! I even noticed I was saying "It's to die for" when I ate something I loved although I'm not sure where that phrase came from. Now I say purposefully, "It's gorgeous" or "It's lovely" instead. I caught myself saying "It cost an arm and a leg" the other day and realised I needed to tap on the memory of the time when my sister Stephanie came back from the hospital after having to have her leg amputated. I was only eight.

Your most common words may be telling you something. Anything that you repeat is something to investigate.

Your most common words may be informing you of some sort of fear, belief (good or bad), or insecurity or doubt and they may be telling you how you developed these as well. Anything that you repeat is something to investigate. What are your favourite phrases? Why do you use them? Did you hear it somewhere before?

The more I delve into my language and that of my clients', the evidence and consistency cannot be ignored. Your words indicate your understanding of your world and beliefs so clearly. Don't discount them, because your selection of words indicates your focus and has a direct link to your future.

Chapter 4
Language Limits in Business
Success, Achievement and Productivity

Whether it's growing your own business, reaching your sales targets, giving a high-level presentation, going for that promotion or breaking free of ME – I've found the process and principles are the same.

Sorry you high-flyers reading this book, there's no getting around it. Our limitations, I've found, revolve around unresolved issues. It's your past experiences that limit your future just like someone who has manifested or exacerbates a physical or emotional problem. Although you might be able to cope with your past experiences better than some (or at least physically better than another person) they are still there in the background, underneath, potentially acting as motivators pushing you to under-achieve, over-achieve or devaluing your true abilities.

These hidden or visible drivers in your history limit your future until you decide to not just look at them, but clear them. Stuffing, discounting, misguidedly or innocently ignoring, or stubbornly out and out refusing to address key 'character-building' events which shaped your life hampers true efficacy. Not addressing the emotional content or baggage you carry (your *luggage*) is a mistake. Overlooking any uncomfortable, even minor undesirable yet pivotal events can only go on for so long until you feel restrained by them. If you are already a shining star in your corporation or industry, just think how productive or successful you could be if you put down the backpack of heavy or prickly memories.

Many of us have adopted the attitude that our emotional bumps and bruises have helped to create who we are today. Accepting that they were important to us even if uncomfortable or disturbing. In some way all the little or big things that happened in our lives have helped us achieve or develop many positive aptitudes including resilience, independence and flexibility.

I agree with this. If it were not for my strong personality-forming life, I certainly wouldn't be writing this book and wouldn't be an American living in England. (I have dual citizenship but originally I'm from the west coast of the USA). So, I'm definitely not diminishing the invaluable lessons of my life nor yours. There's a strength offered and gained through experience and survival, however these same experiences form or contribute to our beliefs and expectations. Often this is exhibited and viewed in successful people as a good thing but sometimes it shows or acts as a double-edged sword. You may be highly compensated in your career yet your personal life is non-existent, or you may just get-by but feel sick in your stomach when you have to negotiate that big deal. I discuss how our beliefs and expectations influence our experience in Chapter 11.

Signs that it might be useful to seek out and find your own *icebergs* in business situations (or otherwise) are repeated lost deals, repeated or constant encounters with difficult or abusive clients or managers, getting fired, bullied or bullying, nervousness or outright panic about speaking in meetings or to groups, fear of flying or driving limiting your territory, difficulty thinking on your feet or confusion when put on the spot in a meeting or presentation, disorganisation, lack of efficiency (with or without an excuse), stalling, avoidance or general procrastination.

If you have difficulty with any of the habits or issues I've mentioned or experience other recurring patterns like being late, not reaching your revenue or sales targets or not setting goals for yourself (I discuss fear of failure, fear of success and fear of change in Chapter 16) then it's likely that you have an *iceberg* or two of your own which you need to demolish or melt!

I remember when I used to do a lot of high-level (or at least high value) presentations when I was in telecommunications long before I knew anything about tapping. I would always break into a slight sweat and begin to shake when I initially started my presentation. It didn't last long but it always happened, even if I was just introducing myself whilst sat down around a conference table. Yet, it never happened when I greeted people standing up and I had always thought that odd.

I discovered that my response was linked to something that had happened when I was in the fourth grade (that's equivalent to being in junior school in the UK. I was nine years old). My teacher called upon me to read out loud to the class just as I was determinedly and swiftly applying pressure onto a stapler to bind my assignment together. Startled, my fingers slipped under the high capacity stapler head and as I stood up to read I forced the staple straight through the index and middle fingers of my other hand. The thick staple not only penetrated my fingers but it went roughly all the way through my two nails to the fleshy underside of my finger tips.

I already dreaded reading out loud because I was so slow and struggled with getting the words right but this was the worst. My mother had worked with me patiently each evening that previous week having me read my textbook and homework to her but all our preparation could not offset the excruciating pain I felt as I read my well rehearsed assignment to the class. As I spoke the words my hands shook severely and I forced myself to hold back my tears. After I'd finished I tried to pull the staple out of my fingers without anyone noticing as blood dripped onto my desk. I wasn't meant to be rereading or stapling my assignment in class, I was supposed to be ready and listening to the others read but I had been so afraid that I'd mess up in front of everyone with my poor reading ability that I had been rereading and rereading my homework so if I were unlucky enough to be called upon I could do it confidently. Just when I felt ready and I decided to staple my work together so it'd be all set to be handed in, I was asked to read. Needless to say I didn't tell anyone what I'd done.

One day, in my forties, before a group business brainstorming meeting, I sensed a growing nervousness inside me and I decided I should tap on it (use EFT to relieve it). I quickly recalled this *stapler event* from when I was only nine and neutralised it. I couldn't believe this had been the reason for all that difficulty for so many years but it had been and as I tapped on the memory that had surfaced my nerves settled down and I broke into a sweat one last time and then it was gone, for good.

The easiest ways to find *icebergs* in business people or others:

1) Listen to your words, thoughts, comments or criticisms of yourself or others. The clues to limiting beliefs or history is not always directed at yourself, they can be conveniently masquerading as critical thoughts, superiority and unwavering high standards or perfectionism. Classic examples are: "Don't be so stupid", "Don't be ridiculous", "It won't work", "I can't be bothered", "Maybe they won't like my idea", "Nothing ever goes right" and "What if…"

2) Evaluate your language for any negative connotations, poor outcomes (expectations), doubt, and unreasonable demands. Phrases like these are not as innocent as they appear and may be reducing or sabotaging your chances of success: "I don't know if he'll like it", "My idea isn't good enough", "She's so boring and unoriginal", "They'll find out I'm an imposter", "Why would they listen to me, after all I didn't study business in school".

3) Create a timeline of events in your life or business career. Include all the things that you wish hadn't happened to you or that didn't go as you would have liked. Include things you would change if you could or things that support your doubts, destructive or non-constructive habits or traits. Determine how you felt about those things which happened to you or those things that you did. For example, what were the dominant emotions connected to these events? Were you embarrassed, sad, letdown, mad at yourself or someone else, did you feel shame or guilt? What did you feel, and why?

4) Decidedly force yourself to go all the way back in your history and add

onto the timeline other periods in your life when you were also letdown, disappointed, felt stupid or failed, or were scared etc. Find all events when you felt similar feelings to your current unwanted patterns. For example if you feel embarrassed or guilty when you have procrastinated find other times in your life when you felt embarrassed or guilty. If you feel worthless when no one asks for your ideas or unworthy to chime in during a brainstorming session or you feel stupid rather than clever when you have to approach a partner, particular gender, title or personality type – ask yourself when was the first time or other times when you felt this way. Could it have been when you failed your first Kent test, froze up in your French or Chemistry exams, GCSE or A Levels, dropped out of high school, got caught skipping or bunking off school and received the belt from your mum or dad, or when you threw up in front of your classmates on a fieldtrip when you were seven?

I've found that no matter what your personal limitation is – it is linked to a belief you've taken on board or an emotion you subconsciously are trying to avoid. Your beliefs and hidden expectations are often interchangeable.

When you feel confusion in the workplace or with a colleague (or even a relationship for that matter) you can find yourself pushed into your 'dog brain' which has limited speech and cognitive function. Although 'dog brain' is not a true technical or biological term, it is so descriptive in the picture it conjures up and easy to identify with that I love using this phrase to explain what happens to many. Your brain is made of different parts dedicated to particular functions. Regular cognitive abilities including decision making, logical negotiation and complex thought is impaired by strong disabling emotions. The intelligent part of your brain, capable of unimaginable computations and commands goes off-line and the primitive reptilian brain often called the 'dog brain' takes over. When a current experience reminds you at some level of a tragedy or scary moment in your life this emotional association or link can cause you to regress and lose cognitive capabilities, especially speech.

Working with people in the United Kingdom (England, Scotland, Ireland, Wales and Northern Ireland) I've seen a deep-rooted desire to repress, ignore and minimise the significance of events in their lives. Additionally if I can stereotype for a moment, although of course there are exceptions many British do not like to show weakness ('stiff upper lip, and all that') and often choose not to express emotions that show sensitivity or vulnerability. Don't get me wrong, they feel them but they hold back and often replace them with another emotion like feelings of disappointment (being letdown) or even anger. I've heard many of my clients say they learned it was unacceptable or better not to show how they really felt for many societal reasons. School seemed to be the number one reason (certainly for those who attended 'public' school which in America would be referred to as private school) along with their parents' expectations. I wonder sometimes if it has a lot to do with having wars on your soil. People 'just get on with it' when things are tough saying "What's the fuss" and "Don't be so stupid, I'm fine". Maybe these are the common mantras of a people who refused to allow fear to creep in and take over when the nightly air raids hit London in the 1940's. So I have immense respect for some of the distancing and coping strategies used but the body nevertheless hangs onto unresolved emotions and traumas and these can cause all sorts of problems when left to their own devices.

England also is filled with a mixture of nationalities owing to its membership of the European Union which for a while now has allowed open migration for all in the EU. Additionally, because of the benefit system including nationally funded healthcare, many risk their lives to come to the UK. I've been privileged to work with people from Poland, Germany, Romania, Czech Republic and France as well as Africans, South Africans and other nationalities each having their own social norms and taboos when it comes to emotions.

Whenever you try or succeed in one way or another to lock your emotions in a compartment or box or bury them deep within you deciding never to look at them again, they are actually still there inflicting an undercurrent of anxiety and damage tarnishing your sparkle. I want you to uncover your true brilliance. Release the limiting memories, emotions and beliefs to allow you to reach your greatest success without struggle or discomfort.

I often see 'successful' business people who aren't as successful, confident or consistent in actuality as they would wish. They may appear totally functional but are not always comfortable with how hard they have to work or what they see unfolding in their professional or personal lives. Sometimes they come to me because they've found themselves burdened with a large debt or money owed to them. They want change. They are capable of great things but haven't been able to find the missing piece of their own puzzle; their internal conflicts causing issues and stubborn patterns.

When I work with business professionals I've found the sessions to be quite extraordinary and they could be best described as rapidly transformational. It's as if they were ripe and ready by the time they found me. We clear their blocks so quickly, covering so much ground that our heads sometimes feel like they're spinning and muzzy. We both feel dazed! This experience is not exclusive to professional people however it happens often at this pace with highly success-ful motivated people. I think this is because they are usually very practised and competent at decision making. They often have a keen awareness of their own self-exposed limitations and have attempted to fix them already, sometimes many times. Additionally if I present an 'odd' yet effective strategy option to them to break an outdated detrimental habit, they normally don't care what it is I ask them to do, they'll do it if I feel it will work for them. High achievers are frequently easy to work with (but not always!) as they actually seem to like hitting their *icebergs* head on, hard and fast versus dancing around, or dipping their toe in to test the water. They just go for it, unlike some who are unwilling to face their *icebergs* or own up to them.

Another big difference is that they aren't sick or ill. Although they may be hindered physically or emotionally, they have not become physically disabled by their problems. They're looking for improvement or identification of what's in their way versus survival. Once we isolate their issues, it can be kind of a 'wham, bam, thank you mam' experience as they used to say in the States as we find the root of the issues (also the solutions) and clear the *icebergs* in record time.

I love working with people who truly want change and are willing to delve into their foundation (business people or not). This is often uncharted or forgotten territory with me acting as their guide to clear the way for a brilliant future. We must clear the past to open unrestricted opportunities. It's always the same for everyone.

In the following chapters I will share with you many ideas and actual techniques that anyone that wants real change can use. It doesn't matter if you are a managing director, a veteran, a university student or professor, a novice sales representative or a chronic rheumatoid arthritis sufferer unable to get out of bed some days. If you'll give me your ear and your mind, I'm confident you'll benefit from the tools being offered in this book. This stuff really works if you are willing to give it a chance.

Chapter 5
A Bit about NLP and Submodalities

In NLP, Neuro-linguistic Programming, a therapeutic coaching and coun-selling method, language is used as a powerful persuasive tool for change. Anthony Robbins is a keen user of NLP as well as Paul Mckenna the famous hypnotherapist. EFT and Meridian Tapping Techniques (MTT) incorporate many of the primary principles of NLP.

The creators of NLP, Richard Bandler and John Grinder observed psychol-ogy and hypnosis and took it to a new level. They investigated why some thera-pists had better results than others (specifically Perls, Satir and Erickson) and realised that most psychologists spent the majority of their time studying mental illness by modelling mentally ill people whilst these three did the opposite.

Grinder and Bandler came to believe that studying highly effective people, successful people, people at the top of their field and those who were able to handle life's stresses with ease would give them a healthy mind model. Instead of applying potentially distorted information and principles of how the mind works when it is ill, (those derived from unhealthy mental patterning), they went about modelling achievers and applying their valuable thinking strategies.

Modern energy psychology or positive psychology techniques like MTT, EFT, NLP, Kinesiology and Thought Field Therapy (TFT) etc. embrace the concept that the mind is working perfectly if you have an understanding of its model of the world, subconscious patterning, motivation, beliefs or intention.

Grinder was a linguistics professor at the University of California at Santa Cruz when Bandler met him. Bandler was a mathematics student. Together they founded NLP. They began modelling the effectiveness of the language patterns used in therapy by Fritz Perls, the founder of Gestalt therapy, Virgina Satir, a successful family therapist and hypnotherapist Milton H. Erickson.

Richard Bandler's later work in the field of NLP focused around this aspect he coined as submodalities which are subtle sensory perceptions and distinctions of our internal representation of an event or memory. Bandler realised that the way a person spoke told you a lot about how they learned, processed and understood information. In general, submodalities in NLP involve our sensory perceptions of our experiences.

He realised that individuals made a distinction in the form of language indicating which sense they felt most comfortable with and used this sense to derive their perception of an experience. He found that, if you determined what sensory sub-categories or submodalities a person used when speaking, you could use the same submodality to encourage a change in them.

The submodalities included visual (sight, images, colours, spatial, movement, distance), auditory (sound, voice, volume and other qualities of sound like pace and intensity), kinaesthetic (breathing rate, temperature, somatic feelings in the body), and olfactory or gustatory (taste or smell, fragrance, sweet, bitter etc).

In NLP observing your sensory style of language tells the practitioner the submodality you use in organising your thoughts and feelings and evaluation of the world around you. They then use your preferred submodality in their own speech to build comfort, rapport and instigate change in you. Using your submodality they can make a greater and quicker impact on you as this is how you order or categorise experiences in your mind.

For example, if an NLP therapist determines that the person they are working with is a visual person they would match their language by using words like "You could see he was never going to understand you" instead of potentially saying "You felt he'd never understand" or "When you caught sight of where the conversation was going you must have felt shock", or simply "I see what you mean". If your client were auditory, you may choose phrases like "I hear what you are saying" or when in hypnosis or visualisations you may suggest that the volume of the sirens be turned down or even silenced.

Matching submodalities in therapy removes a further barrier to building rapport, creates a more comfortable environment for the client and can aid you in changing perception. However, my experiences reveal that the importance of the words we choose goes far beyond this.

The words we choose goes beyond explaining whether we are an auditory, visual or kinaesthetic type of person and building rapport.

My findings show there is much more to what we say and how we say it. It goes beyond explaining your primary way of expressing and contacting your memories and feelings. It goes beyond explaining if you are a feeling person, auditory, visual, and gustatory/olfactory or a blend of these and all that that implies. The words you use tell a much deeper story. They hint at what lies in your subconscious so I've learned to take particular notice of any repetitious words and phrases.

My observations have shown that there is further information lingering behind or below the words people select. There is a reason for the specific words. These words tell me more than just how to phrase my sentences, form my language and hypnotic suggestions, or what words I could use to help them.

Their choice of words helps me not only understand that they may be a deeply sensitive kinaesthetic person, they provide me with an appreciation and realisation of their life experiences, perception and expectations.

Evaluating and thereby truly hearing what someone is telling me, not just saying through their words, has been an eye opener, or if you'll allow me to say it, *a mind opener*.

Chapter 6
What You Choose to Say about Yourself
The Internal Critic

Now that you've heard some examples of how the words, adjectives or phrases my clients selected were tainted by their past experiences let's consider what you say about yourself. How do your words impact on you or reflect your reality (past or future)?

Whether you say something out loud or in your head, it has an effect on you. Often it shows what you really think or believe about yourself.

The words you say in your head can be even more destructive (or supportive) than any others. They have the ability to enable or disable you. They can keep you from trying new things, from achieving or prone to being a workaholic or perfectionist and contribute to depression or happiness. The results can be at either end of the spectrum depending on the risk or danger you perceive around you or how talented or worthless you feel you are.

Like the phrases you select to use in everyday conversation, the phrases and comments you say to yourself usually follow a theme.

I suspect your inner voice, often referred to as *your internal critic*, is even more powerful, controlling, damaging or encouraging than your audibly spoken word. *The internal critic* in your head or how you feel inside has the overriding veto, the power and the final say.

So what do I mean when I say "what you say about yourself"? I'm talking about how you talk about you to yourself; the conversation you have with yourself in your head (your internal dialogue). This is also referred to as *self-talk*. This includes what you believe is true about you; your worth, your abilities, your honour, how good or bad or how lovable or disgusting you believe you are and what you think you are capable of or what limitations you place on yourself. Is it safe to go outside? Are you trustworthy and decent? Or do you believe you are a bore or "too ugly for words"?

Your self-confidence or self-esteem is critical to your mental and physical health as your internal beliefs are reflected in your physical being and world.

In Transactional Analysis lingo, a form of counselling therapy, your sense of self is referred to a sense of okay-ness, whether you feel you are okay or not. This measure of okay-ness is about believing you are safe, loved, important, or worthwhile or not. In the classic groundbreaking psychology book *I'm Ok-You're Ok* by Dr Thomas Harris, he asserted that every child determines they are **not okay** by approximately five years old. This decision is based on their perceptions during these very early dependent years and they've evaluated and recorded (*taped*) all the experiences during this time for later reference.

In *The Road Less Travelled,* M. Scott Peck refers to this feeling of okayness as an internal sense of value. A child comes to understand if they are valuable and loved or not.

In the first years of your life, when you are totally reliant on your parents or guardians to feed you, keep you safe, warm and comfortable, you also need them to pay attention to you so you grow and gain abilities and communication skills. Conditional love (an "I'm not okay" or maybe I should call it an "I'm not okay unless" belief) and feelings of value apparently naturally occur during this period to varying degrees based on the response you receive from others to your needs. Again Harris believes that every child by the age of five deduces "I'm not okay" to some extent. Thus he believes having a totally happy childhood doesn't really exist for anyone and that we all come away with some sort of concern or doubt about ourselves that needs strengthening through our development.

This perceived sense of being not okay can shape the dependent areas of your life until you choose to question the appropriateness and make the effort to change.

If you are not cared for in a loving, attentive way, you may develop a strong belief that something is wrong with you. You are unworthy, bad or terrible, hence definitely *not okay*. The perceptions *of I'm not okay* or *I'm ok* have four options according to Harris: (1) *I'm not okay, you're okay,* (2) *I'm okay, you're not okay,* (3) *I'm okay, you're okay* or (4) *I'm not okay and you're not okay.* These comparisons or conclusions about yourself in certain types of situations can stay with you until you challenge them, otherwise you may live your life, making decisions and actions based on your early foundational years and never really grow up.

Although, apparently, you may continue to modify your rating of *okay-ness* as you experience life's enriching, inspiring or stressful events much of your basis of who you are or who you allow yourself to be is already carved out for you. It was built way back when you were very dependent on others.

Some of the more challenging cases I have worked with were those of people whose distress or upset was pre-verbal. Sadly often people have experienced difficulty from the very start of their lives. So it's no wonder they may have negative attitudes or ideas about themselves and their potential. Depending on spiritual or religious beliefs, perhaps we enter this life with accumulated history too.

The words you say (beliefs you hold) about yourself might sound like:

"I'm unlovable" or "No one will love me"

"I'm not important"

"I'm disgusting"

"I'm worthless" or "I'm crap"

"Everyone hates me and will leave me"

"I'm shameful"

"I'm fat"

"I can't do that" or "I'm not capable"

"I'm too stupid"

"I'm lazy"

"I'm gross"

"I'm boring"

"I'll always be alone" or "No one will have me"

"I don't deserve happiness"

If you are one of the lucky few or you have spent a lot of effort reconditioning your mind and beliefs, it might sound like:

"I can do it"

"I am valuable"

"I can do anything, all is possible"

"I'm okay"

"I'm safe"

"I'm lovable"

"I'm wonderful"

"I'm caring"

"I'm intelligent"

"I'm attractive"

"I'm interesting"

"It's easy"

Affirmations

For twenty years now, I've been an advocate of using affirmations. Affirmations are positive statements about yourself or your life. They are said in the first person and present tense as if you already believe them or have this aspect in your life (similar to steps in the Law of Attraction). Some examples might be to say "I am rich beyond measure", "I have a loving respectful relationship" and "My life is worthwhile". The classic affirmation you may have heard before is "Every day in every way my life is getting better and better".

Affirmations are intended to help correct inappropriate or destructive beliefs you may have about yourself and help create a sense of well-being as well as a more desirable life. I was introduced to them by a wonderful counsellor, Barbara Dennard in 1989, and they can be a valuable tool for those who will use them.

People are usually pro affirmations or against them. Some people believe in affirmations whilst others firmly assert they do not work for them. For many the problem with affirmations seems to be that the positive statement (that which they say they desire) is so very different from the current belief they hold. The divide is just too great. The reality is too far removed from the desired goal so that the affirmation statement simply seems ridiculous. The discrepancy may cause people to discontinue saying a particular affirmation or be strong enough to cause a reluctance to use them entirely.

Let me give you an example why some people may have gone off affirmations. Let's say you currently believe you are unlovable and you've been instructed to say to yourself "I love myself", "I'm great" or "I'm worth loving" even though you simply don't believe it. I've found that if you don't believe the statement at all, rather than having no effect on you it almost reinforces the original negative belief.

If you persevere with an affirmation statement, it can eventually erode and replace a negative or limited belief but sometimes you might give up before this transition takes place. If you start small and take steps to the desired feeling you may have more success. You can say "Someday I hope I'll be able to love myself" or "I choose to allow myself to begin believing I'm worth loving". Pick a statement that you can say without any feedback from your mind. Design a phrase approaching what you'd like to feel about yourself but which your mind, *your internal critic*, doesn't contradict and say "I don't believe that" or "No way is that true" in response to it. Then as you practise using this modified affirmation and get comfortable with it, you can improve on the statement until you reach your goal.

Now to be more productive or make it faster to be able to achieve a better belief or feeling about yourself I encourage you to use tapping with your affirmative statements. When you combine tapping techniques with an affirmation you can make noticeable transitions very quickly. The tapping helps reduce the negative feelings you have for yourself and allows you to migrate to a more positive belief more easily. (Later in this chapter you will find helpful advice on how to create positive and useable affirmations and instructions on how to tap can be found in Chapter 20.)

Some people say that it takes 21 days to change a habit and thus 21 days to start to believe an affirmation. I don't know exactly what it is about 21 days (maybe it's to do with building a new neural network in the brain, see Chapter 18 or to do with biorhythms) however 21 day cycles appear to be used in many religious and healing practises. Whatever and regardless of the reason, I've found that some beliefs can be very difficult to shift and require further investigation and diligence. It may take more than using affirmations alone to release. If you've wrestled with fear or less than generous beliefs about yourself all your life, you can accept it may take a bit of practise to recondition your mind away from that long-held belief and destructive self-talk. Consistency and persistence are important to retraining and reconditioning your mind.

It's beneficial that when you begin helping yourself that you or your therapist or coach become aware of what you believe about yourself. Listening to your self-talk can go a long way and give you a head start in uncovering and recognising your beliefs. Many have not even acknowledged that they have self-talk, mind chatter or an internal dialogue going on in their head at all, or if they have, they haven't tried to change it, negotiate with it, or improve it. They've often just agreed with it and gone along with it for decades.

Observing or noticing your comments is essential.

Awareness is the first step! Often when I ask clients what they say to themselves about themselves, they look at me blankly. I haven't decided if it's because they think I can read their minds or if they feel they've been caught doing something naughty. Actually I think it's more that they really have been unaware of their personal conversations, corrections, directions and self-monitoring, or at least unaware of the importance of it or that they could or should change it.

Usually I need to give them examples or prompting. I ask "Do you say 'I'm stupid', 'I'm ugly', 'I shouldn't contradict my husband', 'I'm worthless', 'It's not important how I feel' or 'It's not safe here'?" Then their heads start nodding up and down as it sinks in and they get it.

I ask people to identify the statements they say about themselves right then and over the coming weeks so we can review them the next time we are together. Their statements usually follow a theme. They may be all about their lack of intelligence for example or feeling they are unattractive or not important. In my experience most people have one or two main themes to their life and self-talk (self-abuse) but they can have more.

Their self-talk themes indicate their beliefs about themselves, the world around them and their possibilities.

What if you aren't talking to yourself negatively?

What if you are not aware of talking to yourself at all and you haven't heard a little voice in your head condemning or supporting you? I've also had clients say they hear their mother's or father's voice in their head chastising them but not their own voice!

If you don't hear an inner voice or commentary after paying attention for a few days, then you can observe how you feel. It's important to note that frequently there is self-criticism going on however you are so used to it that you don't even notice it. It can be subtle too. It can be a grumble or a look. It could be a sarcastic comment or a sneer when you look at yourself in a mirror. It might not be heard but felt or acted out.

Sometimes you may notice that you actually say negative things about yourself to others rather than criticising yourself in your head, you do it out loud. There are those who tell people exactly what they feel about themselves. You may be one of those who tell their friends how terrible you believe you are! You might mutter or pronounce "I'm such an idiot" expecting others to agree with you.

With practise you may observe your internal or external dialogue allowing you to easily spot how you view yourself. If not, there are other ways as a conscious thought is not always discernable because you function mostly from your subconscious. You may just have a feeling. You may feel a particular emotion. You may feel down, angry, embarrassed, uncomfortable, excited or sad. You may have a sensation in a part of your body. It could be tightness in your chest, a pain in your back, butterflies in your stomach or an odd feeling or awareness in your gut. More often than not, both the feeling and the thought are present but the thought happens so quickly it is not always observed. So listen to your feelings. Whatever it is, take notice. This is your voice; the body is talking to you. How you feel is your primary indicator.

We sense, evaluate and perceive our surroundings so rapidly that we simply respond without total conscious awareness. Assessing the environment and determining your subsequent behaviour comes through your feelings, through your nervous system. You may not be aware of having any thoughts at all and your nervous system and mind's conclusions may never be consciously articulated, but there will be a feeling, or a change in how you are feeling that you can distinguish.

Whether you have an *internal critic* or voice in your head doesn't matter because it's about how you feel anyway. What is important is that we begin to recognise what we are feeling. The feeling may be easy to identify or it may be confusing. Often highly sensitive people and those who have succumbed to illness have ignored their feelings for a very long time.

Start to notice how you feel, as negative feelings should be corrected with an affirmation or cognitive counter-statement.

In Cognitive Behavioural Therapy (or Cognitive Therapy), it is believed that the thought always comes before the feeling but if you only notice the feeling that's okay. Our bodies respond so quickly to a thought that we are talking about a tiny infinitesimal amount of time between the two things occurring anyway. The theory is not what's important here.

**'All that we are
is the result of what we have thought.
The mind is everything.
What we think, we become.'**

Buddha

Therefore, I teach people to use their counter-statements or affirmations when they *feel* bad as well, not just when they catch themselves talking poorly about themselves but when they feel uncomfortable, weak or are in pain. Especially when the feeling is one of anxiousness, it's important to attempt to reassure yourself by saying "I'm safe", "I'm okay" or "All is fine".

'I'm safe', 'I'm okay' and 'All is fine'

Creating Affirmations or Counter-Statements to Replace Negative Self-talk or Feelings

So let's try it. Let's design your affirmations or positive counter-statements. Take a look at what you discovered that you say about yourself negatively or what your feelings indicate you believe.

In an affirmation to counter negative thoughts or feelings, you want to create a positive statement that is the opposite of your negative statement or feeling. Remember useful affirmations should be in the positive form using no negative words. What I mean by this is that you do not say "I'm not a mean person" to counter the belief "I'm a mean person". You should never use any form of the word "not" in an affirmation.

State your affirmation in the first person ("I"). Make it current or in the present tense. Do not put it in the future tense if at all possible. The statement should be phrased as if it is in the here and now. For example a good affirmation would be saying something like "I am clever" rather than "I will be clever someday". Use the best possible declaration you can to counter your negativity.

I want to emphasise that your phrase must not be conditional. So often our beliefs depend on something else but a good affirmation is not dependent on anything. It should be able to stand alone. For example, you should not say "I will be lovable when I lose 20 pounds". You should say "I am lovable" and "I weigh x" or "I'm lovable just the way I am right now" and "I am at my desired weight".

Now, perhaps differently than what you may have learned before when creating affirmations I would like you to make the words of your affirmations believable.

If you are used to saying to yourself "I'm ugly", you might decide the opposite of ugly is beautiful but you may not believe you could ever be considered beautiful, so maybe it would be better to create your counter-phrase as "I'm attractive" or if attractive is still too hard to say, you may choose to say simply "I'm okay". By doing this you will feel more honest with yourself and will be more likely to actually say the affirmations.

The most common mistake people make when using countering affirmations is to use a negative to correct their statements. I've even had many clients tell me their qualified CBT (Cognitive Behavioural Therapy) counsellors in the UK have instructed them to say things like "I'm not going to get hurt", "I won't die", "There's no danger" or "I'm not ugly". For someone with an anxiety problem, instructing them to say "I won't die" or "I'm not going to crash" over and over is still focusing them on potential danger. Although I know they are attempting to get their clients to think rationally, it is not reassuring enough, nor helpful enough, in the long run. It may help some but it may also just reinforce their fear and stop short of clearing their worry.

Many years ago I read somewhere that the subconscious mind did not recognise the negative qualifier. Meaning the mind did not pick up the subtleness of your statement "I'm **not** in danger" and interpreted it as "I'm in danger". With an affirmation or counter-statement we want to shift the focus totally away from danger to safety. So, it seems wiser and has proven to be much more effective to have clients say, "I'm safe" "I'm safe" "I'm safe" versus "I won't die". I think there's a big difference!

Another strategy that appears prevalent in CBT (especially in England) is to evaluate how rational your irrational thoughts and fears are. This too I feel is not very effective. I have had clients say that they know their fears are out of control and proportion but that's how they are feeling. Knowing it's irrational almost makes them feel worse about themselves. They need effective strategies to assist them when they are irrational.

Effective affirmations and correctly formed counter-statements are one of the keys to successful cognitive work and sometimes all that is needed to improve your situation.

Whether you call it; CBT (Cognitive Behavioural Therapy) or CT (Cognitive Therapy), the Law of Attraction, Positive Thinking, manifesting, affirmations or counter-statements, I don't care. Just do it. Listen to your thoughts and change those that need correcting or improving. Start paying attention and start replacing your negative or limiting feelings or words with more positive affirmations. Practise 'good mental hygiene' as I call it and do not allow even one negative thought or statement to go un-countered.

Examples of replacement phrases which can be used as affirmations:

Current Negative Statement Disabling or Faulty Belief	Possible Positive Supportive Counter-Statement
"I'm stupid" or "I've always been stupid"	"I'm intelligent"
	"I'm capable"
	"I'm smart"
	"I'm clever"
	"I'm just learning"
	"This is the first time I've done this. I'll get better at it"
	"I choose to see my talents and intelligence"
	"I allow myself to believe I'm smart" or "I'm okay"
"I'm unlovable" or "No one will ever love me"	"I can love myself"
	"I deserve love"
	"It's okay and safe to feel loved"
	"I'm lovable"*
	"I choose to start thinking I'm worthy of love even though I'm not used to it"
	"I will allow myself to begin feeling lovable"
	"Everyone, including me, deserves love"
"I'm sickening"	"I'm okay"
	"It wasn't my fault, I'm well and okay"
	"No, I'm fine just the way I am"
"I'm disgusting"	"Everyone has value"
	"I'm okay"
	"I forgive myself and choose to learn to admire myself"
	"No, I choose to stop putting myself down, I am appealing"
	"No, just because disgusting things have happened to me, I'm a nice person and worthwhile"

*Note: See Chapter 20, How to Tap, for help with disabling this and other limiting or faulty beliefs. Examples of effective tapping statements for correcting a feeling of being unlovable might be: "Even though my mother didn't give me the love I needed, I will someday deeply and completely love and accept myself" or "Even though my mother left me when I was born without good reason, every baby is worth loving, even me, and I can decide to forgive her and accept myself".

Remember never use a negative if at all possible when creating affirmations. If in doubt you can use the catch-all phrase of "I'm okay". You may find it effective to say immediately "No" or "Stop" firmly when you observe your self-abuse to interrupt your pattern, followed by "I'm okay" or your appropriate affirming counter-statement. So instead of sitting with a feeling or thought of "I'm worthless", you recognise you have thought or felt it and then you say "No, I have value!", "Nope, I'm important" or "Stop now, I refuse to think this way, I have worth". In hypnosis or NLP it is sometimes recommended that you use the words "Stop. Cancel" followed by your chosen supportive replacement statement.

Be prepared with statements to counter your common negative or fearful well rehearsed statements.

"Our biggest battle is with ourselves. Our biggest battle is with the enemy that resides within us. We are attacking ourselves more often than there is real danger from outside of us. Our biggest battle is with the mind..."

I ask my clients to keep a list of all the negative things they say about themselves for at least a week. It can be very surprising to see how pervasive self-abuse can be. We are constantly feeling or talking to ourselves and judging and measuring our experience against our beliefs. We are continually taking in information, making adjustments and inferences impacting our reality. We are always making judgements in our heads or body. We are dynamic by nature.

Record all the negative things you say about yourself for a week.

Next week I suggest that you make the effort to listen and record your self-talk, jotting down all the negative things you say about yourself. Once you do this you will have an idea of what you need to work on and combat.

What about criticising others?

I have encountered people who did not say negative things about themselves but were extremely critical about other people. They levied constant criticism or sarcasm on friends, family and anyone else who got in their way. Seeing behaviour or attributes in others which you disapprove of or frown upon is another means of being negative. Although it is not apparent that it is affecting you, the negative statements said or thought about others still have an impact. Just because you don't say it about yourself does not mean that you have not modified your behaviour or are not limiting yourself because of some internally held belief.

Stopping negative talk can be a life time commitment or a simple quick retraining. In my experience, persistence pays off. Once you've noted the negative statements you *like to use* and have written your corrective counter affirmations, you need to put them into action.

I recommend that my clients try to correct every occurrence of their negative words or phrases. "Don't let even one get away" is my strategy and advice.

Each time you hear yourself saying or thinking one of them, stop it by saying "No!" and then say your positive counter-statement.

So it goes like this - you catch yourself saying "I'm so stupid", you acknowledge you said it and then you say, "No, I'm okay" or "No, I'm just as intelligent and quick as everyone else", "No, I choose to believe I'm smart and capable" or "I'm clever".

Be careful not to say any further put-downs when you catch yourself. Some people have been known to say to themselves, "Damn, there I go again. I'll never learn, I can't even do this right, I must really be stupid". Do not further criticise yourself when you start observing your patterns of self-talk. We want to change it and to do that we first must be aware of it. Even if the realisation of the number of times you criticise yourself is startling, praise yourself for catching it and becoming aware. Awareness is critical to change and growth.

What if you see something bad instead of say negative things?

Some people are fabulous at visualising. Rather than saying things or feeling negative about themselves, they see or imagine bad or dangerous things occurring in their mind. What you see or imagine is very powerful. These visions can be handled in the same way as addressing negative non-supportive statements or feelings. First recognise that you are imagining disturbing occurrences, consider the types of images you repeat in your head, and then design a positive or comforting counter-image and statement to use as a replacement.

Then when it happens next, quickly stop the vision by saying "No" or "Stop" followed by an affirmation that is suitable. It might be "No. I'm safe" or "Stop. Everything is okay" and then add in a new pleasant scene to replace the bad image.

An easy way to change a negative image is to recall vividly a beautiful scene from a pleasant holiday or to remember holding your child as a baby. Whatever pleasant memory you can conjure up can be used to replace the *bad* scene. Think about a time in your life when you were truly happy and use this pictorial memory. If you don't have a pleasant memory or can't remember one, then find a pleasant picture of a scene in nature like the ocean surf or a sunset and use this. Just as you create your affirmation statements in advance, I ask my clients to have a picture of a memory ready so they can access it quickly. If you are someone who visualises troubling or unsettling scenes, you already know what they are like and about (the themes), and you can design a replacement phrase and image before it happens again.

What if you moan or make noises?

Sometimes a negative expression is not expressed in actual words or by an image but by a noise or a glance. We all know a person who 'tuts' in disapproval or a person that audibly moans, groans or sighs when angry, nervous or upset. This has meaning to them and an impact on you depending on how you perceive it as well. So if you are a person who sighs, decide what it means to you then create an affirmation to offset it. Or if you don't know why you are doing it but you are uncomfortable when it happens, answer it with a "No, I'm okay" or an "I can relax, everything is okay" reinforcing statement.

A lovely friend of mine began making what she described as a 'binging' sound around the house after tapping had helped her to relieve some of her regrets and doubt after a near-death experience. She is often heard going about the house making this lovely, happy and uplifting sound.

So if you make sounds or grimaces, investigate what they mean to you. If they represent a positive feeling, by all means continue this activity but if they have an air of danger, worry, angst or disdain replace them with safe reassuring comments or statements of acceptance to yourself.

Whatever you do to undermine or support yourself, whether you talk to yourself, see things, grumble or criticise others, it's the intent and the beliefs behind the expression that is important to understand. It's the feeling behind your action or thought which you need to evaluate. Use how you feel as your guide.

Chapter 7
Thoughts & Emotions are Energy
Vibration Matches Perception

It may seem to you that it's simply your style to use certain words frequently or repetitively and you may believe it unnecessary to change them. However, words and thoughts have energy and immediate consequences as your body and the life around you responds to them.

Energy emanates from your every thought and perception of your environment. This energy then directly influences your body, your reality. There are instantaneous as well as a long-term affects to how or what you are thinking (saying), feeling and perceiving within your mind and body.

Your sensing (perception) of the current or future experience is modifying your experience within it.

Perception takes into account what's happening around and within you. Even more accurately, perception is what you believe is happening around you. You also **sense** the current or immediate future experience through comparison of your past.

What you think or feel about anything is derived from an integration of what your sense organs pick up and your own history and ancestral legacy. Therefore, our perception is uniquely ours. It is our very own interpretation based on all the information at hand at a conscious and subconscious level including that of our past.

Your mind and body extrapolates at amazing speed and decides how best to respond to the circumstances. It promptly references your memory bank, any similar events or associations and deeper instincts bringing you to a conclusion; a feeling, a sense, a thought, a knowing, followed or led by an appropriate response in your body. In short, your perception is what you subjectively understand about your current experience or situation. It is the meaning YOU personally attach to it. The meaning you intuit individually.

Everyone's perception is unique. Therefore everyone's reality of the same given moment will differ from everyone else's.

Vibration Matches Perception

Earlier in this book I discussed the importance of your vibration. Well your vibration matches your perception. It is indicative of your perception or interpretation of your circumstances, yourself, and your future.

Vibration and perception are interlinked or you might say one is dependent on the other. What you think is going on in any particular moment, whether correct or not, will alter your energy. Leading experts in modern medicine and science explain how our body responds to our perceptions and creates the world around us.

We Really Do Create Our Reality - It's Proven!

In quantum physics it has been proven that we affect our surroundings. We, as **the observer** are believed not only to influence our environment but we apparently create it as well as our experiences. Science now confirms that we do in fact create our reality.

In highly controlled laboratory experiments when the only variable was the person conducting the test the results were surprisingly substantially different. The results varied according to the observer. The person watching or administering the experiment and nothing else was responsible for changing the results!

Now for once medical, scientific, spiritual and consciousness experts <u>all agree</u>. We really do create our own reality. We control and shape our life. As the observer we have controlling influence on what we experience. This may be a concept that you don't want to believe but it is actually true. You have ultimate power over your health, wealth and happiness.

Using this understanding as a foundation, the importance of my clients' language became that much more evident as it helped me to identify their perception and beliefs and the factors that formed them.

'Truths' (Beliefs and Perceptions)

"In our life we have an opportunity and perhaps a responsibility to enhance and build our personal strength and depth of intention, overcoming our challenges, our self-doubt, internal conflicts and disturbances. To accomplish this we must question our truths – what is true for us (our beliefs and perceptions), relinquish our fear based patterns and find clarity and strength for growth and vision.

Without removal of these blocks true clarity and understanding is clouded. True truth is obscured.

We learn from experiential vision; our wisdom is accessed personally. Each one of us has our own truth alterable by the events we choose to hold close and the events we choose to relinquish. Remember everyone's truth (and wisdom) is subjective, unique and personal. Your truth is changeable by changing your beliefs. My truth, your truth, or the truth of another - are truths of dramatic difference.

However, they are true until a choice is made to change. Changing a truth can take a moment or numerous life times. Welcome unexpected transitions in life as they often reveal deeper inner truths (or beliefs) which are hiding, clouded or obscured by any fear based truths.

Fear based truths are doubtful situations causing a disturbance. A truth of this shape or form is only masquerading as truth...'

Further Evidence

Although I cannot justify my findings with mathematics or microscopes, others have done. Dr Candace B. Pert, a neuroscientist, conducted pioneering research which provided evidence that our emotions create corresponding chemical responses in our bodies.

In her book, *Molecules of Emotions* she explains that our feelings create a cascade of chemical responses. Major chemical changes occur in our mind and throughout our body with our every thought actually. Our emotions, how we feel about something sets off a chain reaction inside of us. Her work in this area of neuro-anatomy and pharmacology confirmed that our thoughts, personal perceptions and emotions have a real, direct and immediate impact on our physiology. The matching or corresponding chemical chain reaction in the form of neuro-peptides (proteins) caused by our feelings can be damaging or improving for our body. They have the power to heal or destroy.

Dr Pert has proven scientifically that our feelings and perceptions affect our health. Therefore it is through our outlook, thoughts and feelings that we encourage our health or illness. In my opinion this places further responsibility on us to be more aware of how we are feeling and to make the effort to improve our emotional state.

To provide further clarity on how important your thoughts, words, and feelings are to your health I'd like to offer a few premises at this point

It is also proven that the mind-body does not know the difference between intensely remembering or visualising something and actually doing it. It does not differentiate, meaning therefore the mind and body will reply in the same way, creating all the same chemical responses!

If you were to vividly recall your happy, sunny holiday in Fiji, your mind and body feel as if you are actually there. Thus now familiar with Dr Pert's findings you know that chemically inside of you your mind-body will recreate that same happy state it experienced in Fiji. Your body will make all the same substances necessary *to recreate the feeling* of being there. You can feel just as you did then just by thinking of it and benefit from the holiday all over again.

You can see the importance of what I'm saying if you consider someone who is in a state of perpetual worry or fright. A person who keeps remembering the attack he experienced in a park twenty years ago has the internal experience of the event repeated. The effect on the body is like being attacked again and again with the body answering chemically to the thoughts. This person experiences the sensations and chemical messengers of their emotions of the terrible encounter each time he recalls it intently. His body creates the chemical equivalent of fear which destroys and damage cells, places undue pressure on his organs and exhausts his hormone glands.

The importance of any event is your perception of that experience. How have you interpreted it? You have made some decisions about what is taking place by reference.

If you enjoy hang-gliding for example, your body creates happy, exited, content or even blissful chemicals that help you internally. But if you dread heights and think you are doomed engaging in this pastime, your body will create harmful or dangerous chemicals. These are destructive molecules, like free radicals that go about causing havoc.

The chemicals we create when we are eager, thrilled, excited or exhilarated are very different than those that we make when we are afraid, ashamed or angry. Each individual emotion has a matching chemical messenger. When you enjoy yourself or are positively excited by an activity or event you will make good, health-giving chemicals like serotonin, endorphins, pain killers, opiates, anti-inflammatories and others. The body has the ability to make everything you would ever need to achieve and maintain health. However as Dr Candace Pert has proven it is truly how we feel about things that matters.

How we feel about something literally causes the feeling within us, our body responds to our perception.

This is not science fiction or positive new age mumbo jumbo; this is fact. It is clear that our perception of our experience influences us today and in our future.

However perception is linked to our past and is prone to being faulty, immature, limiting and distorted as you will see.

Because of this, reviewing our perception to understand *the why* behind the way we feel is fundamental. We not only make decisions and base our actions on our perception, we chemically and therefore energetically change. Our perception dictates how we feel and what we do consequently. It literally changes our outcome.

What's Important to You?

Two or more people can experience the exact same thing and feel totally different about it. Each one weighs the available information against their history and decides how to feel. One person may be scared whilst another feels enticed or even inspired.

Dr Pert says our emotions also decide what we think is worth paying attention to. **Even the thoughts we let into our conscious awareness are determined by our feelings and what we focus on is based on our emotional perception.**

The people from HeartMath have created software to allow you to monitor your heart patterns which are linked to your emotions. They promote tracking your heart rhythm whilst doing visualisation to learn to manage your body.

Perhaps like me, you believed or even learned in your biology class that the brain controls everything in the body. This is now outdated information. Scientists have come a long way in understanding how our mind and body work together. If you still believe the heart only receives and responds to instructions from your brain, you'll be surprised to discover that it actually is more the other way around. The heart is not only sending more messages (instructions) to the brain but it controls and influences brain activity including your emotions, thus our body chemistry, where we place our focus and attention, our perception and even our cognitive abilities and memory.

You can buy the HeartMath software to use for yourself or visit a therapist who uses it in their practice. It may be just the thing you need to do to understand the real power of your thought (and your visualisations) if I haven't convinced you already to pay attention to what you think or say.

Organs and Words Vibrate

As I mentioned, everything is vibrating which means everything has a certain frequency, signal or sound. Each of our organs has an optimal vibration. Dr Herbert Frohlich, of the University of Liverpool showed us in the 1980's that each cell, tissue and organ in the body vibrates or resonates at an ideal frequency. The liver for example vibrates at a particular frequency when it is healthy and the heart at another. Additionally, every single word, thought or image you have has a certain vibration.

Words, as well, can be measured or calibrated for their overall frequency. So just like a radio station being broadcast on 98.1FM to which you would tune your radio dial, you are broadcasting both inward and outward a frequency with your words and feelings. Your body and others receive these oscillations of frequency.

Internally you may be altering your healthy frequency and moving away from equilibrium with your words or thoughts and if you maintain a disruptive frequency long enough your health deteriorates.

Emotions, or the words to express emotions to be more accurate, can be placed on continuums. They may range from love at one end to hatred or from shame to appreciation and gratitude. Moving up or down each continuum shows a change in the intensity of your feeling. There are many words you could choose to express how you feel about something and based on which you select you could feel dramatically different.

According to Dr. David Hawkins, author of *Power Versus Force*, love calibrates at 600 whilst shame is perhaps the lowest emotion a person may feel measuring at only 20 on his scale of emotions.

Dr. Hawkins is a psychiatrist, physician and researcher who conducted a 29 year study using clinical kinesiology quantifying the body's responses to emotions through muscle testing. As just saying a word changes your body chemistry, it can either weaken or strengthen you. A word or thought alone has the ability to alter our physical and emotional wellbeing and therefore can be measured with even simplistic forms of kinesiology.

Dr Hawkins systematically measured the emotions of shame, humiliation, guilt, apathy, grief, regret, anger, forgiveness and all the rest to joy and beyond to a feeling of enlightenment. He asserts that there is a turning point from unhealthy or weakening emotions to strengthening emotions. This point is reached when a person feels courage. Emotions that are an improvement on courage or a willingness to seek change strengthen us whilst any emotion with a rating below courage weakens us.

Although I sometimes confuse my clients when I compliment them or applaud them for getting angry about something they've been depressed about for a long time. They may find it odd that I even encourage them to feel angry if only momentarily about an event in their past. It's easy to understand if you know that the emotion of anger is closer to the emotional midpoint or turning point and only a few steps away from optimism.

Although there are many who try to avoid anger at all costs, it is actually a more empowering feeling than many other emotional responses. It is much better and preferred than feeling despair or humiliation. (I'm talking about a feeling of anger or frustration and not an act of violence or vengeance.)

Try saying out loud the following words, to see how it feels to say them. Say each word or phrase slowly to give yourself time to transition and feel the difference it makes in your body.

Say: "You disgust me." Now stop and see how you feel.

Say: "I hate you". Now stop and see how that feels.

Now say: "I'm ashamed of you" and see how that feels to you.

I expect even saying the above statements may cause you some discomfort. Now say the following phrases out loud or to yourself and sense how they make you feel.

Say: "You are so special". Now notice the changes in you.

Say: "I'm pleased you are in my life." Now stop and let that sink in.

Now say: "I love you" and feel that inside.

I hope you could feel the changes within you with each statement. There is so much to say about the power of words. There's a difference, a great difference, between saying "I'm angry", "I'm furious", "I'm annoyed", or just "I'm miffed" or "I'm a little irritated".

Your choice of words to express your feelings can enrage or calm you.

When you are furious with someone or with yourself, you can change how you internalise your anger simply by adjusting the level of your words you select to describe it. If you become conscious of the appropriateness of the word you select you can influence and change how you feel.

Be more accurate with your choice of words or change them willingly to elicit or influence how you feel.

Sometimes we select a word to express our feelings out of habit and we don't actually feel as strongly about something as we say we do. You can amplify or dampen (decrease) your emotional response if you take a moment to evaluate what would be an accurate or appropriate reaction. You may unknowingly be habitually choosing to intensify your reaction because you have associated or confused experiences or emotions, or you may want a particular response from someone. In the UK this is accurately referred to as 'winding yourself up'! Additionally you may elect to play up the trouble you went to, for example, when speaking to get an acknowledgment, recognition or sympathy.

Sometimes you aren't really furious even though you use that word---but using it creates a more furious feeling in you. For example you may not really be violently furious over the event of someone taking your parking space but you are in the habit of reaching that level of emotion or intensity.

We all probably know someone who is constantly angry or the reverse, perpetually optimistic or nonchalant or not bothered. Emotions like anything else can be habit-forming. Some choose to ignore or tone down their emotional response to things whilst others choose to heighten them into full-on rage or debilitating sadness.

Addicted to an Emotional State

In biochemistry, it's been shown that people can actually become addicted to particular feelings! Each time you feel grateful for example or appreciate a beautiful sunset, your body makes the corresponding neuro-peptides, the chemical duplicate or equivalent to gratefulness. It might feel like serotonin, the chemical necessary for us to feel happy and content.

On the opposite end of the scale, if you feel shameful or disgust or even anger as I've been using in my examples, the body produces a different set of neuro-peptides which match these emotions. These chemicals may cause pain, inflammation, tension and nervousness in the body. Cortisol and other stressful, ravaging chemicals immediately invade the bloodstream and the cells of the body latch onto them.

You may be surprised to hear the principle of being addicted to emotions. Yet just like being a heroine addict who craves more and more heroine to get the same effect, your body's cells crave more and more of the emotion they have been experiencing.

The cells of the body have receptors on them which an individual neuro-peptide can slot into like a key into a lock. The cells create more matching keyholes for the common or regular neuro-peptides they are expecting and less of the specifically shaped keyholes for other emotions or chemical messengers which are less prevalent. This is great if you are addicted to contentment and calm balance because you will seek these emotions out. But if you are addicted to fear, anger or pain due to constant exposure, within or outside your control, you will need to wean yourself off these damaging emotions.

Try Choosing an Accurate Emotion

In this vein, I'd like to make what might seem an odd suggestion. I'd like you to consider modifying your choice of words when expressing yourself. **Try choosing words for your feelings that are more closely in line with the life you want.**

Make an attempt to feel or express annoyance instead of anger when annoyance is the appropriate response or how you would like to feel, or try to feel forgiveness when the idea of revenge finds its way into your head.

For some this advice is not appropriate as they may already minimise their feelings. If you are in the habit of not feeling, or not knowing how you feel, going numb, or ignoring how you feel or are confused and intimidated by confrontation or conflict you may benefit from another strategy. You may need help with assertiveness or feeling safe to express strong emotions. Get the professional assistance you require.

Appropriateness is the guidance I can offer. Try to understand how you feel and question if it is appropriate. Is the intensity accurate for the moment? Is it too much or too little? Is the level of emotion you feel based on what's going on now or something in your past?

A real clue to knowing that you may have a pattern or addiction to an emotion and its chemical partners is if you notice that you fly off the handle and realise your response to a minor situation is over-the-top or highly charged, or the opposite, you do not react when you should.

Some people have a full range of emotions expressed in a few minutes. They scream at the top of their lungs in anger over a 5 year old child dropping a plate of scrambled eggs, swat the child viciously, slam the door and then they may burst into tears. Are they reliving a pattern of their childhood, confused about how to feel, or are they addicted to emotions and drama? Without more information it would be impossible to know but it's clearly out of proportion and up and down behaviour. Over responding, over-reacting or exaggerating may point to unresolved experiences or emotional conditioning just as under-reacting can, the source of which EFT tapping and counselling may be able to clear.

Everything takes practise to achieve consistent results. Whether the result you are trying to achieve is that of plastering a wall or reaching and maintaining a feeling of self-acceptance. What we do well or to a high degree consistently is an achievement that takes practise. It doesn't normally happen overnight or as a unique experience. Even a feeling of sadness, grief or self rejection is practised and habitual. We have exercised our mind and nervous system to reach an emotional state. It may come as no surprise that our self-talk is one of our forms of preparation and practise. We become accustomed and patterned as we rehearse. Speaking kindly to yourself is a great pattern to develop and may require effort.

Dr. Masaru Emoto of Japan shows the importance of kind and appreciative self-talk in his photographs of crystals formed by freezing water samples. In his worldwide study, he took water from various sources and cryogenically froze it. He found that certain water when frozen in these conditions formed beautiful crystalline structures almost like snowflakes, whilst polluted stagnant water frozen using the exact process formed disjointed distorted, even ugly shapes.

Emoto's photographs showed that the more pure or sacred the water was the more intricate and lovely the crystal formations were. Whilst this was not a huge surprise to some, Emoto then began *speaking* words to water. He would write a word or a phrase on the containers of the water samples, including distilled water, before freezing them and this act stunningly altered the subsequent crystalline form dramatically.

He developed his study further and found that if he played music to water or showed it a photograph or even the name of a person or a historic event, that this would alter the structure again when frozen.

The results showed that water had memory and that it could be influenced. The importance of this finding is very significant. It displays that water has some sort of consciousness or if that's too big a leap for you to make, that water has the ability to reflect the intent of words or take on the vibration of them. Water crystals change form based on what is said! If you praise it, pray over it or badmouth it, it is affected. The words change the pattern it creates.

Now for a moment consider that humans are mostly made of water, especially babies and young children. We are on average 70% water, 90% water when we are born slowly decreasing with age. At death we are around 50% water. Maybe affirmations are worth the effort and a try, huh?

Chapter 8
What You Choose to Believe

Whilst the importance of your words may be evident in Dr Emoto's photographs, considering that your body including your brain, heart and blood consist of more than 75% water, but it's not exclusively what you say that matters. It's about what you believe.

What you say, your choice of words is of even greater importance because of what they reveal about your beliefs and intentions.

They tell, point to or highlight for you, what you believe about yourself and your world. One reflects the other. Let me make a clear distinction right now, **it's about what you choose to believe** about your self and your world. That is what is being revealed through your words. More specifically it's what you choose to believe <u>right now</u>. Beliefs change all the time and they are individual and biased. Beliefs are not fixed even if they are old. They can be changed.

Your beliefs are what are causing you to pick your words. Your beliefs are what lie below your words, your thoughts, your feelings and your actions. But your words can point them out to you.

What you say can also inform you about the experiences that formed the beliefs. Helping you understand not just what you believe but perhaps why.

Your words and beliefs not only tell you where you are right now, but how you got there and what you may be attracting. They offer you magnificent insight and the means to change.

"Listen to everything, believe nothing."

"Let me explain this further. If our experience is all about perception (judgment, thinking and choosing), you can listen to everything you hear but you shouldn't accept all

you hear, just as you wouldn't eat all the things that might be on your kitchen table. You wouldn't eat the newspaper or a vase however an apple or perhaps a pear that is on the table is okay to eat and has nutritional value.

The value to you and your experience should be a keen measurement of its acceptability, validity and use. Is it of use? Is it kind? Is it novel? Is it sane? Does this new piece of information resonate as truth? Is it supportive? Is it as good or as grand as it can be? Does it sit with you and improve you? Does it excite and enlighten you? Does it degrade you? Does it denigrate anyone, anything? Does it link to more valuable tools for you? Does it encourage you? Does it push you to deeper conscious introspection? Does it manage to do any of these things? If yes, it's valuable to listen to it, say it or believe it but measure it each time you recall it and ensure it still has value for you.

Each time you take a concept or accept a belief it should be repeatedly tested for accuracy, or validity against today's model with today's standards and today's knowledge. It is important that you measure against what you want in your future – will it fit?

As you grow you need less stringent rules and less dogma; less is really more as they say. Your potential is greater than you know and you need to take time to evaluate each time you limit yourself through your beliefs, your inheritance, your phrases, your catch-all anecdotes, your titles and explanations. Be sure they are not of the past but of the now.

Are they valid now in this critical moment (your thoughts, beliefs), this time? Are they still valid and useful? If yes, use them and apply them wisely, if no, discard them and learn what they offered is no longer true for you although it may be for another. No judgment, just useful observation of your thoughts and application.

Your applicable methods and beliefs today may not be tomorrow. <u>*The more you conceive, the more you loosen your strict adherence to others' rules.*</u> *Be of your own making; be of your own thoughts accepting responsibility. Be original; be full and not persuaded to ignore yourself...Demand choice. Demand growth for yourself."*

As I mentioned earlier, it's about awareness. It's about doing things consciously versus by rote, habit or in fear. It doesn't matter if that's the way you've always done things, if you elect to, you can change through modifying your beliefs and your words.

Let's just review a little. If you create your own reality you can surmise that only what you believe in can show up in your world. So if you manage your language, increasing your vibration, clarify your desires and shift your focus; things miraculously change. It may sound like a lot but it's really about understanding your actions and what you have decided to accept as your truth (what you have decided to believe).

So if you believe *all men cheat* then in your reality or life, they do and will for that matter. What you believe happens. It's that simple. **So change what you believe to what you want to believe**.

It's said that you can only see or interpret those things that you can consciously conceive. This is how the mind actually works. The mind struggles to interpret things it hasn't seen before or doesn't know how to fit them into your current belief structure.

"Have faith in those things you cannot see as they hold the mystery and the key (to unlock you)."

There's an old story which says that when the Spanish armada first arrived at the new world, only the shaman, the medicine man, of the indigenous people could see the ships. The others' view or perspectives were too limited. Only until the shaman told them all about what he saw were they able to form a picture in their mind.

This illustrates why it's important to understand what you believe to be true and possible and why I suggest you clear away those things that are keeping you stuck. **Your belief system holds all the answers to the life you are living and the life you can live.** Only if you can conceive it, can you can create it.

What I am attempting to show you is how understanding your beliefs and choosing to adjust them can bring abundance into all areas of your life. Now, being rich or abundant can mean something different to each of us. It may mean having time to read or simply go for a walk or play with your grandchild, to have a large bank account or to have improved or excellent health. For some, unfortunately, the only importance money plays in their life is to meet the requirements of personal shelter, warmth and food, the basic level of necessity according to Dr Abraham Maslow's hierarchy of man's personal development.

Maslow's Hierarchy of Needs

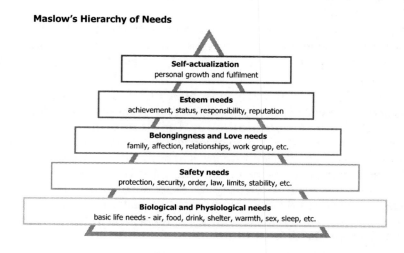

Only after your 'basic life needs' (biological and physiological needs for survival) and 'safety needs', survival and) are satisfied are you able to start considering your psychological needs. This is when your beliefs come under scrutiny and into play either promoting or limiting your expansion towards self-actualisation. Although better defined by Dr Maslow himself, I would define self-actualisation simply as a state of feeling fulfilled, capable and content within yourself – it's when you have the confidence and sense of being who you are meant to be, i.e., reaching or approaching your potential. It's a state of service, perpetual growth and happiness within yourself. You are no longer preoccupied or concerned with the survival and comfort necessities of life but the meaning and joy of life.

Beliefs that affect you are not just beliefs like *I'm not good enough* or *I'm very talented.* They extend to all parts of your life and include those beliefs which you picked up along the way when you were just surviving or staying safe.

Some beliefs like the example I used before that *all men cheat,* women or men may inherit from witnessing their parents' experiences, whilst others come from statements, actual words that were heard or from feelings. Your beliefs can come from many sources and avenues.

Along with your experiences and perceptions of your parents' lives of course, your siblings, teachers, friends, neighbours, acquaintances, bosses, peers, the media, the television, radio, advertisements, books, religious or authoritative figures and other mentors all contribute to your belief system.

What you hear others say when you are forming opinions of your own are often added to your beliefs. So if your family had the attitude that *rich people are greedy, money is dirty* or *you can't be wealthy and spiritual at the same time* you may have trouble reaching any great level of financial success as it conflicts with what you believe.

An excellent way to encourage awareness of your beliefs, which may be acting as a boundary or ceiling for your achievement, or filter through which you deny receiving what you'd like to attract, is to list all the things your parents used to say.

In an educational DVD, the founder of EFT Gary Craig asked the attendees of his seminar to write down as quickly as they could what their fathers used to say and what their mothers used to say. The statements we heard repeatedly from our parents would be stored amongst other memories in what is referred to as *our tapes* in Transactional Analysis (a psycho-therapy method, discussed in Dr Harris' book *I'm Ok-You're Ok).* Our mind is like the biggest computer hard drive in the world. Everything we experience is recorded with the only exception I have heard being the record of an epileptic attack. Apparently as this is like a storm in our nervous system, our electric system, the information cannot be registered or recorded.

My lists of what I heard my parents say would look something like the following:

My Father Used to Say:
"You can do anything if you put your mind to it."

"Grand" (said in response whenever asked how he was).

"You don't have to have an education to be successful."

"Anyone can be successful if they work hard enough."

"Dirty rotten _ _ _ _ kids" (said when he was angry about something we'd done).

"You can fall in love with a millionaire just as easily as a pauper."

"I love you."

"You are special."

"You should always have at least 3 months living expenses in the bank, just in case."

"Don't spill the milk."

"Don't talk back or else."

"Don't be wasteful."

"Don't talk or eat with your mouth open."

"You can tell so much by people's table manners."

"We can always buy more" (said sarcastically meaning we wasted something again and he wasn't happy).

"Money doesn't grow on trees."

My Mother Used to Say:

"You should always have your own money" (so you aren't dependent on anyone).

"You can become whatever you want."

"You can do anything.

"Be prepared because you never know when things can change."

"I love you."

"I'll take care of you."

"Be sure you have enough food in the larder in case things get tough."

"Never go to someone's house when you are invited, without a gift."

"It's rude to be late."

"Women should never slouch, it's very unattractive. Watch your posture."

"Never walk alone down a dark alley."

"Always walk in the middle of the street if you are by yourself."

"$50 of happiness" (said when buying some flowers or a plant for the garden).

I think I'm one of the lucky ones. Although, my parents passed on some beliefs about money meaning security and some beliefs about the world not being a safe place they both told me they loved me and that I could achieve.

Now doing a list like this is very useful and be sure to take it a step further ensuring that you understand what you thought they were implying or meant by their statements. What messages were they sending to you? What beliefs did they have about the world and potentially pass on to you?

Additionally, it's worthwhile to add the perceptions or beliefs you formed from life within your entire family. There's more to consider than only what you heard. Maybe it wasn't something they said at all. Maybe your beliefs were created from something left unspoken or from behaviour you witnessed in your family any versus words or comments. We've all heard the statement that *actions speak louder than words*. This is often true in the case of the development of a belief; they also come from what you observe or sense rather than just hear.

These understood yet unwritten rules and perceptions of what life is like or can be in your environment are just as valid and important to review. Many family rules (beliefs) are never spoken out loud but everyone knows them or feels them and may modify their behaviour because of them.

Although my father spoke about how we could all succeed, he also indicated through his behaviour, directions and criticism that we were inferior or a failure if we did not (or at least that's how I interpreted it). All of my family came away with a very strong work ethic because of this and the ability and confidence to accomplish things, but we also (or I anyway!) felt strongly that we (I) must be highly successful to be acceptable or valued.

We're very entrepreneurial as a family goes. We all have run our own businesses. I expect as well that we all believe we can do whatever we put our mind to. My father showed us it was possible. He could make anything out of a bit of metal or a piece of string not to mention reaching the top in his field in business.

If you choose to make these lists as suggested, don't be surprised if your lists and those of any siblings' vary. They will be different based on perception and your unique experiences. My sister, Claire (not her real name) did not hear the "I love you" comment from my mother as much as I did. Claire's birth order meant that she was born after my sister Stephanie who was born with spina bifida and my brother Sean who was in his own words *the black sheep of the family*. Stephanie and Sean kept our mother pretty busy to say the least and Claire was probably somewhat neglected just because she didn't require so much attention and her birth order. Sean's mis-behaviour can easily be interpreted by a psychologist as a way to gain much needed attention. Stephanie was a hard act to follow.

Additionally, Claire looked just like my mum and my mum's own self-esteem issues and past probably kept her from being close to Claire I think. Looking back now, I expect my mother was depressed after having Stephanie, and then Sean's energy taxed her further beyond her limits. She was probably simply exhausted emotionally and physically and not able to be there for Claire.

So my lists, Claire's, Sean's or Stephanie's lists of beliefs and perceptions derived from our parents repeated phrases and our childhood experiences could have great variations. Though our beliefs around work and earning I expect are the same as I mentioned or similar. We all know earning money is possible for us if we apply ourselves and work hard, but we also have a sense of how necessary money is to survival. Living through the Great Depression and World War II, my parents had an attitude that you must have savings both in the form of money and food supplies (canned and in the freezer). Their philosophy (belief again) that you must earn **a lot** of money and be prepared for the worst to survive was drummed into us and very true for them.

So my beliefs about work, income, security, comfort, safety and survival were all entwined. There was urgency to the earning; it was a requirement. I had put huge pressure on myself when I was in my 20's and 30's to be a top performer in my industry and career. I had determined (unconsciously I might add) that money and what it meant (food, a comfortable home, a dependable car, savings for emergencies, respect and safety) were important and mandatory because of what I learned from my father and mother.

From my mother I derived beliefs about the world being unsafe, the importance of social graces and a sense that I too needed to be independent from men.

All these exercises I'm offering you are opportunities for you to gain more insight. They are to get you to think about your beliefs and how they are directing your behaviour and actions.

Even Illness or tragedy can be a positive pivotal event in your life. It can cause you to sort through things that would otherwise stay just as they are, neatly or seemingly conveniently out of sight. Challenges often cause us to look inside and see what is or is not working or worthwhile in our life anymore. Any significant, dramatic or even relatively innocent event that triggers a modification in your life has the capacity to change you for the better. It gives a new opportunity or forces you to review your viewpoints and clarify beliefs, values and priorities. In retrospect even tragedy and grief has the capacity to propel you forward in your personal growth and conscious awareness as usually you are required to *clean house* so to speak to set your life in better order.

How Do You Decide What to Believe

Many of the beliefs you hold may be faulty, incomplete or taken out of context. Beliefs should change as you evolve, progress and grow but it's not uncommon to hold the beliefs of a child until you analyse your thinking. Einstein said:

The significant problems we face cannot be solved at the same level of thinking we were at when we created them.

You cannot solve a problem from the same consciousness that created it. You must learn to see the world anew.

Albert Einstein (1879~1955)

When you have an experience, perhaps one that contributes to the forming of a belief, your nervous system is bringing in tons of data through all your senses. From this huge amount of information available to you, only that which you choose to pay attention to, will be used to create a belief or perception.

Our perceptions just like our beliefs are not always right.

Our emotional responses are not always right.

We are conditioned by our past.

When you decide how you feel (or your subconscious does for you) about something or someone your feeling is not always right or fitting. Every bit of it is subjective. Even what you think is objective may in some way be subjective and personal because of your mindset.

Apparently your brain or subconscious processes 400 billion bits (pieces) of information every second which it receives through your senses (through your nervous system) but you are only aware or conscious of 2,000 of them! So, what are you missing? What are you choosing to ignore and what can't fit in with your current beliefs?

You perceive or sense all the bits of information on a subconscious level but you don't acknowledge them in the present moment, in the conscious mind. Your body may react even if the information does not *bubble up*, as Candace Pert puts it, into your consciousness. This explains how sometimes a person is unaware of the various triggers that may cause them or contribute to them having a panic attack. Their mind-body observes or feels something but it's reviewed below in the subconscious part of the mind. It also explains how you may sense or intuit that someone is not okay even when they say they're fine or say nothing at all. You have registered and analysed various bits of data through your nervous system, without your active awareness. You sensed it subconsciously and reacted to it.

I want you to start being conscious of what you can do, expanding and questioning your awareness and discovering your beliefs, always considering and speculating that your current beliefs may not be right, because they become outdated, stale and need to be revised. Your beliefs can be changed and modified. You are doing this all the time anyway subconsciously and you can choose to be more aware of the process if you want. Because our perceptions and our beliefs are subjective and not objective this is a powerful activity for change.

Your beliefs and your memories can be your obstacles as well as your strengths. Decide whether they are helpful or not and choose to change them or how you feel about them.

Your past does not have to be your future if you choose. You can tap into your own divinity or divine connection and create what you want to appear in your life. The world does not have to be what you've heard others say or what you have said or believed about yourself in the past. My work has proved to me that speech is belief driven and both beliefs and language can be changed.

Remember of the 400,000,000,000 bits per second we actually receive through our senses in any given moment we filter out and discard from our conscious awareness those that we just cannot accept or cannot believe. This is proof that there can be so much more to our lives if we can only start to think that it may be possible.

I'd like to offer you one more fascinating example of this filtering process in action. In *What the Bleep do we Know: Discovering the endless possibilities for altering your everyday reality* a layman's interpretation of the universe and quantum physics by William Arntz, Betsy Chasse and Mark Vicente, they tell a story of a pilot that had to make an emergency landing on a motorway. The plane landed safely and all was fine until cars that should have easily avoided the plane crashed into it. When the drivers of the cars were interviewed, they said they didn't see the plane. The mind truly cannot see things it does not expect or believe to be there. Think about what you could see if you allowed yourself to broaden your horizons and possibilities?

I believe the possibilities of life are endless and without boundaries. Be that as it may, you must see the potential for this for it to even be an option.

Examples of beliefs I've heard from my clients:

"Life is a struggle."

"I'll never compare with my sister."

"I'm not strong enough to work anymore."

"People shouldn't brag, it's just not right."

"Pride before a fall."

"I shouldn't compare myself to others."

"I'm uncomfortable with talking about money or charging for my services."

"I'm hopeless at marketing."

"Our family has always lived in London."

"I can't change, that's just the way I am."

"I should just be thankful for what I have, it'd be wrong to want more."

"I shouldn't be selfish."

"I can't say what I really think, that'd be rude."

"It's not proper to disagree." (especially in social settings)

"I can't say no, people won't like me."

"I must not draw attention to myself, it's embarrassing."

"I'm not good enough, I should have done better." (a legacy of the British school system perhaps)

"I can't tell them they upset me."

"I wouldn't give them the pleasure of seeing me cry."

"I don't want to make a scene by complaining."

"Family hold back." (a phrase used often by the middle class to denote that guests come first and you must give of others before yourself)

"It'd be just greedy to have more."

It's still fascinating and amazing to observe the many cultural differences between the British and the Americans. So often the practises of 'good social etiquette' keep my clients fixed in self-defeating patterns. Perhaps it's about socialism versus capitalism but I think it may have something to do with the school system and social norms. I mentioned earlier the *'pride before a fall'* comment which I hear a lot but I also hear statements about it being *'greedy'* to want a second tasty biscuit or serving of food (perhaps a relic of post war times). There's often a strong need or belief that you must give always which can cause difficulties if you yourself are in need financial or energetically. The 'pride before a fall' statement I feel represents a terribly disabling belief, one that should be rubbed out (erased) in my opinion. In the United States we encourage and applaud effort and success and feel it's acceptable to draw attention to it as it encourages others to strive. This is not to say that we like bragging or boasting at the detriment of another however it is okay to be proud of your talents and achievements in the States.

I believe as I express my best and the greatness in me, which is in all of us, I allow others to do the same. I lead by example and refuse to conform to this outdated, inappropriate or critical view of pride. To be proud of yourself is not arrogant but empowering for you and others around you.

I'd like to share with you something I wrote. It's kind of a poem dedicated to being empowered and bold.

Uncover Your Brilliance

"Don't deny your brilliance.
Open those eyes around you, be brilliant for them.
Flood them with your light whilst flooding yourself with it too.
Every ounce of illumination achieved,
Illuminates ten-fold in your following.
You create change in all you see and touch and are.
You must not worry, must not dally,
Must not doubt your own ability of oracle nature.
So clear your mind and be ready for it.
Be brilliant, be bold, even arrogant at times if you must,
To squelch the doubt in those around you who gravitate to you for guidance.
Be a beacon, do not hide your brilliance.
Do not sit in the shadows, for it benefits no one including you.
You have been blessed with the ability to take responsibility.
You have been blessed with the ability to create your environment.
You have been blessed with this body, this light body, this body capable of so much more.
Be responsible for what you attract.
Be responsible for what you accept to attract.
What do you want? Be clear. Discover what you want.
Be strong and vulnerable. Let life in.
Stop guarding every aspect from hurt.
Be vulnerable. Be real. Be in this life."

Annie Cap

You will find many effective exercises in Chapter 13, **Uncovering Core Beliefs and Repeating Patterns, Discovering Why You Choose as You Do** to assist you uncovering, questioning and changing your belief system.

Chapter 9
Do We Choose our Symptoms?

What comes first, the symptoms of illness, or the words focusing on them? As I have mentioned, I often think it's like the 'chicken or the egg' debate. I shared with you the words of my clients in Chapter 3 and my thought that they developed their illness or situation because of continuing to focus on distressing life events or beliefs. Wouldn't it be amazing if their words caused the actual symptoms?

Caroline Myss, a renowned medical intuitive, author and popular speaker says "your biography becomes your biology". She believes that when people dwell on the difficulties of their life, their biography or history can create health problems. Candace Pace's work certainly supports this theory as she has scientifically proven that how we feel about things affects us physiologically.

I take this to mean that unless you find a way to shift your focus away from distressing events of your past you become bound by them. You identify with them and are them. You create your on-going life including all the scratches and scrapes left by any unresolved life events, which are inadvertently being included in the design of your future. Those events that you interpret as negative or damaging end up damaging your health or mental state unless you can release them including forgiving yourself and others for them happening.

Myss believed and postulated that people became ill because of negative emotional experiences in their lives which they hadn't let go. She discouraged and highlighted the danger of identifying with your particular damage and speaking about it. She even questioned the long term value of some self-help groups for example incest survivors, believing that these groups may keep you focused on your trauma or damage rather than allowing you to move on and heal.

Myss called it *woundology* when people identified themselves with their issues and their issues became who they were. She stressed how people commonly introduced themselves with a title that incorporated their problematic past or experience, perhaps saying "I'm a survivor too". They used their trauma as a calling card, like a rapport building tool.

Whilst I believe that fundamentally most support groups play an invaluable role providing people with a place to safely review their experiences and express their feelings, it can be almost like joining a social club sometimes instead of a self-help group. Initially the members may believe they have a lot in common with the other victims, of this or that, with the trauma acting as a way to build instant friendships and sometimes unlikely or unnatural bonds. An unhealthy yet new pseudo family can be formed of people harbouring the same theme of damage. (Remember 'like attracts like' as discussed in Chapter 2, *until you choose to change*).

However whilst participating in these circles a conflict may develop and attending the group may become no longer in your own best healing interest. When everyone is sharing their intimate, emotionally charged, sad or horrid details of their past, would you feel comfortable saying that you don't want to talk about your story or journey anymore and that you wish to forgive and forget? There may be a risk involved in healing in this situation. You might have to give up your new friends if you decide not to focus on your *past stuff* anymore.

Short term attendance in a group where you are able to share your experiences with people who will not judge you certainly can be worthwhile but I'd review any long-term association with victim support groups. However hopefully there will come a point in time when you will want to break with communicating about these difficult things in your history to allow yourself to move forward. Although awareness and acknowledging your experiences and feelings is necessary to healing, you also can't release something and move on if you keep focusing on it and identifying yourself with it.

I agree with Caroline Myss when she says "your biography becomes your biology" and I'd even go further to say that your experiences (your biography) not only have the potential to create an unhealthy outcome but that any preoccupation you have with your past is repeated in your language and in your future life choices and encounters, including the choice of illness or pattern of self-sabotage – until you release it. Basically I believe any unaddressed wounding or detrimental memories create more future memories of the same quality. I'll continue to research but my findings to date show a remarkable likelihood that this is so.

About the 'Choice' of Symptoms

My clients with extreme eye problems literally didn't want to see. They didn't want to see themselves or the unfolding events in their lives, so their body-mind helped them shut off their vision either mechanically by closing their eyes (blinking, fainting) or organically or physiologically through cataracts, blurred vision, inability to focus or the inability to process light.

A client who had frightening experiences as a toddler involving knives became a 'cutter' in her words (a self-harmer). It may not be related but why then did she not become an alcoholic, a bulimic or heavy smoker instead? Why did she choose to cut herself when stressed or overwhelmed? I'm not saying that all 'cutters' have experienced events involving knives but this particular one did.

♥Heart problems are so metaphorically understandable to me now. All the people I have worked with who have had heart issues like tachycardia, recurrent and distressing palpitations, congestive heart failure or an enlarged heart (inflammation of the heart) have had a deep sense of being unloved and unappreciated, or an inability to express their love fully for one reason or another.

I had a fantastic and fascinating result with a man that had chronic and severe pain. I'll call him John. Whilst the cause of John's pain was unable to be diagnosed by the medical profession he was living on massive doses of analgesics. He found total relief when using my *iceberg* strategy with tapping I found a link between his pain, his words and his feelings of tremendous guilt. He believed he was a 'total pain' for his unwed mother. John said he was "a pain" and that "her life was painfully difficult because of having him". Many times throughout the session he actually repeated "I'm a pain" and his subconscious mind must have heard this so many times before and interpreted it as a command and complied. Even more startling, in our second appointment, he recalled whilst we tapped that his mother had told him as a small child that her boyfriend started beating her regularly and severely once she told him she was pregnant with him.

Even my sister Claire, who has Lupus, one of the more pervasive and debilitating auto-immune diseases which are expressed by the body attacking itself, admitted that she didn't want to live. She thought about dying or wanting to die frequently, feeling it was a way out of all of her problems. She talked about it for decades. In her case, the disease appeared obviously aggravated and very possibly created by her feelings of unworthiness and longing for the love of our deceased mother. Her emotions and thoughts were noticeably undermining her life. They were killing her literally, attacking every organ.

Claire is known to commonly and consistently say things like "I'm killing myself at work" and she really is, as she pushes herself beyond anyone's normal healthy limits. Her emotional regrets, difficult life experiences, sorrow and self-reprisal keep her concentrating on beliefs that her life isn't worth living and her body is operating in agreement.

We spent some time tapping once when I was visiting the states and I found out later that she had continued doing it alone after I had returned home to England. She had tapped on her emotional hurts surrounding her relationship with our mother. She had been able to release and accept some of the situations of her childhood using the simple straight-forward version of EFT I had taught her. She realised she had been loved and appreciated by our mother and gained a better understanding of the pressures of mum. She decided then that she must start taking better care of herself and stop doing things that were working towards her early demise.

Unfortunately her progress has been up and down. She's still highly sensitive and emotional and (in my opinion) perceives things too strongly and personally to keep her Lupus in remission for long. Claire has more things to resolve when she's ready. At the time of the final edit of this book Claire has had a severe flare up of her disease and again out of her mouth poured phrases centred around death which had ceased for awhile including casually saying to me "Stephanie is dying to tell you about it", "I was woke from a dead sleep" and sadly "Everyone would be better off if I were dead" and "I'd be easier if I were dead". Compassionately and concerned, I pointed out her choice of words to her. She hadn't been consciously aware that she was saying them and then I recommended she see someone to help her.

Do we choose our illness too?
Is our illness symbolic of our issues?

I came to realise that the symbolism of the 'choice' of illness should not be ignored. If not the illness itself, the role of the body part affected or position of it in my clients seemed to mean something.

The literal nature of their illness, the organ affected and/or the symbolism matched their words too. The parallels cannot be denied. Again my clients' attention was locked onto this particular area in their life or body. They were extremely focused on it. The correlation and literal connection to their past or outlook for the future was too amazing to ignore.

One of the more disturbing trends or connections I have observed was that of my ME clients. Every single one of them I've worked with liked to or chose to say "I'm sick and tired of ...." Whatever it was in their life that bothered them, they were *sick and tired* of it. And of course if you know anyone with chronic fatigue, you know that they are exactly that.

They're *sick and tired* and often in pain for years or even for the rest of their lives. So the question one might ask is when did they begin saying this mantra to themselves? Was it before or after the ME set in? My ME clients have been some of my most rewarding to work with but they have also been some of the most trying for me as they may or may not want to apply the techniques that have been found helpful for this debilitating illness. Some of them whom I have coached have regained all their energy whilst others choose to discontinue therapy not willing to change tactics or disturb the past. Some actually told me it was too uncomfortable talking about their history even if doing so could make them better. They would rather choose a life restricted than look at how they got here.

Imagine deciding you'd rather be ill. It happens a lot actually. People, in my opinion and experience, do often prefer to choose illness. There can be many benefits to being ill which I will discuss in the next chapter.

When offered even free or heavily discounted sessions, a few clients chose to stay how they were. No one can make someone heal. It's up to them. It's their *choice*, again. A person has to want to change their life. No one including me can make them do it.

It can be possible with a skilled, experienced coach or therapist using tapping to get beyond chronic illnesses like ME. If you determine to review your life and patterns with techniques like EFT, are willing to consider nutritional supplements, and other lifestyle and dietary changes you may be able to stop being '*sick and tired*'. However, you need to be open to changing strategies admitting that the current systems are not working well for you; something definitely needs to change to foresee a difference in the future. (This includes reviewing how you interact or react emotionally in relationships, social settings and your default way of being.)

It can take a combination of adjustments along with tapping or other appropriate therapies to affect a real change as many things contribute to illness. Although I'm an advocate of tapping (energy psychology in various energy forms: EFT, MTT, Matrix Reimprinting, *The Iceberg Process* or TIPs, TAT, TFT), the particular therapy is not always what's important; it's the energy, passion and skill of the therapist, counsellor or coach who guides and encourages you combined with your determination, willingness and application.

My experience has shown that some sort of giving up may have taken place in my more chronically ill clients and it takes their responsibility and dedication to choose to discontinue patterns of illness. Once they have an understanding that change is possible, a choice must be made.

Are our organs linked to particular emotions?

Further support of my theory that an illness may be chosen in some way by us (by our subconscious mind) or for us by our experiences, memories or emotions is the fact that in traditional Chinese medicine seven emotions are linked to various major organs and their meridians. Traditional Chinese doctors believe an excess of these emotions or psychological factors can cause illness or disease. The seven emotions that they pay the most attention to are joy, fright or shock, anger, worry, sorrow, fear and grief.

The heart in Chinese medicine is linked to joy. Whilst I've read that they're particularly concerned with excesses in any of the key emotions, in the case of joy it's a lack of happiness, an imbalance and a lack of joy in one's life which can impact the heart itself or heart meridian and associated parts of the body. Thus rather than too much joy there would be too little. In all the heart problem cases I've dealt with there has been a lack or severe limitation in being able to experience or express feelings of love with parents, children or partners. Panic or fright is also said to be linked to the heart, which matches my clients who have had problems with palpitations.

Not commonly known is the fact that the heart produces the stress hormones adrenalin and cortisol and has a direct connection to the brain and responds instantaneously, just as our adrenal glands do to external stimuli. Most people think that all stress hormones, our *'fight or flight'* hormones are produced from the adrenal glands exclusively but the heart produces them too (refer to Chapter 7, HeartMath). So when someone feels their heart hurt, it is a real feeling. The heart produces this pain or sensation itself, through sensing your feelings. Again, there is an active connection and communication from the heart to the brain.

Below is a list of the main seven emotions and the organs they are linked to in Chinese Medicine:

Joy – linked to the heart (excessive or not enough in my opinion)

Fright – linked to the heart (panic or sudden fear)

Anger – linked to the liver

Worry – linked to the spleen

Sorrow – linked to the lungs

Fear – linked to the kidneys

Grief – linked to the lungs (extreme grief or shock)

Another valuable reference and excellent book is *You Can Heal Your Life* by Louise Hay. She linked illness and the body part affected to particular concerns and she developed appropriate affirmations and strategies designed to help alleviate them. Hay also believes that each part of the body is symbolic. Problems with the ears for example she says are about not wanting to hear or an inability to hear whilst issues with the stomach represent not wanting to or being unable to digest experiences and concepts often due to fear.

Chapter 10
Do We Choose to Be Ill?

I believe, not consciously normally, but in some bizarre way we choose to be ill. Whether it is to give us some *'me time'* in the case of a cold or migraine that keeps us home from work for a day or two or something more severe like ME or chronic arthritis as I discussed in the last chapter. Do we allow ourselves to become ill or perhaps *will* ourselves to be ill?

You might think, "No way, I don't believe this. No one wants to be ill intentionally" but I think, in some challenged situations and perhaps confused, distorted or protective way, some of us do. It may be because we are *ill at ease* or as the name implies *dis-eased*. Or it may be a choice we've made to work out our karma if this is a concept in our belief system.

I have observed with illness, whether it is mental or physical that there seems to be almost some sort of underlying wish to be ill or method of control gained by it. Even the most terrible experiences of panic seem to be *a choice* your mind is making to help you in some way. In every case I have worked with on anxiety or panic, the panic attack itself or potential panic attack (*the pre-panic episode*) provided the client with a *'get out clause'*. Allowing them to not do something they didn't want to do or feared. It helped them avoid feeling a certain way.

Ironic isn't it? Panic often provides control for the person even though they feel so out of control when it is happening. I'll discuss particulars about panic later in this book.

Now back to the question of whether we choose to be ill. The unconscious or even the conscious mind may be selecting to be unwell. There is a concept called 'secondary gain' in psychology which we use in tapping (energy psychology practises) as well. I call it, having a vested interest. My clients often gain something or have a vested interest in being unwell. They get something out of it. This may seem extraordinary but we usually find that there is a value or even direct benefit to not being fit.

There may actually be multiple benefits to not being well in the subconscious or conscious mind.

This is a very touchy topic to address with people as you can imagine. Someone who is in pain constantly, or has lost their balance and can't walk, or is going blind does not want to hear that they may be benefiting from their illness, or they may be creating or aggravating the illness with their *chosen* patterns and beliefs. I take great care to present this idea in the kindest and best light possible.

I mentioned that in psychology, the benefit you might derive from an illness is referred to as a secondary gain. In NLP (Neuro-linguistic Programming) it is posited that people work perfectly, all actions have a purpose and every form of behaviour has a positive intention. The presuppositions of NLP further state that **people always make the best choice they can at the time.**

My view on physical symptoms, nervous habits and even some forms of illness is that in some way it is helping or assisting us or in the past it did. Whether it is through simple distraction, causing someone to take a break and rest or something more significant, it has a purpose even if that original purpose is now out-of-date. At some time in our lives it was a valid and beneficial choice. It assisted us in some way, albeit odd, strange or inappropriate now. It was a choice made at some level. It was a workable strategy to accomplish something at some time in our life, under the particular conditions of that time.

The Parts Technique

Asking a client if they are aware of any benefits they derive from their illness or problem is sometimes fruitful. But often for a more complete understanding I wait for a time when we can enter into a light hypnosis and use an NLP strategy called the Parts Technique. Using Parts we ask the mind and body why it's doing what it's doing and how it might be attempting to help us. We enquire, as the name indicates if there is a part or are parts of us that are causing this thing to happen or contributing to the way we feel.

This is not about placing blame. We are not blaming anyone for getting ill or causing themselves to faint or panic. We are simply recognising that our mind and body is very powerful and may be trying to assist us with something. Our mind-body does everything for a reason and it keeps doing it if it thinks it is beneficial. But an 'if it ain't broken why fix it' attitude in the subconscious prevails until it is reviewed.

With Parts, we seek to find out if there's a part of us that is creating the condition or reaction in our body (our problem) and what the benefit or advantage might be to us. We are trying to discover and understand how the body and mind are helping or controlling us and what it would take for it to allow us to do things differently and regain conscious control to break the cycle.

When I use Parts I customise the words for each client allowing myself to intuitively find the most appropriate phrases and direction for them, to lead them to their own answers. Sometimes it winds up being a bit of heavy negotiation with their subconscious mind which doesn't believe they can handle themselves effectively or safely alone!

It's as if there are splintered bits of us, these parts, and each of them has an identity and role to play. They have our security and feelings in mind and work diligently to perform their tasks to keep us safe, free from struggle or in control. They feel responsible for our well-being. It can be so surprising and profound; the honest responses people get when using Parts. What they hear, see, feel or become aware of when they sincerely attempt to *talk* to their Parts is highly enlightening and provides a curative springboard.

In some cases I've seen it's not that someone can't heal, it's that their subconscious is refusing because it thinks it's doing a good job for them already and it needs encouragement if it is to alter its' current activities. Whilst the body inherently wants to be healthy and is the most magical self healing system known, the mind wants to protect us from harm and its' strategies may need correcting and updating.

Science has moved on rapidly in reviewing the mind-body connection. Further ground breaking insight has been brought to the public by Dr Bruce Lipton, a cellular biologist, now author and lecturer who taught medical students histology at the University of Wisconsin. In his fascinating book *Biology of Belief* he dismisses or clarifies the scientific connection between genes or DNA as the cause of illness. The often accepted understanding that our health is decided primarily by our genes is not correct. Our health is determined by our perception and by our beliefs – they have the ability to override genetic predispositions.

He explains that there is an error being made when we or the scientific community draw the conclusion that genetics dictate health or rather illness. He discusses how there are scientific reports that state that a particular gene has been correlated to a certain illness but correlated does not mean you are guaranteed to get this illness.

Our genes do not give us a particular disease at all according to Dr Lipton. He shows that it is what we believe which controls our health and that we can actually change our DNA with our beliefs!

He describes clinical trials which show how what we believe governs our health. One trial was that of arthritic patients scheduled to receive knee replacements. The results showed that those who thought they had had the procedure did just as well as those who actually did. You may say, "Ah yes, this is the placebo effect in action" and you've heard many stories about how the placebo effect works *sometimes* and wrongly dismiss this study. However, Lipton further explains that there is an opposite to the placebo known as a nocebo effect. This is when a negative thought or belief changes our biology.

Whether you believe you are ill or you believe you are well the mind-body knows the difference and responds. It responds to your perception or assessment. The words nocebo and placebo are Latin: Nocebo means 'I will harm' whilst placebo means 'I will please'.

One case Lipton wrote about stood out for me. It was a case of a cancer patient who died quickly after his initial diagnosis and treatment, just as expected by the doctor, and therefore by him. The man died within the short timeframe normally seen for someone with the form of cancer he was told he had. He died very quickly, in the window of time the doctor had said and he had expected. The autopsy however showed that the man hadn't had cancer at all. Therefore he died because he **believed** he would.

I quote from Dr Lipton: "The new sciences of epigenetics and quantum mechanics recognise the important role of the invisible fields in controlling life, which includes the thoughts and energies that contribute to our reality. This new awareness changes our old worldview. We now know that we control our genes. We control our lives. Our thoughts are real and tangible. They influence our physiology. Physicists are now beginning to recognise that *the universe is a mental construct*. Knowing these things we become empowered. The programs in our subconscious minds are downloaded as the life we are experiencing. What we have to do is review our lives and identify the things we want to change. The things that we strive for and don't work generally reflect a subconscious program that sabotages our efforts to get there."

Chapter 11
More Clues to Vibration:
Expectation, Attitude and Responsibility

Reviewing your expectations and attitude can be very helpful in understanding why your life may be as it is. If you took on board what quantum physics told us about how you create your experience, you can understand why I believe it's so worthwhile to consider these.

Your attitude and expectations just like your perception are good indicators of <u>your reality to date</u> and of your current beliefs. They affect your body chemically and influence your body's frequency. Your attitudes and expectations are often the easiest signs to spot of your current vibration and probable future outcome.

As Henry Ford said:

"If you think you can do a thing
or think you can't do a thing,
you're right."

A fabulous thing to remember is that what is showing up today in your life was created by the thoughts, attitudes and expectations of your past. So if you notice something you don't like, change your thoughts now. I say "*Shift your focus*". In other words, observe what you are focusing on, find out where you are placing your attention and purposefully, actively shift it, to improve it.

Why would you not want to expect good things to happen, if you knew you had that choice? If you expect nothing monumental or good in your life, does that release you somehow from responsibility? Are you tricking yourself? Is that what expecting failure is about?

If you expect everyone to let you down you mistakenly ignore your responsibility for your own happiness. You can even justify this approach by thinking that people just don't care about you, people are unkind or lazy, you're not worthwhile or that people just can't be counted on so you shouldn't expect better of them. Isn't this dropping the responsibility baton? Isn't this playing a blaming game, a victim in disguise? I want to share with you a true story about expectation.

Some years back, I befriended a lady named Tara whom I thought was very kind and talented. I met her when I first started teaching meditation classes. Tara had a lot of interest in developing herself and wanted to work with me on a personal, non-professional basis. After a few cups of tea together, I discovered her life was a bit of a let-down to her. She wasn't really doing much of anything in her opinion and felt her life was stuck. She didn't feel she could go out and get a job or accomplish anything worthwhile because she had dyslexia as a child and couldn't write a CV (résumé).

I offered to help Tara with her CV and tried to encourage her. She said she wanted to be my friend and to get together often, but I found Tara extremely difficult to contact even though she didn't work and "was always home" in her words. I made the effort as requested to stop in for a chat whenever I was in her area but she rarely answered her phone or doorbell. She didn't have a phone messaging service or an answering machine and she never kept her mobile phone charged and didn't know how to text. The only way I could get in touch with Tara successfully was to ring her husband at his work (which she suggested) and ask him if she was available that day.

I persevered because that's what I do and I guess I found her intriguing. After a few get-togethers I expressed how difficult I felt she was to get a hold of and she commented "she expected nothing of me". At first I wasn't sure what she meant by this. Was it that she was so nonchalant that it didn't matter whether we met up or not or was that spiritual speak like '*if it's meant to be it will happen*' kind of thing? For a brief instance, I thought maybe she didn't like me as much as I had thought. I dismissed this one quickly deciding not to take on her possible issue. I continued to think of options. Maybe it was Tara's way of being detached from the outcome and maybe she was a much more evolved person than me and understood the bigger picture? Maybe I could teach her to text and ask her to keep her mobile charged? I looked for a workable solution.

None of these answers sat well with me. I mulled it over in my head further and realised the comment that "she expected nothing of me" was possibly that of a wounded or even hurt person who was in a subtle victim role without her awareness.

If I hadn't been the type of person I was, she would have pushed me away as she probably did many others, never uncovering her self-sabotaging behaviour. Previously, I suspect, other *would-be* friends, not as persistent as me were successfully avoided and Tara's lack of expectation was granted. Tara expecting nothing of me meant she expected me to let her down, so why bother? It was better not to, safer not to count on me. Everyone let her down. She had been building up a whole pile of examples and evidence that friends and family weren't there for her when she needed them, but she never gave people a chance.

In one of our last conversations, I explained to Tara that I was trying to be her friend and that I was jumping through hoops that most people just would not do and I pointed out her *expecting nothing* comment. Tara didn't see my point at first nor the connection of her behaviour and her feelings of being mistreated by friends and family. She told me that she hadn't put much thought into her comment but that she must have adopted this attitude of expecting nothing as a form of self-preservation. It was not a positive loving detached gesture of an enlightened individual at all. It was an attempt to avoid further hurt.

I explained my view on the importance of positive expectations and in her case allowing herself to have expectations at all. She admitted she had been unaware of the strategy she was using until I brought it to her attention and agreed with me that it was no wonder she had *trouble with people*. Tara had successfully hidden from herself her own damaging technique of blaming and feeling resentment for others underneath her veil of pious, saintly spirituality. I intuitively knew that my being so forward with her would put our friendship at risk but I felt this was too important to leave unsaid. She wasn't used to talking about her behaviour and certainly not used to considering that she might have some responsibility for her own lack of close relationships.

The last time I heard about Tara, I was told she was helping to teach a weekly meditation and Law of Attraction study group aimed at helping the members get through their week. They were assisting each other in being more positive. I was pleased when I heard this. Good for her, she got the point.

Expectation, Attitude and Responsibility

Although your expectation, attitude and perception as well as your ability to take responsibility may be tied to your past, they all influence your future. They represent your over-all internal state and ability to consciously improve your experience. Taking responsibility is imperative and compulsory in taking an active part in the game of life. It empowers and orchestrates. It is essential for positive change, and as you become responsible for yourself, your expectations and attitude will follow.

Attitude

Your attitude is your view, negative or positive about something or someone. It is your feeling, your manner, position or disposition and your way of behaving because of this. Your attitude represents to what degree you like or dislike something.

I might explain attitude as a judgment, an emotional evaluation of how good you view your life or how much you are enjoying it. If your attitude is optimistic, hopeful and excited or if it is at the other end of the spectrum and is apathetic, dreading, doubtful or anxious, isn't this again about your previous experiences up to this point? Isn't it about looking backwards yet you use it and need it to assist you when looking forward?

I believe your current personal emotional rating of happiness is reflected in your attitude. Again your vibration is evident. You'll notice happy people are usually optimistic about their future whilst depressed or angry people are the opposite.

Your attitude influences your expectations. If you have a good attitude, you also expect good things to happen for you. They go hand in hand.

Expectation, Intention

I cannot underestimate the power of expectation. I believe if you expect something to happen or someone to act a particular way they will grant your wish. When you expect or anticipate something you are also setting your intention, they are interlinked and sometimes interchangeable.

If you think back to the first step of the Law of Attraction which is to 'Ask', isn't expecting something to happen basically the same as asking for it to happen? Being expectant is a powerful feeling of strongly asking for something. So you need to be expecting what you desire!

It's easy to forget about the underlying intention in expectation and even easier to not be aware of what you are doing with it. You are always expecting or anticipating something – this is what creates or changes matter. It more accurately foretells your intention.

Do you expect success or do you expect failure? Are you expecting a bad experience or a good one? Remember what you think will happen and what you focus on most will be drawn to you. I've assisted numerous clients who have experienced bullying or even violence at work or from business partners. Due to their background each of them had been unknowingly expecting and preparing for a fight or struggle, exactly what they said they didn't want.

When you change your expectations and make choices that match your true healthy desires, you begin to create wealth in all areas of your life (and remember I'm not talking about only money). However even people who appear to understand their creative force inadvertently put limits upon themselves or operate with undesirable intentions through conflicting subconscious programmes (icebergs).

Do not tease yourself into thinking that you are avoiding problems, like Tara did, by not expecting anything, or not expecting much, think again. I'm not sure it's actually possible to not expect something, anyway. I believe feelings of expectation are on a sort of continuum as I have said, I may be wrong but I don't think so. Either way wouldn't you agree that thinking you are not expecting anything or that you are not expecting much is revealing an attitude of pessimism, distrust or doubt? So you see YOU ARE then expecting something not nice to happen. As I illustrated with the story of Tara expecting nothing of me, your expectations come from your past experiences and frame what's yet to come.

"I am looking for a lot of men who have an infinite capacity to not know what can't be done."

Henry Ford

But you can change your expectation and attitude (along with your beliefs) once you consider them. I offer affirmations or tapping sequences to my clients to assist them in improving their expectation levels. Even without working on clearing the actual past events that may be blocking you, tapping on your expectations can bring rewards. I show you how to uncover and change your beliefs in the chapters that follow.

Affirmations you can use to improve your attitude and expectation:

"I expect wonderful things to happen to me each day."

"I deserve and expect people to treat me with kindness."

"Everyone I encounter is generous and courteous."

"My day is filled with surprisingly wonderful people and experiences."

"Around every corner I find helpful people."

"Everything will go easily today."

Tapping phrases you can use to help you expect good things to happen:

"Even though my life has been a struggle, I choose to expect things to change for me."

"Even though I'm not used to expecting good things, it's time it started happening for me, it's over due!"

"Although I can't remember when I was treated with kindness, I'm going to choose to start believing I deserve it and stop blocking it."

"Even though I have a hard time believing all of this, I am going to allow myself to see the best in others."

"Even though I'm not sure what to expect from people, I am open to the possibility that there are kind people out there and my life can improve."

Note: Complete tapping instructions can be found in Chapters 20-22.

Responsibility

In the coming chapters I will be offering you steps to begin transforming and bettering your life. The first step is that of taking responsibility. Not wanting to jump ahead, I'll just say a few things now about responsibility.

Responsibility can mean a duty or obligation, but with responsibility comes the authority to direct one's self. Responsibility also represents some autonomy (independence and self-sufficiency); the ability to make decisions and to take any necessary or warranted action.

You may think of responsibility as a burden because you link it to account-ability. You may feel that if you are responsible, you are also the one to blame if things go wrong. In order to have some control of my life, I'm willing to risk occasionally being wrong or making a mistake. I want the responsibility. That's the trade-off: responsibility gives you autonomy and control but carries with it ownership. Isn't that how we grow and learn, being responsible?

Often people don't realise they have stopped being responsible and slipped into a dependent position, a potential victim or blaming role. You know what I'm talking about, the feeling that someone else caused you to not be able to have the life of your dreams. Your mother is to blame, your boss is the problem, and the government policies make it difficult or impossible for you to get out of your rut. If you find yourself refusing to take responsibility and blaming another for your lot, the information in this book will be revolutionary to you if you *choose* to use it.

Accepting responsibility and managing your intention (through your expec-tations and attitude) is about taking control and not being a passenger on this ride. They are required to move you from passive reactive living to active living. It's your choice to regain your personal power if you have given it up by accept-ing proactive responsibility. Give it a try; the benefits certainly outweigh any perceived burden.

Chapter 12
Making Conscious Choices for Transformation

Often the illusion that someone has little or no choice in their life comes from years and years of practise of not exercising choice consciously. However if you hold the belief that you have had no say or involvement in want you see around you, this is symptomatic of not accepting and embracing your authority and not taking responsibility. This deception can also come from not acknowledging, questioning or understanding your choices. We actually have a choice in every moment. I remember when I first heard this how mind boggling it was to me. At first, it's easy to pass this off as just new-age rhetoric but as I thought deeply about it I realised it was one of the most powerful statements I had ever heard – if I was willing and able to take it on board and apply it to my own life. Seizing the opportunity to make meaningful choices instead of 'absent' choices in every moment takes some doing and has massive implications.

Learning to make conscious deliberate choices is like learning to play golf. Probably more than anything else the sport of golf requires mental practise and mental correction and conditioning. This is far more important than any other physical ability in order to consistently make your puts or drive your ball straight down the fairway without slicing it into the trees or into a sand bunker. Golf and life are both massive mind games. It's your thoughts and subsequent choices that make the difference.

Even if you adamantly deny that you have choice all the time - it is still actually true. Although choice is a personal responsibility as well as a right and it can take effort, you are always choosing in some way or another whether you realise it or not.

However many of us are in the habit of unconsciously deferring our choices (our decisions) to others especially to our partners, family, employer, friends and social class or clergy. Our choices as well as our desires and beliefs are often dictated to us as we allow ourselves to be guided or ruled by others' opinions of what's right for us, good, and bad or acceptable.

Taking Responsibility for Your Choices

The initial decision that needs to take place is to believe that you do actually have and have had some choice in your life and to stop giving away your autonomy. When you've been living a life where most of your decisions have been made for you this can feel odd or uncomfortable. But realistically, you are exercising your right and responsibility for choice all the time. If this is a new way of thinking for you, or you find it difficult, it may require a leap of faith on your part. If this is an unfamiliar or untested concept (though many of you will already known this) it may help to say to yourself, "Maybe I have chosen my life, even in part, and actually my choices, actions or non-actions have brought me to this point" or "Maybe I have in some way been involved in creating and allowing what I see and feel around me and can learn to choose differently". Imagine it is true (that you always have choice) and give it a try. Accepting your responsibility and agreeing or admitting that you influence your life is vital to changing your future.

If you've already acknowledged that you are responsible for directing your life through constant choices then you may wish to jump ahead in this chapter skipping to the sections which concentrate on reviewing or questioning your choices although you may glean some fresh and useful ideas if you choose to read them.

I'm asking you to be responsible for what happens in your life. Accept it fully, or if you aren't ready yet *just entertain the possibility for now* and observe your behaviour noticing when you give your choice away. <u>Accepting that you helped shape and influence your life and that you are choosing to perpetuate what's happening through conscious or unconscious choices can be a major turning point for many.</u> When you do this, you can no longer be in a state of denial or blame. You move into a position of greater strength, authority and control. By this single mental act the promise and expectation of transformation is initiated and things begin to transform.

Whether it was your own active choice or the passive acceptance of someone else's which brought you to this point in your life, admit that at least you were involved.

As I mentioned at the beginning of this chapter, it is said that you have a choice in every moment. Therefore every moment you have a decision to make. You must choose – you are choosing. You choose whether you want to continue what you are doing or whether you want to change or stop.

It has also been said, and I believe this, that <u>what you see in your life today comes from choices you made in the past</u>. This means the choices that caused or contributed to what you are experiencing right now are old choices and *may not* represent how you would *choose* today. Our experience today is not this moments' choosing but choices made before. What's happening now is from old stuff, old thoughts, patterns and choices. You can choose differently in this moment creating something else if you don't like what's going on. You can correct or alter your choices and make a different future as long as you choose differently.

Practise Awareness Acknowledging What You are Choosing

Becoming aware of the choices you are making in real time whilst they are being made, is extremely beneficial and thought provoking. It is an important step for everyone, even those who have been working with their creative power for a long time. Practising awareness and acknowledging what you are choosing requires that you watch closely your many choices, both those that involve action and non-action. You can learn a lot about yourself when you do this and start to notice why things are as they are for you.

If you have made a non-active choice, a choice made by default by not bothering to alter the current status quo or situation, by not electing to choose or by not recognising and exerting your personal desire and authority or by giving your choice away to someone else – you have in fact still chosen. It's important that you acknowledge this. These subtle non-active choice options are still choices you are making. Because we have a constant opportunity and responsibility to choose you need to be vigilant, especially if your life isn't currently as you'd like. Start being aware, really monitoring and acknowledging everything you choose by saying to yourself "Oh, I'm choosing this!" or "What am I choosing now and why?" You are electing to do something or not do something, to think something or not think something, or to continue just as you are with your routine choices.

It may be shocking to discover what you are choosing. This observation and ownership of self-participation needs to happen before substantial transformation can take place in your life. Once you acknowledge your day to day, hour to hour and gradually moment to moment choices, you will begin to see your options and the enormity of the task of learning to deliberately, consciously choose your life.

Those who view themselves as victims or martyrs often find this premise of personal responsibility of choice a challenging discovery which can be hard to accept. They've frequently been under the impression that stuff just happens to them and other people just do things to them and that they have little choice in the matter. Saying "I'm choosing this" or "I'm choosing to continue this" for someone with an ingrained or long term victim mentality can be disorienting and even disturbing. Do it anyway!

Let me reiterate, you always have a choice to make (you have options and freewill), at least to some degree. YOU are involved in YOUR life. This concept can truly be a stumbling block or hurdle for some. To say "I'm choosing this" when you have been experiencing terrible things takes courage and I implore you to convince yourself to do it. Even if it's difficult – do it anyway.

Decide you can begin to change your future even if you can't erase your past. Allow yourself to become aware of your choices so you can begin choosing differently.

People are often unreasonable, irrational, and self-centred.
Forgive them anyway.
If you are kind, people may accuse you of selfish, ulterior motives.
Be kind anyway.
If you are successful, you will win some unfaithful friends and some genuine enemies.
Succeed anyway.
If you are honest and sincere people may deceive you.
Be honest and sincere anyway.
What you spend years creating, others could destroy overnight.
Create anyway.
If you find serenity and happiness, some may be jealous.
Be happy anyway.
The good you do today, will often be forgotten.
Do good anyway.
Give the best you have, and it will never be enough.
Give your best anyway.
In the final analysis, it is between you and God.
It was never between you and them anyway.

Mother Teresa

Question Your Choices

Decide if You Are Happy with Your Choices?

Now that you are noticing your many choices, I'd like to persuade you to question yourself about them. Asking yourself the simple question "Am I happy?" or "In this moment, am I happy with what I am doing (choosing)?", "Is this okay", "Do I like this?", "Do I feel good about what is going on here?"

Evaluating and determining if you are happy with what you are choosing helps you understand if you've made a good selection for you. This is an extremely empowering part of the process of change.

Other forms the 'Am I happy' question may take are "Am I pleased with this choice?" or "Does this choice move me closer to my goal", or "Does this choice move me nearer to happiness?" Sometimes the 'right' or 'best' choice for you right now is not an easy one but is necessary and in your best interest in the long run.

Asking "Am I happy" is not about being whimsical or capricious. When I ask you to contemplate this question about your choices I am not referring to trying to be hysterically or deliriously happy to avoid commitments, responsibility or effort, it's about doing things consciously. It's about understanding your decisions and staying out of victim mode, and reducing feelings of resentment, helplessness and vulnerability. It's also about understanding your involvement in how you feel and moving towards doing things consistently which are advantageous and healthy.

Sometimes when you ask yourself "Am I happy?" the answer may be "No". Then ask yourself "Is this the best choice I could make today or in this moment?" or "Am I choosing this from a place of fear, power or calm?" and "Would I willingly choose this again?" Questioning your choices in this way creates a shift in you as it acknowledges your input and participation, and qualifies your position and circumstances. Your answers can reveal your real patterns. Pointing out whether you are content with your choices or whether you need to do a bit of work on yourself to improve your lot. I believe we all need to continue to grow and work on ourselves or we stagnate. We can always improve and questioning your actions has the capacity to enrich your life, confidence and self-esteem.

"Do not stagnate. Chances will come for greater happiness, grab them.

Don't stagnate. Watch those in stagnation and their misery. Keep moving, keep changing..."

"Seek joy in the moment of decision and in the thought of the possibilities of invention. Decisions are many and constant and each decision offers you a chance to align with the real you. Decide to be you. Decide and you progress. Stagnation is the killer of joy and creativity and self-realisation.

Decide and it is done in manifest. It's your choice. It's your choice to align with love and joy and others in search of the same.'

If You're Not Happy With Your Choice

If you discover you aren't happy with the choices you're making, before you can choose reliably differently you need to find out why, both why you aren't happy with your choice and why you made it. True awareness comes from this level of understanding and scrutiny of your behaviour.

Knowing why you do something and what influenced you can be annoyingly elusive and a hard to pin-down. Start by asking yourself "Why do I do this if I don't like it?", "Why do I continue to do this?" or "Why do I allow or accept this?" and importantly "What am I getting out of this?" Recognise and admit that you are allowing, continuing, permitting or accepting behaviour and choices from yourself and others that do not suit you or which are even harmful.

When you start activating these sorts of questions into your psyche, seeking honest answers from yourself, you cannot help but modify and enhance your life. You can move from operating in the auto-pilot mode to a higher level of self-awareness of your internal drivers and motivations. Understanding these, *your whys,* the light bulb may come on for you – it can be your 'eureka' or 'ah ha' moment moving you out of numbness and ignorance (or submission) into awareness and active creativity.

I believe everyone has it in them to create an exceptionally satisfying life. Your soul is naturally bright and sparkly and you only need to let go of your tarnish to shine.

Seeking the answers to *why* highlights your inner beliefs about yourself and the world around you. Yet beliefs can be not just out-of-date, they can be blatantly wrong. Thus you are likely to realise your choices are based on faulty beliefs (including thinking that you don't have any choice) and avoiding some-thing instead of seeking fearless desires and true authentic purpose.

When your choices are misaligned with your potential you can assume that at one point in your life the current behaviour (your choice) was useful, even if now it's just a habitual or defeating pattern.

Understanding What You Want - Understanding Your Desired Feeling

Whether you are happy with your choice or not, try to understand the feeling you are attempting to reach. Even if you are making poor or what appears to be inappropriate choices in your life they may be well intentioned. **When you consider and clearly understand what you're unconsciously attempting to realise, through your choices and behaviour, you can be more produc-tive in attaining it.**

Question "What is it that I really want and am trying to achieve through my choices?" and at the end of day "How do I want to feel?" Choices, which on the surface, don't look so great or that generate negative or so-so outcomes can be better understood with this insight. I often ask my clients what they're trying to gain or avoid through a particular behaviour or decision and how do they want to feel. Not surprisingly they frequently respond that they don't really know but they know what they don't want!

At some level they really do know what they're striving for – it's not actu-ally true that they don't know. *Although their behaviour may be unclear to them and even look counter-productive, their conduct is trying to achieve something!* There's purpose and direction behind their choices. All that is necessary is to turn what they don't want around (just as I explained in Chapter Two on the Law of Attraction) flipping what they don't want to know what they do and how they want to feel.

Once you realise what you want or are trying to obtain, what you're reaching for, the next step is to break it down to its lowest denominator, *the emotion - the desired feeling.* How you want to feel is what's driving you.

Understanding the Why behind Your Desired Feeling

When people say they want lots of money, in fact they want what money would give them or what they think it would give them. It's necessary to uncover the desired feeling behind what you want as it often points to something you are trying to avoid or fear which will need to be released. How you want to feel and why you desire something needs to be understood. If it's tainted with defensiveness, reluctance or fear, the items as well as the wanted or prayed for emotional state will continue to be evasive.

This is probably one of the least understood concepts of my clients, especially my business clients. They're sometimes unknowingly actively seeking money to give them recognition, safety, independence, freedom, consistency, or a feeling of calm and control which they lacked as children or at some crucial point in their life. They think money can buy them what they didn't have and now crave.

Once you figure out what you want and understand why (how you hope to feel if you have it), including your history which supports the desire, you will understand the emotional state you're seeking. It's this state, this feeling, rather than the physical item or accomplishment that is motivating your choices. It's the longed for sense or emotion too that exposes your *icebergs* that need clearing, so your *wants* are motivated by sincere unblemished desire and not doubt or fear.

"It is the tangible emotional nature of material wants or needs that I'm speaking of, not the actual things. It is not necessary for example to give up shoes, a stereo or the desire for a large home. It is only necessary however to see them as unnecessary but nice to enjoy. To enjoy an item is fine. To require the item for joy is a less than actualised individual.

Challenge yourself to reduce all negative aspects. Challenge yourself to question "Does this bring me closer to my happiness or does this lead me further from my path of joy?" Avoiding difficult choices because they appear challenging may in actuality be against the path to joy or avoiding unexpected or uncontrollable outcomes may seem more joyful in the moment but in actuality avoid joy as the future unravels and shows that path as being self-destructive. Critique your choices, critique them and accept them and if you choose, change them. Limit the harm accrued by correcting the path back towards the joyful choice.

Your truth unfolds as you develop your focus, your discipline and extinguish your self-loathing, doubt and neediness for external validation."

What I Want Or Don't Want	What I May Want Or Want To Avoid	The Desired Feeling (Desired Emotional State)

Ask yourself, "If I had this, how would I feel? Or what will I avoid feeling? Or what void is it filling?"

Examples (Three different reasons someone may want to earn a lot of money):

1) I want to be rich	I want financial independence	I want to feel safe

Why: I can afford to leave any bad situation. History: Ex-husband was abusive

2) I don't want to be poor	I want nice things	I want to feel proud and accepted

Why: I never want to be embarrassed. History: Friends laughed when they saw her in her father's old car

3) I want to earn £200K a year	I want to know I can pay my mortgage	I want to feel in control

Why: If I can afford my mortgage I feel safe. History: At 9 parents' house was repossessed

Summary of Making Conscious Choices

Knowing how you want to feel represents the real desire. The feeling is the true goal, never the item. It's not the car, house, new dress, partner, ring or even food that you crave; it's the feeling you get when you have it, that's what you want.

Finding the feeling you are trying to achieve, whether it be love, security, pride, safety, respect, peace, serenity or even excitement gives you an even greater understanding of self. It shows you what is currently important to you, again highlighting areas of your life which may need bolstering or improving.

If you find that all the things you think you want show that you want to feel loved, you should investigate this. When didn't you feel loved? Perhaps you have hidden or known abandonment issues or a feeling that you don't deserve love? Perhaps you feel unloved or unlovable?

If you are reaching for a feeling of security, perhaps your life felt (in the past) or currently feels tenuous, insecure, unpredictable or unsafe.

Great realisations can come out of doing these exercises. Taking these steps to awareness will allow you to make more conscious choices and uncover further hidden obstacles limiting you. With this information you can work to

"Shift your focus" and draw what you want to you. Whilst the awareness of lack or avoidance itself may not be enough to make huge changes, releasing the historical reasons for it can. This is where tapping excels. New and improved experiences will begin to appear in your life once these past contributors are neutralised. Then the magical phenomenon called synchronicity or serendipity starts occurring. Some call it coincidence but I've come to believe there are no coincidences.

Things happen for a reason; they happen because we create them through our desires and expectations and through our actions. Once we are pointed in the right direction (in the direction of strengthening and healthy emotional desires), the happenstances of synchronistic occurrences appear more frequently. They increase in speed and regularity as you clear yourself, appearing lucky, timely, guided or even miraculous to move you towards what you want and away from what you don't.

Chapter 13
Uncovering Core Beliefs and Repeating Patterns
Discovering Why You Choose as You Do

The last chapter was to assist you in becoming more aware of <u>all</u> the choices you are making and to get you to think about and understand why. It was intended to enlighten you because knowing why you do something gives you the necessary information to begin to release any issues which may be influencing your choices today.

Self discovery is a process that many people do not actively embark upon until later in life. Many may reach the age of forty, fifty or sixty plus before reviewing the whys and wherefores, unless circumstances forced them to look more in-depth sooner.

I'm thankful that I began looking at my decisions long ago, when at twenty-nine I had a divorce and found myself unhappy and depressed. I realised I selected my ex-husband for all the wrong reasons. He appeared the opposite of my father in a few significant ways! As a youth and as a young adult I had thought my father was the root of all my problems and only just before my mother died did I come to realise it takes two to have an argument. Then later after my mum's death and some supernatural happenings I realised I was the author of my entire story and experience! These were big concepts that kicked off huge belief shifts within me. The ensuing changes were massive in fact.

Discovering I had chosen inappropriately was one thing, although it was hard to admit, (meaning my ex-husband wasn't as nice a guy as he appeared on the surface and he could actually have benefited from some of my dad's good traits). I could deal with that. However then admitting that my incorrect choices were my fault all along and not the fault of my parents (who I had blamed) and that in truth I was totally responsible for everything was a huge paradigm shift!

Somewhere along the way, perhaps after my mum died, I discovered my many poor decisions in life were made from a place of fear. They could more aptly be described as my attempt to avoid fear, insecurity or punishment. I was making some pretty poor choices, although many of them appeared to me to be good at the time. They were inadvisable and just bad. When it came to men, I was making a choice for who I thought would be a 'safe' or 'calm man', and for a man that I thought I'd feel comfortable settling down with, a man who wouldn't cause me to fear him.

I became a very monetarily and organisationally successful telecommunications professional. Spending many years of my life earning in excess of £100,000 a year in a time when other women (my peers) were earning £20k and many men around £35k. I thought nothing of buying a bottle of wine or two in a restaurant for £30-40 when out to dinner or paying £400 for a designer good quality suit, but I was doing this ultimately because I was afraid! I was afraid of being vulnerable, limited or controlled by a man or by a husband.

I listened to my mother's stories, her 'reality' and in a way it brainwashed me by setting my beliefs of how the world was based on her experiences and not my own. She told me in not so many words or those exact words even that "Men couldn't be trusted" and that "You should always have your own money so you will never feel trapped".

I was a 'runner'. If my relationship was going bad, it was me that called it off. I had enough cash to be independent and I was watching for the signs my mom had so diligently and innocently warned me about. So was I expecting to be hurt or used, or was I expecting men to be disloyal or unworthy of my affection? Of course I was! I was absently choosing men who I would eventually find were not up to my standards or they would fulfil my subconscious low expectations of them and I would have to leave. So my other fear of being alone or left was fulfilled or granted. My thought that men were not trustworthy or would take their love away was assured so I'd find exactly what I was afraid of happening. This may be interesting in theory but 'the light bulb didn't come on' until I repeated my mistake enough times that I got it, but when I did get it what was I to do about it?

The same goes for you when you find out why you do something and if you discover it's not for the reason you thought, how do you change it? I'll show you later, I promise.

The Whys in Your Life

I'd like you to consider now all the *whys* in your life. Why do you want a big house? Why do you stress over the dishes not being done? Why do you laugh when you should cry? Why are you afraid of changing jobs? Take all the choices you identified in your earlier reviews and really ask why you made these decisions. Why do you stay with a man who ignores you or has had an affair? There may be good and valid reasons but you need to know why. If it's because you believe all men cheat or you believe no one else would want you, or that you are boring, then you have uncovered what we call core issues or beliefs.

Beliefs, as I've said, are what normally drive our choices. Core beliefs are at the centre or root of your decisions and behaviour. Therefore they are shaping your life. They create your reality. They are your overruling or overriding convictions and principles. They are your understanding of yourself and your world and they are directing your actions. Often beliefs, although different than your values, can be intertwined with them. Values are what are important to you whilst beliefs have the ability to govern you perhaps even more than a value. My most important life values are to be honest and kind and this differs dramatically from my beliefs as I do not believe others will always be kind or honest however I will always strive to be. My expectations of them, my belief how the world is, is different and I am actively working on changing this!

If your core beliefs about life and yourself are soiled with fear, lack, non-acceptance, hatred, guilt, blame, shame or another lower weakening emotion your behaviour is compromised. Your actions (choices) may be to avoid conflict, avoid pain, avoid embarrassment, avoid stress and these limitations may conflict with your desires. Remember if only the things you believe in can show up in your world, your beliefs may be narrowing your opportunities greatly.

We choose accordingly; our choices match our beliefs and reinforce them. Each experience that upholds our beliefs whether faulty or helpful etches it deeper into our brain making simple change more challenging. Subconsciously we choose to fulfill and confirm our healthy or unhealthy, helpful or destructive beliefs.

An interesting point that must be made now is that beliefs come from many sources including from your ancestors or relatives. Like me, some of your beliefs may have been established by your mother's experiences. By her telling you about her life or expressing her concerns whether it was out loud, through her actions or body language, cautions ("Look both ways when you cross the road") or energy.

You can inherit fear, as I have mentioned previously. Sometimes the feelings and beliefs you inherit will seem just as real and valid, maybe even more than those that you have accumulated from your own interpretations of your experiences. Contentment or limitation can even come from when you were in the womb as you received and felt the 'chemical cascade' from your mother's thoughts and emotions throughout her day to day life.

Fear can come to you second-hand. It can be handed down to you just like an old piece of clothing. You try it on and if it fits your thoughts, you create the same feelings and beliefs as the person who passed it on.

Now beliefs that are passed on to you can be super beliefs as well. Fear or the thought that 'the world is a scary place' is only one of the possible beliefs that can be bestowed on you. You could have inherited great skills and encouraging or unflappable beliefs. You may have benefited from unwavering, unending confidence and self-esteem of those around you.

In contrast, along with the beliefs about relationship troubles, wanting to avoid conflict or wanting to earn a lot of money to 'assure' independence, my father instilled in me many empowering beliefs for which I have thanked him. My father taught me through his actions and his speech that I could do anything I put my mind to. He always created solutions from nothing. Showing me that there were answers and fixes always available to most problems and that things could be improved with a bit of persistence or thinking outside the box. My father could make something functional from a pen cap or a matchbook! He'd turn a coat hanger into a decorative latch (not only functional) for the fence gate or make an automatic watering system for his hanging fuchsia baskets from a damaged hose pipe long before watering systems were available commercially.

Dad showed me that it wasn't your education or book learning that made you a success. It was your application, your desire, your action, creativity and follow-through.

So whilst my mother was instructing me on many practical things like how to handle my money, budgeting and even posture, my father was telling me I could make as much as I wanted if I applied myself and worked hard. Weighing the many contributions to my big belief system from my parents, I'd have to say as an adult the overall net result was very good.

If you were to ask my dad how he is, even today, at almost 86, he'll answer "I'm grand". Not "I'm well", "I'm okay" or "I'm tired or aching today" but "I'm grand!" I get my *glass is more than half full attitude* from him and my determination and can do spirit from both my parents. Only after my father had had numerous serious debilitating strokes which left him unable to speak and walk did he say once to me "I could be better." He then decidedly worked to regain his movement, handwriting and speech and the next time I rang he was "Grand" or "On my way to grand" again.

After months in a residential rehabilitation centre once he was back home and able, he joined a watercolour class in his community centre in order to force him to use his hand, asked his doctor to refer him to a local physiotherapist to learn more exercises and did laps walking around the superstore (grocery store) perimeter aisle pushing a trolley (shopping cart) for stability. Recently he bought a home-gym he saw on TV and he uses it each morning. His strength is building and he is determined to see my home in England.

When you look at what you choose and why, your parents' beliefs may reveal themselves. As children or adults we often say "Oh, no, I sound just like my father (or mother)" and of course you do unless you choose to change that. You listen and record everything you see, hear, sense and experience and that includes what your parents passed on to you through their words, emotions and actions. In Chapter 8, **What You Choose to Believe**, I asked you to consider what your parents used to say and what it meant to you.

The things you heard your parents say can affect why you make certain choices but as I said before, it's also the unwritten or unspoken beliefs and the associated feelings that can influence you most. These unsaid rules (beliefs) are accepted and ingrained; the consequences are understood without needing to be articulated in words now. These can often be tough to identify and bring to your awareness. If you are acting or making decisions from a hidden understanding or from a belief that came into your make-up before you had words, you may find it hard to change let alone know it is influencing you.

It's quite common to not know you have particular beliefs even though they're ruling major parts of your life and modifying or diluting your purpose. There may be beliefs of a very destructive nature in you, as well as those that are enriching. It all depends on the belief. So it's extremely valuable to understand what rules you are choosing to live by. Like the rules of any game, you need to know them to play it effectively.

I have come to understand that although I had what appeared to me quite bad experiences whilst I was growing up and I took on board beliefs that may not have been the most helpful at times, some of it could have been viewed either way, dependent on my interpretation and perspective. I was driven to success by a fear of being in someone else's intimidating or mercurial control but I travelled the world, experienced tremendous times over and above any bad and now have the courage and determination to write books. Again in retrospect, I think I fared quite well especially when looking back with the knowledge I've gained over the years and in comparison to many other people.

The most challenging of my possibly inherited or adopted beliefs was that of fearing being physically and brutally attacked. To date, I still don't know where this came from. Even though beatings were a normal parental tool of discipline in my day (some might have called them spankings but that was too nice of a term for them), this is not what I would consider being attacked. Perhaps it was from hearing my parents or brothers fighting when I was in my crib or bed or being a witness to some aggression which I've suppressed, or hearing a story (real or fictitious), or even from scenes on the TV. I still can't watch if someone is hitting someone else on screen, especially a woman. I've started to believe this must have come from a past-life or my mother's childhood fears as I've speculated that she had been attacked and raped as a youth. Even with clinical hypnosis, tapping and Reiki regression I've been unsuccessful in resurrecting any relevant memories of my own that would constitute this sort of apprehension. I may never know now if this came from mom but I regret it may be true.

With my clients, often the beliefs that have the greatest impact on them are those that were forgotten or easily ignored *as normal* or *just how life is*. These beliefs are difficult to isolate because they came from simple every day patterning that was non-dramatic, not tragic or noteworthy, possibly regular repetitious feelings or pre-verbal recurring feelings.

The day to day stuff, the patterns and routines, the unwritten or unspoken ways of doing things and the expectations of how life can be or should be in a family environment are very powerful. They become a part of our normal way of being. Even small criticisms or directions, any repeated behaviour no matter how minor, which may look innocuous, can be very significant to shaping judgment and decision making. It's not always the massively traumatic events that leave people challenged, although they certainly can. Even little things that appear non-consequential leave an imprint on you or a residue which can be easily overlooked. It's sometimes the forgotten details, the details that weren't that bad, were okay or just average, yet perpetual, that form beliefs.

I can't tell you how many times I've heard my clients say "But I had a good childhood", thinking that their uneventful lives couldn't have been the cause for feeling flat, depressed or unmotivated.

You may deduce from regular, non-exciting, everyday experiences and reinforcing patterns that you are worthy or unworthy, loved or unloved, or that life is fun or a duty or that there's nothing special going to happen. Events do not have to be punctuating to make a mark. It doesn't require a shocking or harrowing memory to stain.

EFT (tapping) first became known as a therapy which was used to release or cure phobias. However phobias are often caused by the emotions surrounding traumatic or disturbing events in one's life, so it's great for almost any stress related problem or anything aggravated by how we feel, belief or think (which is everything really). EFT is just as effective in changing non-dramatically derived personal barriers and incidents that helped form your beliefs about your world that aren't necessarily bad or painful. They may be happy memories, common occurrences or highlighted events like the birth of a brother, moving home or changing schools.

I'd also like to mention that significant or traumatic events don't have to be life threatening to leave a mark on you and your future. What's traumatic or important to one may not be to another. Some trying events may be a car accident, a failed entrance exam, a fight in the house, vomiting on a plane, an embarrassment falling off your bike, your first uncomfortable kiss or lovemaking experience, the day you were given a kitten, your graduation day and the list goes on.

Repeating Patterns

Although your undesirable patterns may be easily or sadly identifiable, they may be stubborn to shift. Why do you keep making the same mistakes? Why do you find yourself experiencing the same old thing or feel you are beating your head against the same old wall? What does it take to change a life-long pattern or cycle? Are you stuck with them? No! Is it your karma? Maybe but you can change that too. Awareness of the pattern is the first prerequisite to being able to change it. Not liking the pattern and deciding you don't want it to continue is the point at which you might seek help from someone like me. Your patterns like everything else you focus on or do match the feelings and beliefs you have about yourself. Your experiences are cut from the cloth of your beliefs and expectations.

If you feel you are disgusting, you will keep encountering events that cause you to feel disgusting. If you feel you are talented, you will continue experiencing things that prove you are talented. If you have healthy thoughts and beliefs about yourself, that's great, but your life can be disastrous if not. As your history may show, bad things may keep being repeated until you resolve the origins. The cycle continues until you clear the past and unsupportive beliefs.

I woke yesterday thinking *"In order to move something through consciousness you have to act it out....you have to experience it."* You are trying to do this each time you make the same mistake – so you can see it.

My belief and experience with my clients has shown that until you sort out the things in your past that harmed you, your mind will keep trying to present them to you – to offer you a chance to fix them. You recreate *like events* or situations that provide the same feelings as the originals and the derived destructive beliefs (and expectations) continue to be reinforced until you release the emotions around them and any accumulated episodes. Basically, simply put, the same stuff will just keep happening until you settle them.

These similar events, stimulating the same emotional response or state within you, also provide a justification for you to repeat the unresolved feelings. They continually validate and confirm your beliefs until you alter them.

The things we don't want to talk about or hide away from ourselves are desperately trying to be dealt with. The pattern may seem nasty but in reality it is only YOU trying to fix YOURSELF. The hurtful belief or pattern keeps being shown to you in order for you to do something about it. It can get pretty bad before you decide you've had enough.

"It's lightning amongst the chickens sometimes. But it has to be to awaken many. Subtlety is no good for everyone. Be sensitive to what it takes to make change and progress in some. Be calm and patient. Be breathtaking and exciting for others. Be what you know for each. People see contrast and shades of grey or darkness more than they see light if they have no comparison."

Our souls are trying to point out what we need to work on to progress. Once you resolve your past problems, you begin to create more constructive and optimistic events. The cycle of continuity happens in positive patterns as well.

Repeating patterns are about what we experience and choose to do. Both what we do and what we don't do, like what we say or don't say, follows a pattern. There's usually (perhaps always) an underlying theme to spot if you look hard enough. Just as I first starting observing the repetitive words of my clients, an awareness of a trend will begin to unfold for you if you pay attention. At first it may be masked and not apparent until you genuinely want to see it.

Noticing the symbolism, metaphors or literal themes in your behaviour as well as in your words will help you discover how you believe and therefore, continue to create.

As I indicated before patterns can come from uninteresting, subtle or even tedious repetitious events which can be much less obvious and difficult to pinpoint. Take for example being ignored or isolated as a child in a family where no one interacted with each other, or where *'children were to be seen and not heard'*, or being raised in an environment where only boys were allowed opinions and women were always cared for but not expected to accomplish much or work outside the house, or a home where no one ever raised their voice but it was clear there were undesirable repercussions to misbehaving. What beliefs would a child from these upbringings form?

We create beliefs around our experience even if it is calm and unmemorable. We may determine women are to be taken care of and never learn to make our own way in the world, have difficulty expressing ourselves or making decisions, not think we have an opinion or we may feel alone or out of place thinking we are in some way inferior.

We decide back in our past what we believe and we may not even know we chose to feel a particular way about the world and its' possibilities.

We are constantly building beliefs from our experiences (from our interpretation of our experiences, our perception). Whether it's a new exposure or a supporting experience, it is documented in us – in our recordings and potentially finds its way into our belief system. However luckily and beautifully we can choose to alter our beliefs. Even beliefs that have been with us since we were two can be changed when we choose to do so.

Sometimes simply realising that you have inappropriate beliefs can be enough. However sometimes it takes much effort and assistance to change them. Understanding your beliefs and believing your have choice though makes change possible. You don't always need to know why you have a belief to change it. Beliefs can be changed because you want to change, and using some of the energy techniques it can be made easier.

Gary Craig, the founder of EFT, explains beliefs as 'writings on your walls', like graffiti I suppose. He says that we all live or have the potential to live in a 'palace of possibilities' but often we only feel comfortable living in a few of the rooms of our palace. We limit ourselves. On the walls of the rooms we do occupy are all the rules or beliefs that we hold about our life and our possibilities. Rules/beliefs like: "I can't do that, it's not lady-like" or "I shouldn't do that, I might get into trouble or hurt myself".

I interpret his concept like this: all that is written on our walls guides us or distorts our life interpretation. **Instead of creating a life that matches our**

dreams, we create a life that fits within our beliefs. For many this is more of a surreal nightmare than a life. Sometimes we don't even know who wrote the rule because the belief came from someone else or from something we interpreted with the eyes and mind of a child.

Instead of creating a life that matches our dreams, we create a life that fits within our beliefs.

The people who we let write on our walls or assist in forming our beliefs are many. Our parents as I've indicated influenced us profoundly as they were normally the guardians of our survival and intimately involved with us.

Remember beliefs come from many sources, Let me reiterate some sources mentioned earlier plus a few more: our parents, sisters, brothers, our grandparents, aunts and uncles, other relatives, teachers, friends, our community, peers, colleagues, the television, the newspapers, the radio, the Internet, lovers, sport coaches, politicians, ministers or priests, iconic figures, musicians, artists, cultural norms, our environment, idols, our gender, and more. Let's not forget our therapists and doctors too. And if you believe in reincarnation, then it may have come from someone or something you encountered before this current life.

Our interpretation of our boundaries, what is right or wrong, our values, what we believe is respectable or safe, all these and more become part of our belief system and guide our actions. We make discernments and key value judgments adapting our choices and life around them. As they are frequently created by an immature dependent mind it's a good idea to review them.

If you interpret some action as dangerous or potentially uncomfortable or stressful you may change your life to avoid it. This may be the beginning stage of acquiring a variety of coping mechanisms, problems with anxiety or even a phobia. People strategise, often below their awareness, to manage life's expected or unexpected events.

Managing your beliefs is key to your success whatever that means to you individually; whether success means having the time to garden, or being wealthy in terms of the number of friends you have or the amount of money you have in the bank. Being open to reviewing and changing your beliefs and your interpretation of the world will usher in the ability to create something new; modern beliefs that work for you. Then new, different and effective choices will start to emerge.

Below and on the following pages I have provided a list of questions to help you uncover your beliefs. Although some of these may sound similar they are provided to stimulate thought in different individuals.

My Beliefs & Other Peoples' Beliefs

Step 1: Complete the following open ended statements, as many times as you would like to help uncover beliefs.

I am:

I am not:

I believe:

I believe I can:

I believe I can't:

I believe I should:

I believe I should not or should never:

I believe it's impossible to:

I believe it's impossible for me to:

I believe I'll never:

My father believed:

My mother believed:

What I heard my mother say:

What I heard my dad say:

My teachers said I was:

I believe it is right to:

I believe it is wrong to:

My religion tells me it's right to:

My religion tells me it's wrong to:

My family or community says it's right to:

My family or community thinks it's wrong to:

I could never be:

I'm afraid to:

Step 2: Then answer the questions below for each of the above beliefs you have now documented.

Was this true?

Is this true today?

Does this limit or expand me?

Do I wish to continue believing this?

Is it serving me well?

Is it timely and appropriate for me now?

Does it keep me from being who I want to be?

Should I choose to change this belief?

Uncovering More Beliefs (or Values)

This exercise will help uncover beliefs or some of your values you may or may not be aware you hold.

Step 1: Complete the following open ended phrases with as many things as you can think of that apply to you.

I'm uncomfortable with:

I'm uncomfortable being:

I'm comfortable with:

I'm comfortable being:

It's embarrassing to:

People are so:

I will never:

I don't ever want to:

I wish I could:

I hate:

I hate it when:

I love:

I love people who:

It's impossible for me to:

I refuse to:

Life is:

Money is:

People with money are:

Money means:

Our government is:

Authority figures (police, council members, teachers, etc) are or represent:

It's not safe or it's dangerous to:

It's not safe to be:

It's safe to:

Girls should:

Boys should:

Men are:

Women are:

Mothers are:

Fathers are:

Family is:

Friends are:

Children should:

Children are:

Education is:

I always feel.. when or if ....

I always should .... when or if ....

I could do .... if ....

It's okay to .... if..

It's not okay to .... if..

Step 2: Digging Deeper for Greater Understanding

You can always dig deeper into your beliefs by asking yourself *why* or adding *because* to your completed statement. This can show you what lies underneath or behind this belief, if it isn't already evident to you. For example if you completed the phrase 'I should never' with "I should never walk alone at night" you might find yourself saying "Because it's dangerous" then ask *why* again, "Because I might get attacked". Keep asking *why* till you have an understanding of the meaning for you.

Then you can ask "And why do I think or believe this?" and you might respond "Because my Sister was attacked" or "Because I've read about walking alone at night as being unsafe". Finding out more about your beliefs like this is useful for evaluating and adjusting them. By looking at what you believe you should or shouldn't do, your 'do's and don'ts' you can often uncover your beliefs and values.

Uncovering More 'Do's and Don'ts' in Your Belief System & Values

Although many of the following appear in previous exercises it is useful to view them together to see your self-imposed perimeter.

I must:

I must not:

I must be:

I must not be:

It's right to:

It's not right to:

It's wrong to:

It's not okay to:

It's okay to:

People shouldn't:

People should:

It's good to:

It's rude to:

It's nice to:

It's important to:

It is not important to:

I can't live:

I can't accept:

I must not:

It's okay for me to earn a living doing:

It's unacceptable to:

My Values

What is most important to me? (Example: Honesty, Family, Adventure, Health, Love etc.)

1.

2.

3.

4.

5.

6.

7.

8.

9.

10.

Note: Once you've identified what's important to you (your values) you can attempt to list them in order of the priority or ranking (1-10). You may find more or less than ten things that are really important to you.

Chapter 14
Choosing for Yourself What You Want To Believe

As I explained in the last chapter, your beliefs and the rules you govern yourself by can be added to you all the time and from lots of sources. However many of them have been with us since our early beginning and are outdated and certainly need verifying and updating. Adding or changing beliefs can be like adding software to your laptop or PC (or an app to your IPhone or IPad) but these programs control the behaviour of your mind and the performance of your life. Therefore, I'd like you to consider how appropriate your beliefs are for you today because although beliefs act like 'truths', they aren't always true or useful! Similar to software applications they can have bugs or flaws in the programming or not do what you want or expect.

Beliefs, your 'truths', are often obsolete, past their 'sell by date', inadequate or even useless for you. You are always changing and so can your beliefs. You can swap them for better programmes and choose what you want to believe. Rather than running on autopilot or antiquated software, you can replace, update or delete non-functional beliefs **once you uncover them.**

In the last exercises you identified some of your beliefs and possibly their sources. I also asked you to question these beliefs to see if they were still helping you. The next step is to decide if they make you happy or if you want to continue believing and living this way (just like in the Chapter 12, **Making Conscious Choices for Transformation**). Basically I'm asking you to consider if this belief is working for you.

It's obvious when I work with agoraphobics with their complex web of beliefs, limitations and contractions placed on their lives to help them feel safe, that their beliefs are out of control. Their routines and beliefs no longer serve them well and they want to be released from the restrictions which originally seemed so useful. They want to be free to choose differently, to navigate or negotiate through their days and nights more easily. They want to feel in control of their decisions and body versus having to choose the lesser of two evils.

Updating your beliefs is about shaping and changing your future by modifying beliefs built in the past. Whether they were developed in childhood or from recent life-altering events as an adult like going to war or experiencing great loss, I want you to be able to choose beliefs you prefer. Don't just accept what is not working for you. Rub out (erase) the beliefs you no longer choose to embrace or hold.

Some people are dedicated and disciplined enough to alter their beliefs through affirmations alone as discussed in Chapter 5 but a more thorough and fast way to make substantial strides in shifting detrimental beliefs is by using tapping. You'll find various tapping strategies in Chapter 20-22.

Altering beliefs causes dynamic changes within and around you and even reticence or conflict in others. As I mentioned in Chapter 3 when I talked about Sally's friend who wanted her to keep saying she was hopeless, you will encounter friends and family responding to your modifications. Any change in an environment causes others to adjust or to try to avoid it. If you watch for their response and are ready and prepared for it, you can spot it easily and won't be taken by surprise. Reluctant responses to your attempt to break free of your chains of old outdated beliefs and ways may come as remarks like: "Why do you want to do that?", "But you've always been that way", "You shouldn't do that", "You can't afford to go back to school to retrain", "Your too old to take up skiing", "What if it doesn't work" or "I don't think you have the energy".

Changing yourself for the better can have an immediate positive result on everyone although whatever your alteration or new choice is, if it varies from others' expectations of you or crosses their comfort zones (or beliefs) about **their** world they'll feel uncomfortable and may tell you so or act differently towards you. They'll tell you through body language and actions too if not through words or comments. They may choose not to be around you even. They may tell you through objections, throwing their own fears at you. See their comments as a reflection of their own limiting beliefs and not a truism. It's about them and not you.

When you embark on a process of personal growth and change, it shakes things up and people sometimes get upset. You may lose a friend or two but maybe that's what it's going to take for you to have a better life.

I teach Reiki as well and this is a topic I continually explore with my initiates into this healing method. People normally will feel uncomfortable when they sense the status quo altering and the energy changing. Many fear the disorder or disruption of change (the feeling of losing control), some more than others. As your energy moves up and out of denser emotions you will attract others of a similar level and attitude to you. Those at your old level can be unwelcoming, discordant or even angered that you elected to, and have changed.

Personal growth is what we are here to achieve in my opinion, so it's worth the risk of losing a friend if they are holding you back from reaching peace, joy and fulfilment. Remember that the truth is that we are continually changing and evolving. It's unavoidable. It just happens and can't be stopped. Don't be so afraid of change. Change is essential for life and must be accepted as part of our life. Our cells are recreating themselves constantly and every seven years our entire body is new. If you can accept and even be appreciative of change, knowing it's natural and normal, things can be much easier. You can then get on with creating what you want whilst expecting it will take change to accomplish it.

When it comes to the process of change, if you allow your friends, family, peers and acquaintances responses to your change to alter your choosing you are withdrawing or compromising. You are then acting from a place of worry or avoidance of disapproval or fear of loss. If your change is too great for them and they choose another friend as their confidant, I ask you to allow that to happen. Try and persevere. They may adjust to your change and it may motivate them to change but even if they don't, try not to abandon your choice to regain the old balance if it hadn't been working for you.

Anytime someone changes by choice or even if the change came about from something seemingly outside their control like a redundancy (a lay-off), an illness or a divorce, things will teeter or be in flux for awhile. Things may be unsettled for a bit or even downright uncomfortable or horrible. After the dust clears though, in hindsight you will more than likely see it was necessary to improve your life.

It's this fear of change and disturbances, wanting to please others or need to avoid conflict that you must release to make meaningful progress. I want to enlist you to begin choosing change verses avoiding it, but choose yourself and choose for yourself and not only for others.

Although I am encouraging you to be flexible and welcome change, I'm not saying you should take any change just for the sake of it, just to be changing. Your change should be done with thought and reason whenever possible.

"You must be active but you need to know what you are trying to do...directed activity...purposeful activity."

Whilst some people have trouble with change, there are others who make even radical changes quite easily and well, and still others that change without thinking things through.

I'd like to point out something I sometimes come across that may not be so obvious. I have coached people who made poor quick decisions because they had what I call *partnered* or *paired-up beliefs*. They had beliefs that were contingent or exclusive, meaning that they believed some options were all or nothing.

They had restrictions and ties built into their belief system. For example they may believe "I can't have a wife and family and be an international speaker" and therefore may then decide "I'll have to abandon the idea of ever having a speaking career or I'll have to abandon the wife and family to accomplish this dream". Some people believe you can't have both and they chime in with "You can't have everything" and there's me saying "Why not?"! Also some believe, if you achieve or have one thing that it will always come at a price and potentially with another problem or set of problems. These are contingent, exclusive or opposing belief structures which may need to be untangled. I believe you can have whatever you want but you might need to be a bit imaginative or inventive and adjust any limiting contingent beliefs.

Dr Abraham Maslow, Wayne Dyer's mentor was reported to have said - **the highest quality that a human being can reach is to be independent of the good opinion of others** when speaking about man reaching the pinnacle of his individual human development.

As you become aware of your choices and beliefs and start to change them, people who have tightly managed coping mechanisms that can't tolerate disruption or interference can be greatly intimidated by your change. You have chosen to move forward but please don't ask them to do the same or expect them to be totally happy for you.

Having the courage to change comes from within but it impacts everything and everyone around you. What I believe Dr Maslow was pointing out with his comment was that to reach personal fulfilment and self-awareness (to be a self-actualised person) – **we must attend to ourselves and not to the thoughts of others**. We need to be immune from others critical and judging eyes. We need to choose for ourselves what is important to us through great understanding and through deep thought.

Personal awareness into why we do things, why we make our choices, is a major and necessary step towards self-actualisation. It takes a high level individual to want to look at these things. Many never achieve this level in their lifetime owing to many fears or simple ignorance.

The human entity ignores often those things most important for its growth. It ignores for so many reasons, it accumulates these reasons and they become its armour; the armour of safety which in turn is ignorance. This armour appearing as safety is the limiting factor of your potentiality.

Why wear such thick armour, why not become stronger? Why protect yourself constantly from abuse when the main offender sits within thyself?'

"You must be aware of what you think – always.'

Make choices that encourage you, enchant you, expand you and build your strength. A good measurement or way to check your choice is to ask yourself "Am I making this choice because I'm afraid what others will say?" or "Am I choosing this to avoid disapproval?"

'Eliminate this desire to focus on drama. Remove the addiction of drama from yourself. There is a tendency to want excitement, and wrongly sought in terrible excitement, instead of joyful excitement. Wean yourself off of negative excitement. It comes in small steps, it comes as you determine that you will not allow negative to last in your mind for long periods.

It is practise that makes it work. Slowly, you will find that you do not enjoy trauma and drama. Slowly you will find you enjoy happiness and you will seek it only.

The first step, though, is just making the mental transition to choose happiness. This means sometimes breaking the binding ties to people that refuse to choose happiness even when presented with two options. When offered peace, joy, love, excitement and encouragement they would rather choose to be unhappy and dismal. These people will eventually either learn that they can choose differently or they will be settled with this hell.

You have the choice and you have the blessing to know you have the choice - so start choosing. This is the only real way of changing. Every choice you make, even if it is a choice to be quiet, is a choice. If you choose to be idle and allow the unhappiness to be around you, you have chosen. So start choosing more wisely. And simply encourage yourself to understand that there will be, almost as an addicted heroin addict goes through, withdrawals. You will have withdrawals from the excitement of pain. You do feel quite alive with these emotions. There is this thought that happiness is boring. It is not. However, the immediacy of pain and suffering sometimes outweighs the waiting for the happiness in its urgency and immediacy.

Be patient with thyself and make choices and if you choose wrong, change it again in that moment. Do not penalise yourself for choosing incorrectly for the immediate thrill of adrenalin. But change it as quickly as you recognise that you have turned the wrong corner. This is the answer. And with every wrong turn and correction, you will eventually learn to steer your car directly towards happiness.'

Disapproval by others should not be a consideration when you create your life. The major consideration should be: does it bring you closer to joy and to your source. Does it build you up or tear you down?

Some think I'm saying it doesn't matter what you do. Some interpret what I'm saying as selfish and that you can do anything to make yourself happy. This is not what I'm saying at all. I'm not saying discard compassion, courtesy or your personal morals. I'm not saying harm others with irrational or poor decisions. But I am saying, that you need to make choices for yourself - do not let another make your choices for you. You choose, you decide and you determine your next move. You determine the right move *for you* (which may be to stay as you currently are).

The less you focus on the judgment others may have about your decisions, the quicker your life can transform. Consider and minimise the impact and power you give others over your life and choices. Be aware that you may be letting another rule you through their approval or disapproval of your decisions. Also, Wayne Dyer says knowing *what you are **unwilling to do*** is very important. He feels if there is nothing on your list of what you are unwilling to do you are able to accomplish anything.

People often talk about waiting for divine guidance verses acting under their own steam. They want assurances and they want to be told what to do. This isn't how life works in my opinion. You may or may not believe in guides or divine guidance however either way, believe it or not, you are the one who needs to act. If you are inspired or have a gut-feeling or an intuitive hunch, you must still choose to do something. You may be pushed or nudged in a particular direction but you are the one who needs to take the next step.

When I have been asked about waiting for guidance from spirit guides or waiting for intuitive confirmation about or before doing something, I say what I heard one time during meditation: *"You must act. Waiting for it to be given to you on the proverbial silver platter does not happen…you must seek. And seeking is acting."* You must act even if this action is only expressed internally as a simple yet subtle decision, an almost in-discernable openness representing a lack of resistance rather than an outwardly visible action. In regards to guidance coming from outside of you or from within you, I believe this happens and that you should *'…listen to nudges, observe the accuracy, appropriateness, then you decide…the point is that you have choice. And if you exercise choice, you will be given many…opportunities of synchronicity and guidance.'*

Another question you may wish to ask yourself to check if you are basing your decisions on other peoples' opinions or judgments of you is "Would I choose differently if I were living on my own?" Questions like this can crack open the door to change and creativity. Who are you really? What do you want for yourself? What does your soul want you to be? Who are you able to become? Who are you denying?

Remember we are always becoming. We are always growing if we allow it to happen. Try not to fight the flow so much by clinging on to old ways or dogma.

Answer the following questions and see what might be waiting behind the door. Are your answers indicating that you would thrive with a change or you are doing the best thing for you right now?

More Questions to Ask Yourself:

What would I do if I had unlimited funds, time and energy?

What would I do if I were guaranteed success?

Do I act the way I do and make decisions I do to please others?

Am I confident I am living the life I want and not the life which my father, mother, husband, children or community expect of me?

If I were able to do it all over again what would I do differently?

If I could be, do and have anything at all, what would I choose to be, do and have?

Am I holding back or stopping myself to conform or meet others expectations?

Where would I be living if I could wave a magic wand and live anywhere?

What haven't I done or accomplished that I wish I had?

What are my dreams for the rest of my life?

Once you get the creative juices flowing and any blocks removed (including being tied up with beliefs that your actions need to be respected or approved by others) you can run with this. This leads me to my next advice for you. Realise your power to create and begin each day consciously choosing what you want to happen.

Designing Your Day – 'Programming Your Day'

Each day when I wake I 'design my day', or 'programme my day', if you like. I purposely fill my mind with good expectations for the day.

When I first wake up, I start becoming aware of my surroundings. I notice all the things my senses are taking in and start evaluating them. I notice if it's cold outside or in my bedroom. I might hear the wind or the rain against the windows or on the roof. I then may question and assess, is it raining, is the sun out already or is the sun going to be out at all? This process of appraisal continues. All sorts of thoughts and calculations start running about as we come-to. What time is it? What do we need to do today? Do we feel rested from the nights sleep? Do we hurt anywhere? Are we stiff? The list goes on and on.

Along with all the evaluations we are making about our surroundings, our body and how we feel, there's a building of anticipation, a building of our attitude and expectations. We quickly start jumping to conclusions. "Dang it, it's foul outside. Tennis will have to be cancelled." "My back hurts worse today than yesterday. I wonder if this is going to become the norm." "I overslept and don't have time to eat before the train." Etc. etc. etc. STOP!

I choose to literally stop the mind from rehashing all these things. I choose to stop the escalating auto-suggestions of my self-induced morning trance. Then I start over and I begin making my first conscious choices of the day. I choose to decide how I want my day to play out. I design my day, thus programming my mind to behave the way I want it to. I quickly stop myself if my thoughts were not the best and say "No, today will be super. Everyone will be kind and helpful to me. I have all the time I need for everything. Everything will be great. I'm grateful for the kind treatment I receive today. I will…etc."

When I say '*self-induced morning trance*' I'm referring to the hypnotic-like effect which occurs from the habit or ritual many engage in, especially at the start of their day. They take in the environment and current situation and immediately default to making worst case scenario suggestions to their mind and body expecting to experience the worst possible outcome and so they will.

When you wake, you may choose to instantly feel blue or glum about what you are sensing as you fast forward and see the many possible implications for the upcoming day. You extrapolate what you think it may mean for you and your family. Before your day has even had a chance to start you have planned out all the upset or problems you'll encounter.

It doesn't take much to decide to stop setting yourself up for a lacklustre day if you are aware that you can do this. All you need to do is stop and restart your thoughts with a new twist to them. It's very rewarding and the outcome is well worth the tiny amount of effort required. I believe through your thoughts we create our day so let's start out on the right foot.

Even pain and stiffness can be reduced by the way we think when we wake up. It's normal to be stiff after sleeping all night and once we move around things normally improve. Just saying and acknowledging this can make a big difference and if you did some tapping well that's even better. I might say "I'll move more freely once I'm up and about" or something like this. This whole book is bringing your behaviour and thoughts to your attention as consciousness is the answer. Be conscious of your thoughts in the morning too and make a conscious choice to programme your day.

A few examples of things you could say in the morning:

Today will be exciting and fun. I'll move easily and comfortably throughout the day.

Everyone treats me with kindness and courtesy today.

Today I will encounter wonderful people and have quality time for myself.

Today I will enjoy myself and feel confident and at ease.

Today I choose to be relaxed and feel at peace. I expect wonderful things to happen today!

I'm grateful for this beautiful day and all it has to offer.

Chapter 15
What Other Choices Do You Make?

I'm sure you are now realising what happens in your life is not random. Your choices and experiences have brought you to this point. They've made you what you are, and you continue to act and believe as you do unless you decide otherwise. Think again about the trueness of this statement: *'Every thought, every action accumulates. Every thought, every action sets into place a chain of events.'*

How you spend your time and occupy yourself including what you do for a job is also not accidental nor is it fated. What you do for your living like how you speak, what you read, how you spend your free time including what TV shows you like and what you think about or worry about is pretty consistent.

What do you do to earn money, as a job or vocation?

What you do for work is often about what you achieve by doing this job, what you get out of it (or avoid), how it makes you feel or even what it represents to you. Again, questioning your actions and what's behind them (your choice of employment or income) is fundamental here. Are you a police officer because you feel the world is dangerous and you never want to be at risk again? Do you see the police as being in charge and armed? Are you a social worker because you had a terrible childhood and want to keep others from having the same? Or are you a social worker because you have a vendetta against your mother and want to protect other children from neglectful parents?

The decision which led you to your current work may seem warranted and appropriate but I'd love for you to consider if you would have selected this same job if you hadn't had your particular life issues and most importantly, do you enjoy what you do? Often people select their careers by default or they just happen into them. Thus it is common to see people make radical career changes as they approach 50. It might be due to burn-out or could be blamed on a mid-life crisis. However, hopefully big life or career changes at this point have something to do with having grown-up and resolved many issues including having processed fears that were holding you back or driving you and being confident enough to make a choice to do what you really want now.

When we reach our late forties or early 50's some of us are entering a time of maturity and mastery. More than half our years have been lived and if we are mentally healthy and consciously directing our lives we may choose to shift. We have progressed to being more focused on achieving happiness and giving back through service and contribution. If our basic needs have been continually met, we were capable of growing and may no longer be interested in achieving status, power, security or wealth; that's left for those younger than us. We want to give back and enjoy ourselves more.

I'll use myself as an example to give you an illustration. I would categorise myself as an ex-workaholic high achiever. As I've said, in my 20 and 30's I was always motivated to earn a lot of money in order to feel safe. If I did this I felt I never needed to be dependent on anyone. I could maintain control and leave any uncomfortable situation if need be. This requirement to be financially independent from anyone else was hard to achieve but I thought it was essential to keeping me safe. So I was successful because inside of me there was no other option. I wasn't successful purely because I was enjoying my sales roles although I did like the creativity and relationship aspects of the work. Subconsciously it had been necessary to keep up the pace and income to protect the illusion of a sense of security which I gained from having money in the bank and flexibility.

Only when I lost a tremendous amount in a stock market crash and had the entire contents of my home stolen did I realise money and assets weren't the answer! They don't guarantee security. My sense of safety had to come from within me. I had to eliminate the causes of feeing unsafe to free myself. I hope that my honest example explains that what we do is always about a feeling, achieving it or avoiding it and links to any unresolved past and our less than supportive beliefs. It's important to understand what emotional state we seek and why to reveal why we do what we do.

Like many, at one point I thought my life's calling or purpose was connected to my early struggle or my success in getting beyond it rather. When I first started doing therapy work I came to strongly think this way. But now I think my change or choice of a new vocation indicates a change within me – a maturing and a healthy step and not that I was made to help people with tough childhoods!

People often link their purpose to the strength, knowledge and empathy they can offer once they have survived severe difficulty, illness or tragic loss. Learning to be compassionate is also considered by many as a desired life purpose. I think now that **we are confusing the barriers and obstacles to our purpose as our purpose, and the obstacles were only there for us to**

get beyond them to reach our true purpose. They should not be mixed up as the same thing. Basically I now think that everyone's life purpose is the same, and is to find and maintain joy. *"The challenges we experience are obstacles to joy."* These obstacles may help us in some way by perhaps deepening our personal understanding or providing further clarity of our purpose but they should not be confused with our purpose. Each time I change jobs now, and that includes my writing endeavors, I believe I'm passing through another threshold to a new level and to a new understanding of me. I must have freed myself from some internal barrier that kept me doing what I was doing before and not what I want to do now. I believe my personal changes in career (and living conditions and location as well) highlight my progress and personal growth. Our choice of career may just be another stepping stone on our path to find our purpose even if it does involve helping others it may still be only for our personal development that we choose it.

"The purpose, the main, paramount goal of this particular life, the human element, the human experiential life purpose is reaching, striving for and enjoying joy. We view challenge to joy as a lower consequential, subordinate goal or step to joy. The confusion resides within. If you perform in joy, you are potentially living on purpose. If you knowingly select otherwise (you are not). Meaning if you, your choices prepare you to find further additional or consistent joy you may be said to be living your purpose and we say on purpose. So you are on track. This is to say that there are numerous, multiple potential tracks available to each entity. Finding your one life purpose, as so referred, is we will say ignorant. And ignorance as some say is bliss, we determinedly disagree."

Some believe and many spout ideas of our life purpose coming from or being linked to an emotional deficit which we must come to reconcile, for example: learning grief, surviving grief, learning humility, surviving abuse to learn self-worth. However if our life goal or purpose is universal for all and is the acceptance of joy then directing your life towards joy, learning to steer towards joy in any condition is a valid path or purposeful conquest.

"Life is about enhancing and building your personal strength and depth of intention, overcoming your challenge, your self-doubt and disturbances. Relinquishing fear based modalities and patterns of self-crucifixion, self-denial, self-mutilation and self-disturbing patterns must be broken for further anticipation of clarity and strength, growth and vision. Without removal of damage true clarity and understanding is clouded. True truth is obscured."

Consider Everything You Choose

From our birth or before, our life is comprised of a series of choices. Everything we choose has an impact. Everything we choose to do has a reason and a consequence. In some philosophies it might be referred to as *cause and effect*.

Consider where your mind and energy is concentrated. Know what your focal point is.

Reflect on:

- What you choose to say, think and believe
- How you choose to feel
- How you choose to behave (your actions)
- What you do as a past-time
- What you watch on TV, your choice of movies and programmes
- The papers you read
- Is it helpful for you to watch the news
- What you listen to on the radio
- The music you select to listen to and the lyrics
- The people you choose to surround yourself with
- Your choice of friends
- Your choice of partner
- What you do for a living
- Your hobbies
- Where you holiday
- What activities you prefer
- What you read for fun
- What you study
- What interests you
- What you eat
- How you dress
- What colours you choose
- Where you live
- What your home looks like
- What you believe you must have or should have to feel comfortable

Conversely, but just as important in revealing where you are focused, you should consider what you don't do and why. Please refer to Chapters 13-15 where the importance of our beliefs is addressed along with exercises to help you uncover them. Briefly to remind you:

Reflect on what you choose NOT to do:

- What won't you do? Why not?
- What can't you do? Why not?
- What shouldn't you do?

Remember what you won't do or think you shouldn't do may be the reason you are kept from achieving what you say you want in this life.

Further Questions to Ask Yourself and Things to Consider:

Am I happy?

Am I enjoying what I am doing right now?

What do I get out of this feeling or way of being?

Am I repeating a pattern?

What do I believe about myself and the world around me?

Am I living my life and making choices because I fear something or doubt myself?

Am I achieving my true potential?

Am I limiting myself?

Could I do more or better my life?

Is my job right for me? Or is it satisfying some internal void, worry or craving?

What do I like, love and want?

Do I do things that I don't want to do or do not like?

Am I doing things out of obligation or because I feel I should or have to?

Have I adopted coping strategies to avoid pain or panic?

Am I manipulating situations to get what I want, or so I don't have to say no or be the bad guy?

Does my job tell me anything about myself that I should clear?

Chapter 16
What Stops You From Improving Your Life?

What stops you from improving your life? What stops you from feeling happy or getting better? What keeps you from having a wonderful relationship, home or career? Maybe you've given up? Maybe you don't know what to do or are afraid to rock the boat? Maybe you are too busy trying to please others? These are all things that can keep you stuck in your ways. Settling consciously or subconsciously or deciding it is better or easier to keep things as they are is often the reason.

Sometimes it's the pessimism you have acquired over years of dealing with problem after problem. Sometimes it comes from listening and accepting bad advice from professionals who didn't know how to help you.

Discouragement, compliance, or thinking "this is just the way it's going to be" can lead you to a place of apathy and hopelessness. Even family members and friends, as I described, may be keeping you stagnating.

When a client tells me their doctor told them they have an incurable condition, my ears perk up and I get excited. Odd as it may sound, I know I immediately have an opportunity to uplift someone. Explaining how powerful the mind is and how YOU can positively affect your life through your thoughts, attitude and tapping is an amazing gift to offer someone. Curing something is not what I'm promising; it's about improving the quality of one's life and well-being. It is true that I have helped people get over *incurable* things before and I continue to guide people out of dismal situations. So I have a contagious genuine optimism.

Choosing to believe there is no way forward, or choosing to believe you don't deserve abundance or joy in your life has disastrous effects. The mind is so powerful; I believe there is always an answer out there or at least some way to change things for the better. My lovely husband thinks that the most significant discoveries in the coming decades will be about the power and capacity of the mind. I'm sure he's right.

Often people are stopped from improving because they get used to coping with the conditions of their lives or they don't think more is possible. After the professional said and everything they've read confirmed it was unavoidable. It's all they or their family has ever known. How could they change? Why should they expect it? And do they even want to change?

Be aware too of ill-experienced although good-hearted therapists. I can't count how many times I've heard that a complementary or alternative therapist, counsellor or doctor told a client of mine that they were too difficult or their problem too complex. Unfortunately one might take this to mean that they are incapable of getting better. I've even had clients blamed for their lack of success when a therapist's advice, remedy or strategy didn't work.

Sometimes the therapist or doctor themselves cannot see a foreseeable positive outcome or are uncomfortable or never encountered the client's particular condition. Then rather than referring the client elsewhere or saying they're out of their depth they sometimes shift the blame to the client. This is not to say the client is always right and the therapist is always wrong. I have had clients who decide not to get better. They decide sometimes that their situation or habit works well for them and decide not to change. As I said earlier, no one can force someone to heal or alter the way they choose to think or live, they have to do it for themselves.

If your therapist or consultant thinks you're beyond help or you aren't seeing any positive results after honestly working with them perhaps you need to try someone else or a different strategy. Although the responsibility for change and healing ultimately comes from you, having a guide who can help you see new possibilities is wonderful.

What does it take to gain health and prosperity?

The major requirements for healing and prosperity in my view are simple - *a willingness to take responsibility and a willingness to change.* If you combine responsibility for your actions and thoughts with a sincere unrestricted desire you can improve any situation. You may need encouragement by means of a talented and optimistic mentor or therapist, some techniques and practise, but it is possible.

My success rate with clients exceeds 85%; it may even be closer to 90% if I can be this bold. The only people who have had no improvement were those who refused to try and those who refused to talk about their past.

Some have a lot of their current beliefs, habits or patterns to alter whilst others only need to amend a few things to see results. Your lifestyle and environment may need some tweaking too, as it needs to be supportive of your desired change as well. But the mind is the real culprit. *The most important restrictions come from within you; your mindset impacts your choices and motivation. "Your thoughts are you."*

Restrictions from Within – Resistance

A very odd thing happens with many people who come to me for help. At some stage in the therapy work we hit a turning point. We reach the crux where a decision must be made. Do they really want to get over their problem and have what they say they want or do they want to continue the way they've been? Are they willing to break with the cycle or pattern and what it gives them?

We may have encountered some resistance before but there is an acknowledgeable point when the person realises their involvement in maintaining the current limitation or problem. They realise, too, it may be possible to get beyond it. They understand the restrictions are being created by them and that they must choose. They know they'll have to give up particular beliefs and ways of being and they may not want to do this.

This may sound silly to you. You may be thinking "No one wants to have anxiety attacks" or "No one would knowingly restrict their healing or wealth" but they do. It happens all the time. Although the pattern may have snuck up on them unknowingly and been continued unconsciously, it has now become apparent.

As Sue Stockdale, the dynamic woman who was the first woman to reach the North Pole explained to me, some people decide to stay consciously incompetent. When they first came to me with their *problem* it was an unconscious incompetence and I helped them shift it into consciousness. Now they have the power to choose, it's their choice to deal with it or leave it alone.

In almost every complex case I've worked with, the client reaches the realisation that they've been benefitting in some way, no matter how bizarre, from the life situation or condition they've originally come to see me about. It comes as a shock and even embarrassment for many. They may even deny it when it has become crystal clear and evidenced in our work together. I'll explain more about this stage in Chapter 17, **Breaking Those Tough Patterns, Moving to Acceptance and Forgiveness**.

What form does resistance take?

First of all, everyone who comes to me initially does so because something in their life isn't working. They say they want help. They say they want change. Actually, I think people find me when they have been attempting change for a long time and are truly ready for it. But they have some sort of resistance not allowing them to easily change. The resistance is a conflict between what they say they want, what they believe (their belief system, I've spoken so much about, which structures their life) and their coping strategies.

Over our lifetime we have been developing and honing life strategies. In order to change, we must push our current boundaries. Accurate awareness alone can help remove many obstacles and self-imposed restrictions but using some of the energy therapy tools now available can promote more rapid cognitive shifts in how you think of something or perceive it, managing to alter what we thought was unalterable and fixed for good. Flexibility and expansion with more rational thinking is a common outcome of tapping.

Whilst some hesitance to change may be apparent, I often encounter unconscious resistance operating in my clients. They usually aren't aware of what's holding them back or may be in denial about it. Although some know what's stopping them and actively choose to continue to resist change often my clients really feel it's outside their control.

Working at a level that accesses resistance can be very empowering, especially when previously there has been a limited understanding of their feelings, their focus on the past and little if any recognition of beliefs and how they affect their state of being. So when the source of the restriction or resistance is revealed, it comes as a big surprise. Most resistance I have encountered with my clients involved aspects of fear, or a lack of love and acceptance, personal responsibility or forgiveness.

Common Pitfalls, Reasons You Don't Succeed and Self-Sabotage

There are many things which contribute to a happy, healthy, abundant life just as there are many things which may keep you from it. Finding your patterns and the way in which you sabotage or positively influence every outcome is what this is all about.

There are contributing factors to any self-sabotaging pattern or behaviour. I've discussed how beliefs, contradictory beliefs, secondary gains (vested interests or benefits) and the past can stop you from succeeding. Destructive sabotaging behaviour does not have to appear that way (destructive) to be wrong for you or keep you from achieving your aim. Whatever you are doing *wrong (or right)* in your life, you are electing to do it and electing to keep doing it. Maybe you didn't have the best role models and like to blame others but at some point in your life you have to draw a line in the sand and say you are ready to move into the future and learn new ways.

With some effort you can find your disruptive or interfering style and choose to stop derailing yourself. You can find out what you are doing and why. In Chapter 18, I look closely at the subconscious mind and how it thinks it is helping us even though sometimes the result is something we don't want in our life.

Wanting to please others

One of the more common pitfalls I see is that of wanting to always please others. A need to please others can be innocently incapacitating. Even though it can appear altruistic and helpful it may not truly be for you and a desperate need to please at all costs can be extremely detrimental. Always having to behave in ways that you think will please others, to gain favour or love is taxing in so many ways. People who are continually trying to please often look to others for their approval or recognition and usually alter themselves and their behaviour forgetting who they really are. They often think it is selfish or self-centred to think about their own needs but become reliant on the response or happiness of those around them. In the end their efforts sometimes work in reverse and actually shift their burden on to those whom they seek to please.

People who look to others for their self-worth through pleasing have trouble identifying their own needs and desires. They have convinced themselves they're putting others first yet they've deferred the responsibility for their own emotional state and keep looking externally for love and acceptance. It's a great feeling to see others happy but the cost may be too great if you forget yourself.

Fear of failure, fear of success, fear of change

As you would expect, I encounter many people sabotaging themselves because of a fear of failure. These fears are almost always linked to beliefs and not always linked to a past failure as you might assume (although they might be). Often it's about what you think you have to do or be to get where or what you want. It's not only what you think will happen if you fail but what will happen if you succeed. Fear of success and fear of change is also widespread.

What are the ramifications of success or failure? How will you feel and how will others feel? There can be fear of the unknown, fear of embarrassment, fear of loss, fear of standing out, fear of not being good enough (not standing out), fear of letting people down, fear of getting tired, fear of jealousy, fear of not being liked and reprisal from others and fear of being different than others in your family or peer group. What will people think? How will you be treated? There are a multitude of possibilities and reasons why you may stop yourself. Although you can overcome them if you choose, you must understand your reasons first.

Not succeeding at something may also actually indicate that you never really wanted it, or you wanted something else, or you are used to feeling differently than how you think you'll feel if you accomplish it. It's also easy to say to yourself "Oh, it wasn't meant to be." when in fact you've sabotaged your effort.

Your desires may be in conflict with your religion, upbringing, cultural norms, family, friends, education, past experiences or history. You may not be able to imagine it could happen for you. Or you may not know how to go about it, so give up too easily. You may be too busy surviving to plan. You may know what you don't want and haven't ventured to dream about what you do because you are too caught up in your current drama.

In Chapter 15, I briefly discussed some of the many choices you have in your life including your work, what you watch on television and your beliefs in Chapter 13, **Uncovering Core Beliefs and Repeating Patterns, Discovering Why You Choose as You Do**. If after checking for any limiting beliefs you still don't see what you want beginning to show up in your life, and the prospect seems doubtful, you should consider a few more things. Take a close look at your lifestyle, your environment and your food. Additionally, as a tapping coach I want to present the concept of energy toxins and how they block or jam us later in this chapter.

Lifestyle

Lifestyle refers to how you lead your life. It's about your diet (what you choose to eat), how you sleep, what you do for exercise or if you exercise at all, if you smoke, if or how much alcohol you drink regularly, how much water you consume (do you drink the recommended 2 litres a day), do you get outside each day and any other of the many day to day choices which affect your body, mind and spirit. This includes whether you are in a loving relationship and whether you do things which are fun and pleasing to you and supportive of your goals.

Your lifestyle has a direct impact on how you feel and may require some slight adjustment, supplementation or radical change to match what you want. Meaning you may need to eat a balanced diet instead of living on packets of crisps (potato chips) and chocolate bars, you might need to cut down on alcohol and cigarettes and modify your social schedule taking a break from your heavy drinking mates to allow for a walk in the woods, quiet contemplation or exercise.

Environment

Your environment, your home, your workplace and the people you choose to have around you or associate with have a massive impact on you. Your environment frequently is reflective of your beliefs and past, mirroring your feelings about yourself and your self-worth.

Notice if your house is tidy or a tip (dump or mess), is it comfortable and welcoming or unpredictable and potentially dangerous? Who do you live with? Are they kind and loving or angry, controlling, or intimidating? Can you be yourself in your own home? Do you have space for yourself? Do you have any privacy? Are you at peace and at home there?

Sometimes your place of dwelling or partner is not supportive of your goals and it's necessary and worthwhile to change or move homes to achieve what you want including good health. Some environments are just not tolerable or sustainable. However, I have seen dramatic changes occur in someone's environment exclusively because of their own personal change. Often I witness that when my clients make improvements in their own beliefs and clear away the damage or upset they've been holding onto, their environment and significant other fall into place miraculously.

Change yourself first and the environment may change on its own. As you become more comfortable your living space or work will begin to match your internal feelings. Many times this happens without a single word or complaint ever being spoken.

Depression

Sometimes a person is clinically depressed or unbalanced and they aren't able to bring themselves out of it without some assistance. In this case anti-depressants, mood-stabilisers or anti-anxiety medication may be necessary and effective. They can elevate the mood enough to allow change and improvement. Seek medical help is you believe you may be helped by these medications. When the brain does not have enough serotonin or has a chemical imbalance in the neurotransmitters (dopamine and serotonin) it may prohibit feeling contented or balanced. Natural or pharmaceutical medications, herbs, vitamins (B-complex especially B3, B6 and B12, Vitamin C, Zinc), Omega 3 oil and mineral supplements (Calcium, Magnesium and others) can be extremely beneficial. Sometimes the natural alternative to prescriptive anti-depressants, St John's Wort provides enough needed support.

I always recommend that using anti-depressants should go hand in hand with working with a tapping coach or therapist and/or a psycho-therapist or counsellor to get at the cause of the depression.

Depression is very common these days owing to our intensely stressful modern lifestyle. There are also hereditary and environmental factors, sunlight and nutritional deficiencies to consider. Be sure to seek out the proper medical professional to help you.

Many people can find themselves depressed in the autumn and winter when there is less daylight which causes the body's serotonin levels to drop. SAD or Seasonal Adjustment Disorder is a form of depression which is more prevalent in the higher latitudes which have shorter days and receive less sun than the lower latitudes. Regardless of your latitude, it is possible to suffer with SAD if you work in an office with little access to natural light. Serotonin is released as light passes through our eyes to the brain so it's important to get outside every day or use a SAD lamp to stimulate this release if you are susceptible to winter blues.

I hear a lot of objections from my clients to taking anti-depressants because of the stigma associated with mental illness or the potential side effects of medication. Many benefit from being on them on a short term or seasonal basis whilst others may require them permanently. Be sure to ask your doctor for advice if you think you might need some support in this way.

For those with occasional mild to moderate depression I often recommend my clients try St. John's Wort first, especially if they are reluctant to discuss their situation with their doctor. Whatever the option they select, I have seen anti-depressants provide relief and an essential window of opportunity in many cases for improved results with tapping.

Severe Depression or Mental Illness

Those who are dealing with various forms of serious mental illness, severe depression or other complex conditions like OCD (Obsessive Compulsive Disorder), various personality disorders, Schizophrenia and Bi-polar Disorder should seek guidance from mental health professionals and a therapist experienced and comfortable with working with their condition. They can benefit from tapping and other cognitive work but need to find the right methods for their individual condition.

Hormone Imbalances

Hormones can have a major effect on mental well-being. Women who suffer with mild premenstrual tension (PMT in England or PMS in the USA) or the more severe Premenstrual Dysphoric Disorder (called PMDD in the United States) may experience difficulties with consistent results with tapping during these times. PMDD is characterised with marked mood swings that resemble major depression. It may be necessary or desirable to seek medical assistance to stabilise the hormones with some sort of birth control pill, HRT (Hormone Replacement Therapy) and/or anti-depressant which is used throughout your full or partial cycle. Men too can experience hormone fluctuations or conditions which can contribute to health problems. If in doubt see you doctor.

Energy Toxins and Food Intolerances

Ignoring how we feel physically and ignoring our feelings may have similar roots. Food intolerances may have started at an early age so we may have become used to feeling unwell or dealing with digestive upsets. Something so basic as a food intolerance, whilst it may be able to be ignored, can cause havoc in our lives and may have caused us to stop paying attention to our other 'gut feelings'. If your stomach hurts often because you are intolerant to milk but you keep drinking it, it is hard to pick up other indications your mind-body is trying to give you including intuitive messages and nudges.

I have seen food intolerances be a cause for phobias and depression, even trigger a panic attack. Sometimes it's to do with the chemical response or histamine reaction in the body pushing the body into the classic *fight or flight* instinctive self-preservation mode or an immune system response, but other times it seems linked in with bad memories.

There has been tremendous success using tapping to clear (eliminate) intolerances. Although I'm not a specialist in this area, I have found that by eliminating the offending foods, my clients have had breakthroughs in areas of their lives seemingly not associated with food.

In EFT and TFT (Thought Field Therapy) and other forms of the Meridian Tapping Techniques (MTT), energy toxins are considered when we fail to make significant change. An energy toxin messes with your energy system making it very difficult and sometimes impossible to experience the typical fast and often dramatic improvements and shifts we can experience with tapping.

There are eight specific foods or products that can be eliminated to produce greater change when tapping. I recommend eliminating them all if my client continues to suffer with their problem even though they are being dedicated and persistent or if I cannot help them shift an inappropriate belief when we are working together. They are corn, dairy, wheat, chocolate, perfume, alcohol, tobacco and sugar.

I have found using muscle testing that every one of my clients with panic problems had an issue with one or more of these energy toxins. Energy toxins are not the same as a food digestive intolerances or allergies although you may also be intolerant to them. Because the body's response may not be obvious, often my clients are not conscious that they could have a problem with these items.

I have worked with people who had panic attacks triggered simply by eating chocolate. After someone has been off the offending items for a while they get to know how it feels to be well and when they ingest or expose themselves to their energy toxins they know it. Sometimes they are able to reintroduce the energy toxin without any problem but other times they are not.

Although I use a simplified form of muscle strength testing (kinesiology) to ascertain if my client is affected by an energy toxin and which of them (as do many tapping professionals), it's not necessary to have this test performed. If you are trying to tap on your own and are having poor results simply consider eliminating these eight items from your life for a while. This may enable you to have better results.

Dissociation

Some people find it too difficult to discuss or work on their issues. Sometimes it's necessary to use calming or dissociation techniques to reduce the intensity of your emotions surrounding particularly hurtful or frightening memories. There are many effective ways to accomplish this and most professional tapping therapists will know how best to help you. Tapping or Meridian Tapping Techniques are continuing to evolve and we have more and more advanced tools at our disposal. With these techniques and a skilled therapist, gone are the days of being continually re-trauma-tised through therapy or counselling without results. Get assistance from an expert on the more difficult issues you may have.

Persistence

Another reason some have limited success with tapping or other strategies for that matter is that they give up too quickly or without adequate help. Everyone is unique and you may need a different approach or may require more attempts than someone else. What works for one does not always work for everyone. If you continue to try and search for new ways to help yourself I believe they will appear for you. Don't give up. If necessary find someone to support you in your endeavour.

There are many tips available about using EFT, NLP and the family of Meridian Tapping Techniques on the internet now and you can download free manuals or workbooks from many reputable sources. There are also books, videos on practitioner websites and YouTube, DVDs and courses you can invest in or you can spend some time with a professional and you'll learn a lot from them even in only one session. I always teach my clients to tap for themselves and most all of my peers do the same.

This book can start you on your way. I am sharing with you my many successful strategies and exercises to improve your thoughts and choices along with easy to follow tapping routines. Although it takes time and practise to become an expert at these techniques, you don't need to be an expert to experience immediate improvements.

I wanted to help guide you to a greater understanding of your beliefs and feelings so you can feel you have a choice in your life. My intention was to open your eyes and start your search into why you do what you do. Only then can you change it if you want. If the basics of tapping coupled with my other advice is not enough to make the changes you want, seek help from a qualified and experienced coach or therapist.

Chapter 17
Breaking Those Tough Patterns
Moving to Acceptance and Forgiveness

Can we be too responsible? Yes we can. Just as denying responsibility can stop our progress in reaching our true potential, acquiring too much can do the same.

Taking on too much responsibility can take various forms. You may inappropriately take responsibility for other peoples' feelings, care, and reactions to your behaviour along with your own. Or you may refuse to forgive yourself for something that was in or outside of your control. Holding yourself responsible or liable and not wanting to release blame, guilt, or shame about something that you've done or experienced can have a similar result as the opposite of not being accountable. Not allowing yourself to let go of the strong emotions of self-reprisal can limit you too. Surprisingly, it can be as limiting or almost as continuing to view yourself as a helpless victim.

Either strategy (too little or too much ownership) can keep you locked into your past and any difficult emotions which resulted from it. So ironically, either way, you continue to suffer!

Just as you can't ignore responsibility, you can't harbour ill feelings about yourself or take on the others' problems or blame if you want to create a genuinely happy life. They all have the ability to eat away at you if left to stew. The person who chooses the victim role has elected disempowerment whilst the person choosing to be overly responsible may be choosing punishment or something else also unbalanced. Continuing to think harshly about oneself also weakens, dilutes or limits ability.

In essence if you refuse to forgive yourself, you are refusing to allow yourself to heal and move on. You are choosing to stay stuck if you reject offering forgiveness to yourself or to another person. You may even compound it. Ironically, more than likely you will keep having 'unforgivable' experiences at the hands of others or yourself even though you desperately want to avoid them until you release the hang-up through forgiveness.

I listed some points of resistance in the last chapter for you to think about. Now I'd like to highlight a common hurdle that many of my clients, especially those suffering with anxiety, have had to get over.

People don't want to relinquish the disapproving feelings they have formed for many reasons, and they continue to make questionable choices and adopt patterns which act as a form of self punishment or self regulation or governing tool.

I encounter many people who hold themselves in exclusive reproach for their conduct even though others were obviously in control and involved. The details and reasons for this are personal and their own but they tend to follow a pattern. My clients have shown a small selection of reasons why they knowingly feel they should not, or don't want to, release responsibility and forgive themselves for something which has happened to them or which they have done.

The reasons they express are:

1. They don't feel they deserve to release it.
2. It does not feel safe to release it.
3. It's frightening to attempt to release it. (This is not the same as item 2 above. This is about the fear around talking about the event or action for worry of being re-traumatised.)
4. It doesn't feel right to release it (ethically or otherwise).
5. They don't know how to release it.
6. They don't think it is possible to release it.
7. They don't think it is necessary to release it.
8. They feel releasing the emotion is contingent on something or someone else.
9. They feel it's too soon to release it. (They need to suffer a bit longer!).
10. They can't release it because they can't forgive (or think they can't).
11. They don't want to release it because it somehow provides a benefit to them.
    a. Possibly provides control over them or others.
    b. Provides an excuse for the other failures or problems in their life.
    c. Provides a real or perceived benefit (financially, emotionally or otherwise).
    d. Provides an excuse for getting out of something or not doing something.

e. It allows them to say "No" without having to actually say it.

f. It allows them to avoid confrontation or conflict.

g. Etc.

12. They don't know how their life will be if they release it.* (They identify with it and don't know how they personally will feel or function without it. They've had it for so long it's become a part of them.)

    *Reaching this point (as indicated in number 12) is usually a very good sign and indication that the transformation, the shift is happening. We're very close to releasing or *releasement* as I refer to it. (One of my made-up words I found in meditation that you won't find in the dictionary).

It's not uncommon for me to move a client quickly through each of the main barriers to release in succession until we come to the benefit barrier or objection, i.e. don't deserve to, don't feel safe to, don't know how to, don't know what I'll be without it, it appears unforgivable. When they realise they get something out of it, the shock or denial can sometimes be palpable.

Clients are only too pleased to reduce the intensity of uncomfortable feelings bound to an event. They'll happily work with me to drop the emotional sting down to a manageable level. But often they then are satisfied with this adjustment and want to stop then. Some don't want to get rid of the 'bad feelings' entirely. It never stops surprising me but maybe it's just the process of healing emotions; maybe we have to go through these various stages even if very quickly. Because I've found any reluctance to clear it away for good is usually because of one of the eleven reasons I've listed (there may be variations but these are the primary reasons).

Often I see reticence to completely release something when the cause of the event or the event itself has been interpreted as largely their own fault. Or I see this when events and actions were viewed as so disgusting that shame is involved and their self-worth has been distorted or destroyed. It seems that holding on to self-directed hatred or distaste somehow seems appropriate to them. There's a part of them that sees it as useful. (Refer to the *Parts* technique and negotiation explained in Chapter 18, **How to Handle the Subconscious**).

They may feel it helps them monitor and control their future behaviour. Believing or fearing that without the self-criticism or admonishments they would make the same mistake or 'be bad' again, be hurt again or worse. Sometimes they feel they wouldn't be able to trust themselves, so holding on to the terrible feeling is used to keep them in check.

It can also be an issue of justification for the consequential or subsequent events in their life. People sometimes want to accept a bit of shame or disdain to give an excuse to others for their life choices and outcome. You know "What would you expect from her, she had it rough?" or "He'll never change, his parents were drunks".

Sometimes the benefits to holding on to a problem can seem very compelling and real. I've seen people decide to hold on to pain because they get parking privileges and housing benefits and I've seen people choose to stay ill in bed because they don't want to try to be assertive as it risks conflict. People have told me they worry they'd have to go to work if they got better. These may sound trivial but many of the reasons I've heard are far from that. Their fears of change or loss of love, money or attention can keep them trapped as much as anything. People's coping mechanisms in this case have taken over their lives.

I've spent many an hour explaining the value of releasing the dampening emotions of humiliation, shame, guilt, despair, regret, disgust, fear and all the others. The lift you get from reducing these heavy emotions is freeing, and that's the worry for some. If they didn't have these negative thoughts about themselves how would they behave? How would they be? I can be very persuasive but I can't help someone who refuses. Some simply decide it is better left as it is.

My experience and client feedback tells me that they would feel better. So I believe it's worth the time explaining my concepts to everyone. Then they can choose.

I separate acceptance that it happened with the forgiveness stage of release. I explain why I think they'd benefit from releasing it. I explain that it does not mean that I or they condone the behaviour if they find forgiveness; also forgiveness does not mean making excuses or overlooking what happened. We accept it happened and it need never happen again.

Acceptance and Forgiveness – they aren't the same thing

Some think acceptance is the same as forgiveness but they are two separate and very distinct things. Acceptance is acknowledgement. It is appropriate recognition of what happened. It may incorporate a more thorough understanding or recollection of what actually took place; what actually happened including who was involved and the chain of events.

Acceptance involves moving from a place of numbness, denial or shock into a place of awareness, feeling, identification and discovery. Acceptance is no longer hiding an event in our deep recesses hoping that if we don't look it will resolve itself; it will go away and can't hurt us. Acceptance may involve taking credit or responsibility too.

Different than acceptance, forgiveness is reaching a state beyond it. It is, in my opinion, real clarity and release. Forgiveness is found when we reach true understanding. It accepts we are human. It does not condone malicious behaviour and does not right a wrong but it provides kindness, empathy and compassion for one's self and others. Forgiveness does not release accountability but changes our view; it is more appreciative of our human condition and the wider perspective.

Forgiveness is reached when our comprehension and perspective shifts to a more understanding level.

So, real forgiveness represents the infamous and elusive 'letting go' thing people speak of so casually. Letting go can be tough. It might be the Holy Grail for many! It takes insight. With traditional therapy or self-analysis it can take years to reach acceptance and forgiveness. It can take a day or two or just minutes when you tap. Using my tapping techniques has been essential for my clients to reach this point, providing a perspective and calmness they may have long thought impossible.

I think changing beliefs, perspective and forgiveness go hand in hand. We actually see the experience in a different light when forgiveness is reached. It may be that as we see it in a different light we can forgive. Maybe that's why Marianne Williamson who is known for *A Course in Miracles* says you'll know when you reach forgiveness. In my experience, there is something important which happens when someone finds true forgiveness. A weight is lifted – there's an actual feeling of this occurring, a feeling of becoming lighter and of freedom which can be accompanied with tears of gratitude.

Forgiveness has a huge place in the healing arena right alongside of love. Perhaps one is the barrier to the other, especially self-love. Forgiveness incorporates in my view, forgiving yourself for the action/s (the creative endeavour), forgiving others for their involvement in your perceived trauma, and forgiving yourself for harbouring any ill-will or scorn and releasing all of these.

Forgiveness has an important role to play and is an essential part of the *'releasement'*. I have seen clients who said they'd accepted and forgiven on an intellectual basis but they still vibrationally or subconsciously held disabling beliefs or grudges about the logically forgiven event. I'm talking about emotional (energetic) forgiveness and not lip service. Often we can think we have forgiven but we have not. Forgiveness is critical to unbridled growth and happiness.

When I asked myself in meditation what is the difference between acceptance and forgiveness, I heard the following. *"Huge disparity, massive difference (between acceptance and forgiveness)...acceptance is acknowledgement where forgiveness is the release of the limitation or limiting feelings about the action. One is just saying "Yes, I did this" or "Yes, this happened" even if it was beyond your control or within your control. The other is about not harbouring ill-will towards the perpetrator or the thing in you that caused it to happen, allowing that release and that to be quelled or squelched so the antagonist behaviour towards yourself is eliminated. (It's) different than accepting that you did something and taking ownership and responsibility and liability and it is not releasing liability and responsibility that we have forgiveness, it is without ignoring accountability but without harmful feelings surrounding it any longer."*

When it comes to letting go one way is to: *"Take it as a lesson, take it as a transition. Forgive those people involved because they are just lesson-givers. They just bring you to where they need to...If you can try and remember that the purpose of the lesson is (to)* propel you forward and to try to forgive, you can do more. And you need to look to the future. You have so much available to you but you are stuck looking at the past and no one can help until you make a decision to go forward. Decide today. Let it go. This is just a small, small piece of your life, just a lesson-giver.'

Chapter 18
How to Handle the Subconscious

I've been showing you how making practical adjustments can achieve dynamic change in your life. Actively making *better* choices, observing and altering your language or put-downs and taking responsibility can offer extraordinary improvements, but let's say you've done all that and you even took it further by discovering your limiting beliefs, forgave yourself and others and you are still stuck. What if after all your attempts you are still having the same failures or problems? Perhaps you feel your mind is your enemy and is working against you. No matter what you do nothing seems to change significantly.

Let me explain my experience and understanding about what is happening when it seems difficult or impossible to change. Usually it's not that the techniques don't work, although you may require some help to ensure you are doing them efficiently. Normally it's because your conscious mind is not totally in control. The subconscious mind is in control.

As mentioned earlier, the subconscious picks up through our senses at least a million times more information as the conscious mind in any given moment. The subconscious is using this information to make decisions for us along with our past experiences which have taught it about living our life including our dangers (perceived, real or instinctual for survival).

The subconscious mind is super efficient and does things out of habit by creating and consistently performing programmes, repeating things that work or have worked for us in the past. Whether it's processing our food, putting on our clothes, driving the car, breathing or causing us to have a panic attack, the subconscious mind has a programme for it. These programmes make most repetitious outcomes in our lives predictable and easy for us.

Our subconscious controls most of what happens within us and to us on a day to day basis. It does this by following pre-set routines from our past. If you have ever driven or commuted to and from work and found you didn't remember much of the journey you've experienced your subconscious taking over for you. It knows the route. You've done it before many times. You can safely let your subconscious be your auto-pilot. It will alert you when a new decision or choice needs to be made! Even things like your dad's phone number or your mobile (cellular) number sit in your subconscious mind until the conscious mind wants to access it.

Although the conscious mind can control all the functions of our body if we focus on them (even the so called involuntary functions) normally most bodily actions and our behaviour are in the control of the subconscious. The programmes or pre-set routines run by our subconscious mind, our own super-computer are intended to help us in many ways. They allow us to do things like effortlessly walk, brush our teeth, digest food and lift the telephone receiver to our ear when answering a call.

Our body's responses, intelligent decisions and instructions come about quickly and easily because the subconscious mind has learned how to perform these tasks. We have learned how to do things and the subconscious remembers all it needs to do to assist us. It now knows what to do so we don't have to consciously think about it. It recognises extremely subtle clues or triggers and knows it's time to run a particular programme and then performs the complex series of messages along our nervous system to alert our body of what is necessary.

Neural Networks

The brain creates what are called neural networks. In my layman's terms, these networks associate or link our experiences with our feelings (both physical and emotional). Our memories, feelings, beliefs, values and subconscious programmes are all connected through complex networks allowing us to think, feel and act quickly. It's not just about efficient or prompt response but it's about repeating what the mind feels would be an accurate response as well.

As we learn we are training our mind and recording our entire experience. We keep practising, getting better and better; teaching ourselves what is accurate to do in any situation we encounter. With every new experience a neural connection is made and each time we repeat it or something similar the neural connection is strengthened. I visualise the neural networks as tons and tons of spider-webs or cobwebs in my mind, or like a map of greater London surrounded by the M25 with its' complex network of connecting roads. The neural networks with their many associations and connections help us to make quicker decisions and make it easier to do things (if the association is appropriate).

Very importantly also, these neural networks inform us how we should feel about our experiences. More than playing an extremely functional role, activating rehearsed programmes for our body, they are linked to the recorded emotional reactions we experienced before in similar (therefore linked or associated) situations. Each time we repeat the similar event or experience, we are prompted to have the same consistent emotional responses as well as the same physical reactions.

These networks have to be changed if you want to create new outcomes and new responses. New neural networks or connections must be created and the old non-serving, out-dated or destruction connections must be broken to change the old patterns. These neural networks neurologically or physiologically represent or form our beliefs and response to current stimuli and experience. They can be totally inaccurate and inappropriate for you today and hold the key to corrective improvement for your future. Altering mis-associations and associations that are no-longer helpful is accomplished with tapping techniques and awareness.

Affirmations and cognitive self-talk are intended to help you over-ride the neural networks and the pre-programmed responses. However sometimes you've practised the thing you desperately want to change so many times, rehearsing it over and over, that the connection is like steel; extremely hard to break.

A helpful metaphor I use to explain this is that of a crevasse. When you first experience and respond, emotionally and physically, to something new a very tiny thin connection is made to an existing network made up of similar events and feelings (or a new network is birthed). It's like scratching a tiny little line in the ground, making just a light mark. Then each time you experience or practise this same thing, you scratch or dig a bit more soil away from the same place. Keep repeating it and the little break in the ground starts to look like a small trough. Continue practising it and the trough starts to appear like a trench. Persevere with the same behaviour and response and the trench gets even deeper. Soon it becomes so deep and large it's like a crevasse. Once you have created this crevasse it's so easy to fall into it and very challenging to climb out or to change your deeply etched programmed response. You need a rope thrown to you and some crampons to pull yourself up and out.

My analogy of the *iceberg* in your mind maybe should be extended to an icy sea and land with icebergs, ice mountains and crevasses that you need to navigate or successfully scale. One of my friends told me I must not forget to include '*icecap*' in my analogy (making a clever remark and pun on my surname, Cap)! All of the techniques in this book are intended to help you fill or cross your crevasses and create new beneficial paths for you in your mind. As I've said before the more you experience or repeat the same thing, practising the same thought, the stronger the connection is made. Your goal is to avoid the default *easy* route which causes you to fall into the crevasse again and make your way consciously by another *preferred* route by choice. It takes practise and minding your mind as discussed in Chapter 6, *The Internal Critic*.

You may have played out the same poor or wrong response to something 100,000 times over the past fifty years. Your particular reaction is fully embedded and automated but you probably never tried to change it with tapping techniques.

Although I'm totally convinced you can change anything with consistency and diligence if you want to, with tapping it can be so much easier and faster. With EFT or MTT and the other energy psychology tools we can change a belief and create a new neural network connection literally in minutes, providing you with a new option for perhaps the first time in your life. Then you must reinforce the new choice and higher perspective gained by the cognitive shift through practise and conscious management. This new and desired way of responding can become second nature rather than the old default way of coping or not coping of the past.

In Chapter 3, I mentioned counter intentions, *blocking*, or *rejecting* intentions. These are sitting behind the scenes in the subconscious mind as are all your beliefs and personal rules derived from your perception of your experiences. They all form part of your neural network system influencing your actions.

As your beliefs are formed from your experiences and interpretation of your world they too are impacted when you stimulate the brain to make new options, new neural pathways. When you change how you feel about something or how you react, you can change beliefs. This is extremely powerful.

Dealing with Severe Anxiety

Chronic anxiety or panic can result in severe phobias and huge lifestyle modifications to avoid triggering off another attack. In my experience, panic and modification are products of the subconscious (and sometimes the conscious mind as well) diligently and benevolently trying to help you stay safe. Strange way of doing it you might think by causing anxiety but the subconscious mind doesn't think so. It's trying to notify you to (a) avoid the trigger or situations that scare you and (b) avoid an emotion or feeling like embarrassment, loneliness, shame, or pain.

If you suffer with severe anxiety working with an expert may be preferred. Although you may be able to make progress and manage on your own, it can be more effective and comforting to be guided by an experienced expert. The tapping I do, has been indispensable for finding a doorway into the subconscious and negotiating with it and lasting real change must take place in the subconscious as well as in the conscious mind.

There are thirteen key premises in NLP (Neural Linguistic Programming) which we also use in tapping. Three of them are very appropriate when discussing the power of our subconscious mind. These are 1) *Every behaviour has a positive intention*, 2) *People work perfectly* and 3) *All actions have a purpose.* Additionally NLP asserts that the subconscious mind is not malicious in any way. Everything it does is intended to be in your best interest.

I sometimes have to explain these premises when coaching and tapping with people. They can be resistant to these ideas and surprised by them but as we begin to work with their subconscious attempting to gain its' acceptance to changing its' behaviour it becomes evident that they are true. Odd as it may seem, the subconscious mind thinks it knows better than we do (our consciousness). It may also think we are not equipped today as we currently are to stop the particular coping mechanism it has adopted.

A variety of techniques can be employed whilst tapping to overcome more challenging cases. There are many available and one of my favourites is the Parts technique which I discussed briefly in Chapter 10, **Do We Choose to be Ill?** and Chapter 18, **How to Handle the Subconscious.** This technique involves entering a state of relaxation or a light hypnotic trance and asking your body or mind if there is a part of you which is trying to assist you with your specific symptom, behaviour or limitation. Being observant of what you sense as a response (you may hear something, feel something, know something etc.) you then entertain a conversation with that part or parts of you which claim to be causing the reaction. You might ask the responsible part: "Why are you doing this?", "What are you trying to tell me?", "In what way are you helping me?", "Are you trying to alert me to something?", "Are you trying to warn me about something?", "Why do you behave like this?", "What would you need to feel comfortable so you can stop doing what you are doing?", "Can you suggest a few more productive, easier or better (more comfortable) alternatives?", "What do I need to learn to do differently in order for you to agree to stop this response?", "Would you be willing the reduce the intensity of your response if I paid greater attention to you?", "Why did you start doing this in the first place?" Etc.

The information you receive is extremely pertinent and personal. This data can then be used by you to progress further. Often the first time something happened to you the subconscious mind's response was effective; meaning there was a useful or good result (it did the best it could at the time for you). So your subconscious continues repeating the pattern as it worked so well before. Until you challenge it or retrain it, you will continue to do the same thing. You have to insert a new functional programme into the subconscious so that the pattern can be broken.

I also use my own forms of Timeline Therapy, regression hypnosis and my invention of *'rapid Reiki regression'* (the other three 'r's') with tapping to move the client's mind back to any difficult events in their lives to help heal them today in the present. It's often extremely helpful to go back safely to the past in the imagination. I often suggest my clients visualise taking me along with them to provide further confidence, protection and comfort. They can even imagine that I am tapping on them as a little kid or their inner child if it makes them feel more comfortable and confident. I also like to use a highly effective technique developed by Karl Dawson which he calls Matrix Reimprinting. It involves tapping on your younger self (in your mind) during a visualisation. This represents another excellent energy psychology regression tactic to create change in the present. These strategies require my clients trust and although they may each sound a bit strange when appropriately used they have provided excellent results. Some clients of mine have stumbled upon Mr Dawson's strategy on their own in our sessions or whilst tapping alone. Again my experience and feedback gives me the confidence to suggest trying all of these especially if you are stuck. I don't care if my clients or you think I'm off the wall or *'out there'* so long as the techniques are effective.

You have tons of patterns running in your subconscious and there are many ways to make corrections to them using the growing varieties of modern energy psychology. Some of your patterns are better than others and you can decide to overwrite them and the rules you live by through these amazing new methods.

Chapter 19
Using *The Iceberg Process* (TIPs)

Throughout this book I have expressed the importance of your language and how I believe it is revealing what your mind is preoccupied with and focusing on AND **what it is actively trying to resolve or create**. To recap, your words are exposing your programmes which are interconnected with your beliefs and history including any impressing or unresolved memories. As well as this, they may be pointing to any physical symptoms either exacerbated or formed by them and unfortunately all too often, your words represent your deepest fears.

Many of your programmes, beliefs and memories may be highly construc-tive for you, but the destructive ones also dovetail and tie in with your habits and patterns and most importantly your expectations and intentions which are setting up and creating your future. Using the wealth of knowledge and power the *tips of your icebergs* and modern energy psychology have to offer you, real change is not only possible, it can be rapid.

This chapter is intended as a summary and brief reminder of how you might identify and use your personal *tips* to uncover and clear your *icebergs* for a better life. Remember your words not only reflect or reveal your past but they greatly impact your health, opportunities and any forthcoming events. It's for these reasons they are so important.

The iceberg programmes you are running are the real key or secret to achieving your potential because they are showing you what you may be summoning (as discussed in Chapter 2).

Your words and emotions are acting to modify the field around you, main-taining, changing and participating in forming your own particular *morphic field* (as Dr Rupert Sheldrake refers to it). This field or energy cocoon, representing your energy vibration or pattern is what influences what happens to you and continues to happen to you internally as well as externally. Even Dr Pace's studies that confirmed that our bodies create and experience a matching chemical reaction (of neuro-proteins) based on our personal perception and how we feel about something is now considered only part of the puzzle of our personal participation in our well-being. The people at Heartmath have now found that our underlying intention and emotions (based on our beliefs) cause an instantaneous effect on our DNA through electro-magnetic energy transmissions travelling at the speed of light. This energy moves at 186,000 miles per second – that's equivalent to going about three and a half times around the earth in only one second! This is much faster than Pace's neuro-peptide model (when neuro-proteins are released due to our perception and feelings) travelling at only one centimetre per second.

'…their 'energy signature' is that which attracts and encourages…'

Granted some of us have physical or mental limitations and have had to make adjustments. I'm not ignoring this but accepting this, and wish to bring you back to the issue of attitude. Your emotional expression is contained in your energetic field; it controls the 'cosmic' or 'divine ordering' (which the Law of Attraction is sometimes referred to) and brings experiences and opportunities to you. Once you see *the tip* of your personal programmes, you are in a much greater position to create change, even if this only means an enhanced sense of well-being and fulfillment. **Your words should reflect your dreams and not your damage or unresolved issues.**

I'd like to repeat my statement made in Chapter 13 because it's so appropriate for this summary chapter explaining the significance and use of *The Iceberg Process* (TIPs).

Instead of creating the life that matches our dreams, we create a life that fits within our beliefs.

Summary of using *The Iceberg Process* (TIPs)

Briefly, the stages and steps of *The Iceberg Process* (the protocol if you will) are:

(1) Identify your own programmes by observing your repetitive language or thoughts (*iceberg language*), recurring feelings and patterns of behaviour.

(2) Uncover why you choose your words, phrases, statements or patterns by reviewing your unique and personal past. There are numerous exercises and strategies you can use throughout this book, Acknowledge if they represent possible '*iceberg words*', '*iceberg phrases*', '*iceberg beliefs*' or any undesirable '*programming*' etc.

(3) Become aware of what you may be summoning or calling into your reality with these language patterns and behaviours (including and

especially your *default* way of feeling).

(4) Identify the underlying beliefs and expectations these words or phrases may represent for you.

(5) Identify any conflicts between your current beliefs and your past, and your *stated* desires (of course this means you must know what you desire first). Any conflicts may represent *blocking or rejecting intentions* you have within you and represent what you are really *asking* for or expecting.

(6) Check that your actions (as well as your words and thoughts) are aligned with your goals and desires.

(7) Use my tapping techniques and many exercises (or any other methods you have at your disposal) to deliberately begin to resolve and change any sabotaging or non-supportive words, memories, beliefs or conflicting intentions you uncover.

(8) Use your power of *choice* to consciously correct and substitute any negative or weakening words, thoughts, beliefs and behaviours for those that are more empowering (refer to my various cognitive exercises). This conscious mental activity will reinforce your personal awareness and help you establish consistency in being more positive. This is intended to support any progress you have already achieved through tapping, solidifying your results and encourage more.

(9) Continually monitor your *self-talk* throughout your day practising '*good mental hygiene*'. Try not to let a single self-depreciating or negative word or thought escape without you countering it with a positive affirmation or *counter-statement*. This will help you to identify where you need to concentrate your efforts, as well as begin altering your brain's neural networks forming new *default* routes for more positive opportunities in your future.

(10) Optional - Seek help from a professional if necessary. Remember you can often make massive strides by working with someone who is skilled at tapping (EFT and the many energy psychology techniques that fall under the MTT banner).

Review and identify your words and phrases:

Because becoming aware is always the first step to any change, including being aware that you want more out of life or could be happier, I'd like to remind you of some simple ways to spot your own *icebergs* or *tips of your icebergs* in support of the fundamental point (1) in my summary.

Although, much of this book has been dedicated to explaining my concept and providing exercises and examples to help you see (or hear) your own patterns and sabotaging beliefs through analysing what you say, think, feel, believe and do, the following is a list to remind you of the areas of your language to consider. This list also includes a few new areas to review as you attempt to identify your own programming.

What do you choose to say or think...?

♦ When someone asks how you are. (For example: "Not bad", "Pretty good", "I'm grand", "Super", "So so", "Fair".)

♦ As your favourite and common phrases. (Examples: "Money doesn't grow on trees", "Nothing ever good happens to me" or "My life is so boring".) These may pin-point *'iceberg beliefs'* or negative programming.

♦ As your common or repetitive word or words which may be visible in many phrases and is often heard said alone. (For example: "Brilliant", "Frightfully", "Terribly", "Lovely", "Afraid", "Shameful", "Super", "Damn" or "Hopeless".)

♦ As your common expletives or phrases (the words you use when you are really angry or letdown, happy or excited etc. They may even be swear words. Some examples are: "Shit", "Why me", "Oh, no", "Oh my God", and "I knew something would screw this up"). NOTE: Remember statements like "Oh my God" are often followed up by more thoughts indicating some belief. They themselves may not be a *'negative iceberg'* but point to one. "Oh my God" might mean "Oh my God, not again, I'm so terrible" and then the person may experience feelings of shame or embarrassment.

♦ As your favourite adjectives or descriptive words. Examples: "It was *surprisingly hurtful*", "...such a *painful* idea", "That's *stupidly* simple", "and It was *chokingly* hot". These may represent your *'iceberg adjectives'* that are likely to be linked to your unresolved past or beliefs.

♦ As your common verb choice (*'iceberg verbs'*). Often you have many verbs you could select to use in any given situation however you may choose to use one or two verbs, over and over again. If this is the case, these are likely to be connected to something back in another time of your life. Some examples are: "It *drives* me crazy when she...", "I want to *hit* it hard"; "I'm *abandoning* all prospects of ever..."

♦ When you criticise or admonish yourself (*'iceberg put-downs"!*). ("I'm so stupid", "I can't do anything right", "I'm worthless", or "I'm rubbish really".)

♦ About others critically or what bothers you about them. ("She's so ugly and rude", "Martha is so arrogant", "He'll never succeed" etc.). These could indicate *'icebergs'* or a faulty belief.

♦ Phrases you have heard repetitively in your life or childhood, (which you may or may not use yourself). Examples: "Nothing comes easy"; "Men always do better in business". These may have created a belief or doubt within you.

♦ About life, your work or relationship. (Perhaps you say: "Life's crap", "Works unbearable", "He's suffocating"). These may identify further beliefs, expectations or *'iceberg memories or experiences'* to review.

♦ If you must decline to accept an invitation ("Ah *shame*, I can't make it",

"*Forgive me*, we're already committed", "*Life's so unfair*. I can't come I have to work that day", "I *regret…*", "I'm *afraid* I can't…", "and It would have been *wonderful* however…").

♦ When you are pleased or thank someone ("It was nothing", "Thanks a million", "That's brilliant").

Other things to consider:

♦ **What you believe, in general.**

For example: "Children should be seen and not heard", "I shouldn't eat with my mouth open", "Women belong in the kitchen", etc. See Chapter 13, **Uncovering Core Beliefs and Repeating Patterns, Discovering Why You Choose as You Do** for more information and help finding your core beliefs.

♦ **Your name.**

Your particular name itself often carries with it a certain connotation. It may refer to something positive or negative and perhaps even match one of your interests or something you love or indicate your potential. Additionally, your name may sound like something else or have another meaning when used in another context,

Consider for a moment the following names. Hussein Bolt who is currently the fastest man in the world. He runs like a bolt of lightning as far as I can tell, although Michael Johnson (who previously held the world record for the 200 metre dash) says Hussein's speed is extraordinary and that he wouldn't have expected Bolt to be able to run as fast as he does with the inefficient style he'd adopted. My thesaurus lists these words as entries for the word 'bolt': 'to make a dash for it', 'to run', 'run off', 'to take off' along with a few others.

Then there's the wonderful chiropractor I had when I was living in London named Dr Back who helped me when my back went out, one of my client's defense lawyer was actually named Mr Crook and my girlfriend who adores hot, sunny weather who changed her surname to Sun. Also, I laughed out loud recently whilst watching the BBC news as they reported on an MP (a member of parliament) named Reckless who found himself in serious trouble after he'd been caught drinking on the job.

Now if you look at my surname, Cap (which is Czech or Bohemian by the way) perhaps it's not a surprise that I ended up doing *tapping* (sounds like Cap, doesn't it) and creating a strategy for it that I've decided to call '*iceberg*'; perhaps below the surface of my brain I'm thinking '*icecap*'? And then there's Tapas Fleming, another famous fellow *tapper,* she too developed another tapping technique which she has chosen to call TAT (Tapas Acupressure Technique). See any similarities?

Your first name as well as your surname may hold some secrets or influence on you. They have underlying meanings which can be fascinating to discover. Ann for example is of Hebrew origin; Hannah is apparently the English version for it. Ann is said to mean 'grace', 'favoured grace' or 'by the grace of God'. It's a name loved by royalty as well as most societies in general. I feel blessed in a way and even privileged to have been given such a name because some of the other names I've researched have meanings like 'to be challenged' or 'to overcome', definitely not as positive as mine! Now, Susan I've found out means 'Lily' like the flowers, Lily of the Valley and the water lily or lotus blossom, but more importantly Lily means 'joy'. Doesn't this cause you to wonder about the whole water lily thing which is used as the symbol of enlightenment in many eastern religions or philosophies? How powerful really is a name?

But it's not just the meaning of a name that interests me. I've noticed people's behaviour, their vocation (as in my examples) and even their problems sometimes literally match their names. For example, two of the top Michelin starred chefs in the world are named Roux and Kitchin. One of my clients by the name of Bill had real debt problems and tons of bills. It causes me to really wonder and sometimes cringe when I hear some of the names people have given their children.

◆ **The nicknames, pet names, or the terms of endearment you may go by or use.**

Consider the nicknames you prefer to be called or accept people calling you. Also reflect on the slur words or derogatory phrases kids use to taunt or bully each other. They all may have an influence. Whether it's the nickname you use for yourself, a friend and a family member, this word is being repeated frequently and some thought should be put into it. Some examples might be: "My little monster", "Baby", "Sweetie", "Lover", "Worthless", "Loser", "He's my little angel", "He's a terror, "Thunder thighs", "Little Miss Hard Done By, "Chubs" or "Chubby Cheeks". I can think of others but they are a bit crude so I'll leave you to imagine or review some for yourself. If you call a child a 'Little Terror', 'Bruiser', 'Monster' or 'Trouble' (you know, "Here comes Trouble" or "Billy no mates" for that matter) does that reinforce in him or her undesirable or unhealthy behaviour and beliefs which may ultimately affect overall confidence, self-esteem, self-worth and potential?

Your Words Can Reveal Your Positive Nature and Patterns

These lists, although brief, highlight some of the areas where paying attention may be rewarding. Be aware though that *iceberg language* is not just about bad things or programming. It can also display very healthy habits, strong successful patterns and an excellent belief structure. It's not always about negative matters or negative *iceberg memories or words – it's ultimately about your focus, what is drawing your attention and what is most important to you, in a positive or negative way.*

Your analysis can reveal extremely beneficial mental patterns and ways of being. People who are often called *lucky* probably have wonderfully clear and positive thinking trends and language. (Please refer back to Chapters 3 through 8 for more complete explanations or instructions on some of the summary points I'm making in this chapter).

I've found that very successful people or those who at one time in their lives had what I'd consider pretty major financial success, also tend to use words that appear to indicate monetary goals (almost like an unconsciously driven affirmation) or a positive *tip of an iceberg* representing their past achievements. For example whilst my father responds "I'm grand" whenever asked how he is, which has always been a constant source of optimism for me as I thought it a fabulous attitude and positive statement, I've begun to consider that whilst it appears innocently optimistic, might it too be tainted in some way? Could it indicate as well his steady focus on the need to accumulate wealth to support his large family including his 'baby girl' who required tremendously expensive health care? My dad surely saw finances as critically important for the safety and care of his kids. 'Grand' might be wrapped up, even if only in part or just a little bit, with his beliefs about what it means to be a 'good' father.

Thus it may not only be his excellent affirmation and unconscious use of the Law of Attraction drawing to him his 'grand' health, lifestyle and displaying his expectations. It may also indicate 'a grand' which is slang for a thousand dollars, and point to negative or positive *icebergs* within him. It had to have been extremely difficult to come up with all the money needed for our family of seven and Stephanie's treatments and surgeries. My dad's life must have been filled with much personal sacrifice to keep us comfortable including having to travel constantly to maintain his high earnings.

One lovely woman I know, who at a very young age made a million pounds a year, uses the word 'million' just like someone else might use a less buoyant sounding *iceberg word*. I've heard her say things like "I have millions of ideas", "Thanks a million" and "I feel a million times better". Again, this word use could be showing her bright and confident nature which continues to bring her success and, or it may be identifying something more.

Then there's me, who believes that every one of us has within them an internal and everlasting brilliance that just needs to be found and released! Our natural sparkle or spark sits trapped under any of those dang negative *icebergs* that represent our disappointing or lacklustre memories that are just begging to be processed. My favourite and common words are, of course: brilliant, sparkly, gorgeous, wonderful, shiny and stunning. My husband and I often talk about how we love spreading our fairy dust!

Using Words and *The Iceberg Process* to Speed Therapy

I've come to believe all word choices, anything we repeat to ourselves or to others, are worth investigating. I try to ensure that what is said is aligned with what I really want or what my clients' desire. I've also found my clients' repetitive words truly hold the secret within them to release their issues, no matter what they are or how they're presented. Their words are telling me the priority of their mind and what is and was important to it at one time or another. This goes way beyond conscious thought but is clearly visible if you looking for it.

Your subconscious minds' point of focus is being highlighted and if you concentrate on where you're being led, the words often point directly to the most important issues in your life or the most critical *aspect of* any given experience or similar experiences. This can mean the difference between breaking a pattern and healing, or not. It can be what activates the final release of trauma and improves the speed of and ability to change.

The chief advantages of observing and using the *tips of your icebergs* as directional signposts, or sonar for your mind are major improvements in both the time it takes to modify your thoughts and behaviour and increased odds of successfully doing so. You are more likely to be able to unlock and release stubborn and complexly formed destructive patterns and beliefs acknowledging these words. I've found I'm always being guided by my clients' words, whether knowingly or intuitively, to the areas that need their attention. They have become indispensible in providing far-reaching change in even the most difficult cases.

I offer you now two true examples of how my clients' words (their personal *iceberg language*) helped me narrow down their issues and identify the beliefs and specific aspects of their personal traumas that had held them back.

A man came to me seeking help in writing his book. Although he had a wonderful idea to write about and the time, he swore he had writer's block and found himself unable to get his thoughts down on paper. Each time he sat at his computer all ready to type, every time again excited about the prospect, he just couldn't do it. Something stopped him. In our one session together when I asked him what he wanted to accomplish that day he said "I want to abandon my habit of procrastination". As I had been working with my idea that all our words were telling the story of our past (and our future for that matter) for some time by then, I immediately noted the odd word choice or use of the word 'abandon' and wrote it on my piece of paper in tiny illegible letters that only I could decipher.

We worked to identify why he felt he was blocked by looking at what might happen when his book was finished or why he felt he couldn't or shouldn't write it. We quickly investigated various beliefs about capability, fear of failure, etc. and then I asked him to tell me a bit about his childhood (privately knowing I'd never heard anyone use the word 'abandon' in their goal statement before although I certainly have since). He proceeded to tell me what I had suspected. He was raised by his elderly grandparents after his very young mum and dad had abandoned him. They had left him one summer morning on the grandparents' doorstep with a note when he was only four. We hit the goldmine! This was it. We then focused our attention on this abandonment issue. Using tapping we uncovered his writer's block came from a subconscious worry that he'd be rejected again just as he was when he was four when his book came out. He was inadvertently avoiding the risk of rejection by stopping his creativity.

My second example is about another gentleman I'd like to call Mark. Mark was referred to me by a friend after he was told by another conventional therapist that he'd need to commit to two lengthy sessions a week for a minimum of a year to see results. He wanted quicker results and his friend had heard about me and about tapping. When Mark drove down to see me I was impressed immediately by his professionalism, honesty and pacifist nature. It was saddening for me when he expressed that he'd lived in fear all his life and was constantly worried about his decisions and his future. Again, I listened for and acknowledged any odd or repetitive word use. As I noted them it was obvious to me that he'd been abused. I then used his very words to guide him to the areas of his life that I felt might be contributing and holding him currently in his stressful state.

This very articulate and handsome professional in his mid-thirties had had a life that you might expect to see in the cinema. His mum had been a heroin addict when he was young and now she was an active alcoholic having replaced her heroin addiction for drink. His father had taken him away from his mum when he was little but having stopped using heroin himself his dad was angry and frustrated and used to beat Mark for just about any reason. Mark would get beaten if he spoke out of turn, if he forgot his gym kit, if he overslept or if his dad just wasn't in a 'good' mood that day. It was totally unpredictable but all too frequent.

Mark was amazing though, he didn't carry any resentment or ill-will towards his father. At a very young age of ten or eleven he had made the decision to forgive his father and from then on had adopted a profoundly wise state of forgiveness and gratitude for this man who had taken him away from his negligent absent mother when she had been unable to care for him. She was too preoccupied and out of her head to be bothered with proper parenting.

He was or is actually a very productive man but was being limited by fear. He didn't want to wind up like his parents. He worried constantly about his choices and sought financial gain for security and safety. He was always fearful about what was coming. Whilst I listened to him I determined the beatings were the biggest part of the problem rather than other possible issues linked to neglect, shock or embarrassment. He openly told me how he could handle the beatings but couldn't understand how anyone could do that to a child. I'd noticed a significant word in the session and saw him visibly struggling with his breath as he told me his story.

I encouraged him to speak (if he could) about the worst or most memorable beatings that stuck out in his mind. Mark said there were so many but there were two that he remembered most vividly. I listened, watching for the word I'd identified earlier which had been somehow out of place in his sentences and there it was in his second example.

The first beating he described was of having his head smashed against the wall until he went unconscious simply because he'd forgotten one of his football shoes and his dad had had to go back to the house to get it before a match. The second beating story involved Mark being kicked in the solar plexus numerous times. He was kicked so hard that his small body moved across the floor with each impact. His father only stopped kicking him when Mark could no longer breathe. As he discussed this second beating story he had to clear his throat continually and his breathing difficulties became noticeably worse.

I had noted that when he initially started to speak about his father's beatings he had coughed a few times, just little coughs almost more like clearing his throat and his breathing had been ever so slighted disrupted for a short period of time. The change was to such a small degree that the untrained eye would most likely have dismissed it as nothing. I'd also written his poignant phrase "I want to kick the habit of worry" and had circled the word 'kick' in my notes.

So, I looked at Mark and apologised and asked him if he would be willing to talk about the kicking beating with me. He instantly began to cry and with his chin almost touching his 40inch chest nodded in the affirmative. This was the lynch pin, the critical beating in perhaps a hundred beatings that kept Mark in fear. As we worked through this particular memory, relieving it, Mark's breathing improved, his body posture became more erect, his tears subsided and the discomfort in his chest and stomach eased and then ceased. Mark explained that he'd been kicked because he had been sick with food *poisoning* (vomited) although his dad thought he'd just eaten too much chocolate. After releasing the *'kicking' iceberg memory*, we concentrated on uncovering some of Mark's core beliefs and concerns about life during that session and were able to reduce his fear significantly.

Whilst Mark's *kicking* had been announced in his language, his mind's attention wasn't so much on the pain he had felt during the beating; remember he said he could handle that! It was that he had thought that time he was going to die and he could not reconcile nor understand how someone could do such a thing to a child, let alone their child. I have worked with quite a few people who have experienced severe abuse in one form or another; some of their words focused on the pain they felt and I've heard them say things like "It pains me not to be able to attend my niece's graduation" or "I hope it won't be too painful for you if..." (replacing pain for 'difficult' or 'sad' etc.). I never assume anymore that the most crucial or central aspect of someone's abuse is physically based – it can be, but also and in my experience always is an emotional component which often is more impressionable. It's not always about the pain itself though it can be. It can be about embarrassment, disbelief, shock, fear of intimidation, fear of the next time, neglect, resentment, regret, uncertainty, sadness, feeling unloved and unappreciated or any number of other physical responses or emotional factors associated with the physical, emotional or mental abuse.

When using EFT or other Meridian Tapping Techniques it can sometimes be a time-consuming or difficult hunt for the missing or most important bits (aspects, parts or elements) that made a particular experience so stubborn to shift. As you can see in my last two examples, noticing the odd or repetitive use of a single word can help you expedite the process. Use your words to isolate pivotal events (or a single aspect of an event) or to focus in on specific beliefs or fears. You may design a tapping phrase either using the actual words or they may simply help draw your attention to the area or specific time in your life which needs resolution.

When I'm dealing with clients with phobias or anxiety the *iceberg words* have proved invaluable as they show me the priorities as they are in their mind (the part of any issue that was the most impactful or damaging for them or what their subconscious is trying to achieve through its actions). These *tips* help identify the most important *aspects* in a phobia (see Chapters 20-22 for a more thorough explanation of *aspects* in regards to tapping.)

Another Value of Using Your Words

Much of what I've written about in this book talks about awareness and self-understanding, uncovering the *why* behind our behaviour (and words) but sometimes finding out why we do things is not possible for us right now. This is another reason seeing or hearing your words is so valuable. With your words your mind is showing you something important; it's showing you what you are (or at least it is) focused on even if you can't find out why right now.

Sometimes you're not able to completely understand *why* you feel as you do or *why* you believe what you do about yourself and that's okay. You may release limitations or issues anyway and reinforce healthy and supportive choices through observation, practise and dedication. We don't all have some deep, dark, stinking, lurking secret to unearth, thank God!

I've had many occasions when clients never found any significant, specific or traumatic events that needed to be released and other times although they had a feeling about something that definitely happened, they could not verbalise a reason or describe the cause of the feeling. Perhaps this is because the experience or emotions were felt in the womb, pre-birth, or in a previous life or perhaps their mind knew they wouldn't be able to handle knowing about it. More often I think though, there simply isn't anything *big* or shocking to remember. Although, there may have been continued negative reinforcements heard and felt as a child and youth or adult there may not be a definitive repressed memory just waiting to get out! Even without finding a *big* contributing memory we were able to make major improvements by tapping with their words and altering their day-to-day language including their self-talk (their inner dialogue of *the internal critic* that I spoke of earlier in this book).

Tracking Your Progress Using Your Words

As you progress down this path of self-discovery and change, please be sure to compliment yourself and acknowledge your progress. It's very easy to forget where you started from which is why I often provide a small journal to my clients and encourage them to use it if only for our sessions together.

I was reminded recently by one of my clients of her own particular progress.

She had initially come to me suffering with debilitating depression, ME and unresolved anger from extreme long-term stress. When I first recognised the connection between words and our internal beliefs and experiences, she was saying "No trauma" as a general response to almost all queries. I'd say "Would it be possible for us to change our appointment next week?" To this she'd reply "No trauma, I can do another day". I'd asked once how the teacher's meeting went about your granddaughter and she'd reply "It was no trauma". Lately she says "No problem" and we have both commented on it, jokingly because it still has an air of negativism. She rightfully reminded me that it was a vast improvement and although not her ultimate goal, it was so much better than her saying 'trauma' all the time. I'm trying to get her to say "It's okay" or "That'd be fine" or "Super". One day soon, she will, I'm sure.

So acknowledging where you have come from can be encouraging. Even if you aren't quite there yet, keep observing and changing and you'll get closer and closer until you're there. Continue to question your choice of words, thoughts and phrases especially if your life is not as you wish. Question all your choices, not just your language. Synchronicity speeds up as you become more in tune with your potential and your words may well be the answer to uncovering your inner sparkle.

Chapter 20
How to Tap

I've been referring to tapping throughout this book, so what is it? Tapping is the generic term I like to use for the expanding Meridian Tapping Techniques (MTT) often referred to as EFT (Emotional Freedom Technique) or Energy Psychology.

It is a group of extraordinary therapies which offer long-lasting relief from emotional and physical issues. They work on the cause of the problem helping to eliminate, neutralise and change the way you feel about the origins and any supporting beliefs that are keeping you stuck, limited or unwell. Using these therapies is not meant to be a sticking plaster (band-aid) although it can be if the use is limited to only focusing on clearing symptoms rather than addressing the cause. Energy psychology can provide real lasting change.

Tapping incorporates hypnotherapy, NLP (Neural-linguistic Programming), kinesiology (muscle testing), psychology, counselling and coaching techniques with well respected Chinese Medicine and neuroscience. It involves applying finger tip pressure to the body's acupressure points (on the energy meridians) whilst focusing your attention on any physical or emotional issues you may have.

People are successfully using tapping for almost any and every physical and emotional issue there is; from weight loss to cancer and dealing with the side-effects of chemotherapy, and from basic stiffness to the fear of spiders or even public speaking. It helps with serious chronic illnesses, simple and complex phobias, mild to medium depression, grief and trauma (including Post Traumatic Stress Disorder, PTSD), addictions and physical limitations including pain as well as self-esteem, confidence, relationship issues and any number of personal challenges.

As I've indicated, it can improve your attitude, change your beliefs and help you break a life time of destructive patterning. Tapping can help you reach your goals, gain abundance in all areas of your life and be a more fulfilled and positive individual. Whether you want to make minor changes in your life or you have some serious problems you are dealing with, the techniques used are the same.

Who's Tapping?

There's a growing community of *tapping professionals* called EFT or MTT Practitioners and Coaches. But you can tap for yourself or use the services of an expert or pro if need be.

This revolutionary therapy is being embraced by all healing professionals due to its non-discriminate and all encompassing high degree of effectiveness and speed. I commonly receive referrals from medical doctors owing to my success and growing reputation. Traditional counsellors, GPs, clinical hypno-therapists, psycho-therapists as well as other complementary and alternative medicine therapists are performing or recommending tapping to their patients and clients.

Why Do We Tap?

The EFT premise or *"discovery statement"* says:

"The cause of all negative emotions is caused by a disruption in the body's energy system."

Negative emotions cause an imbalance in the body which lead to disease, weakness and decreases in the effectiveness of our immune system. It is accepted now by the medical profession and common knowledge that stress contributes to more than 80% of all illness. Additionally I've shown you that it is also scientifically proven that your mind and body are connected. They cannot be separated. As Candace Pace discovered, your emotions cause instant chemical changes to occur within your body and Dr Bruce Lipton found that we control our expression of our genes by our thoughts and beliefs.

Unresolved emotions are the major contributor to your problems, whether physical or otherwise. Even pain is amplified and can be created solely by your emotions. I've been aware for a long time that pain is highly subjective and influenced by how you feel. However I am still startled by the display of the incredible power of thought and emotion when in my practice something which appears to be a *purely physiological* is totally cleared dealing only with emotional aspects. I now believe pain and many illnesses stem entirely from our thoughts, memories, feelings, beliefs equating to our energy.

Tapping corrects the energy disruption in our system and the effect is to adjust and then neutralise the negative emotion linked to an event or belief. When the negative emotion is transformed, the intensity of the symptoms, feelings and even the associated memories are altered. I can't tell you how many times my clients have laughed about an issue that only minutes earlier had daunted them for years or even decades. Both physical and emotional complaints can be released or improved when the causes of any problem are addressed.

How to Tap and How I Tap

Whilst the techniques I'll be describing for you are based on my original training in EFT (Emotional Freedom Techniques), I will also provide information that represents a culmination of my experience with my clients and my progression in the field of Meridian Tapping Techniques (MTT) in this and subsequent chapters. My style varies from that of Gary Craig, the founder of EFT and represents my ideas, insight and techniques from my successful practice as well as other experts in this field.

Seven Quick Steps to Tapping

An Easy to Use, Short Effective Method of EFT

Here's a quick method of tapping (the abbreviated form of EFT I use regularly). I've provided an explanation of each of the steps just following the description of the **Seven Quick Steps to Tapping** to give you a better understanding of what you are doing. In the remainder of this chapter, I provide **A Full Length Method of Tapping (EFT)** immediately followed by my personal advice and strategies from thousands of hours working with real clients. If you achieve good results using the quick method, keep doing it (it will save you time). Otherwise use the longer version and perhaps some of the in-depth suggestions and variations you will find in the following chapters.

Step 1 – Decide What You Want to Improve or Change

Tapping can help just about anything. Decide what you want to change or improve. You may have many things but pick just one for now.

Step 2 – Make a Tapping 'Set-up' Phrase for It

Insert what you want to work on in the underscored part of the following sentence (the classic EFT *Set-up Phrase*):

"Even though I have this problem or issue, I deeply and completely love and accept myself".

Example: "Even though I'm nervous about speaking tomorrow, I deeply and completely love and accept myself".

Step 3 – Make a 'Reminder Phrase' for It

Use all or a portion of the words that you have inserted in the underscored area of your tapping phrase as a *Reminder Phrase*. For example: "I'm nervous about speaking tomorrow", "I'm nervous" or "nervous about speaking". The *Reminder*

Phrase helps your mind-body stay focused on what you want to change whilst you tap on your body.

Step 4 – Measure How You Feel (0-10)

Ask yourself how you feel about this problem and rate the intensity of the feeling from 0 to 10, ten being the worst. For example, you may feel sad, angry or any other emotion; rate this. In the case of physical pain measure how bad the pain is right now with zero meaning you don't feel any pain at all (the pain is gone or non-existent) and ten being the worst it could ever be. If you have some other physical restrictions or limitations measure them in whatever way you can, i.e., how far you can turn your neck.

Step 5 – Tap on the 'Karate Chop Point' whilst Saying Your Phrase Three Times

Tap continuously on the *Karate Chop Point* (indicated by the circle on the photo below) of one of your hands using the fingers of your other hand whilst you say your complete *Set-up Phrase* three times (the 'Even though...I deeply and completely accept myself' phrase). The speed of the tapping doesn't actually matter, just tap continually. However I tap at about 100-120 beats per minute (the same as a baby's heart beat, about twice the speed of an adult. Which interestingly, I've been told matches the speed of the drum beat a Shaman or medicine man uses).

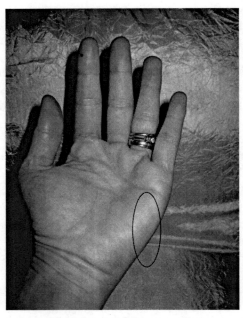

The Karate Chop Point

Step 6 – Tap on the Main Body Tapping Points whilst Saying Your Reminder Phrase

Now begin tapping on the tapping points on the body (as pictured on the following page), one point at a time, starting with the first position on the top of your head and continue through all ten points whilst saying your *Reminder Phrase*. You will tap on each of the points approximately 6-7 times whilst repeating your *Reminder Phrase* at least once. This is normally done simultaneously however you can speak your phrase and then tap or vice versa if that is easier for you. It also doesn't matter which side of the body you tap on; you can tap on either side, both sides or alternate if you wish.

Once you have tapped whilst saying your *Set-up Phrase* (the 'even though' phrase about the issue you wish to address) and tapped on the other main points on the body whilst saying your *Reminder Phrase* you have completed what is referred to as a *round* of tapping.

Note: The pressure of your tapping should be gentle as some of the positions are quite delicate, especially around and under your eyes. Contact just needs to be made with each of the points. Tap gentle enough so that you do not bruise or hurt yourself. However be aware that it is normal for some points to be tender. It is also possible to tap without touching the body at all through intention (using just directed thought).

Step 7 – Measure How You Feel Now (0-10) & Repeat

Now that you have completed your first **round** of tapping measure again how you feel (your level of discomfort) then compare this new rating to your initial measurement to see if the intensity has changed. If the rating is coming down (it has decreased) simply do more *rounds* of tapping (repeating Steps 5 to 7). If the intensity has not reduced, you may: (a) repeat another *round* of tapping saying your same *Set-up Phrase* but more convincingly and firmly (or louder), (b) revise your *Set-up Phrase* and/or *Reminder Phrase* ensuring that they are as specific as possible (starting at Step 2), then do a few more *rounds* of tapping incorporating these changes before checking the intensity of how you feel again. If there still isn't any improvement in your measurement try using the full length method.

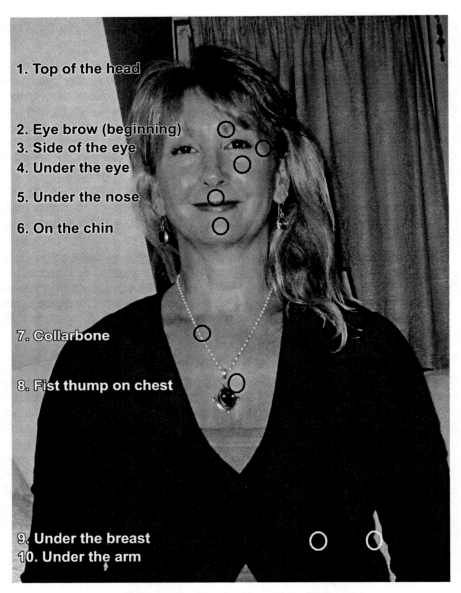

1. Top of the head

2. Eye brow (beginning)
3. Side of the eye
4. Under the eye

5. Under the nose

6. On the chin

7. Collarbone

8. Fist thump on chest

9. Under the breast
10. Under the arm

The Main Body Tapping Points

Note: The ten points shown above are used in both the quick (abbreviated) and complete tapping routines provided. You may tap on either side of the body although I only show one side in the picture for clarity. You may tap in any order however it is regularly done from the top down simply for ease. You may choose to leave out some points if you feel so inclined, however, you may get better results using all the points listed here. The *top of the head* point (1), *fist thump on the chest* point (8) and the *under the breast* point (9) were not always shown in some earlier versions of the EFT sequence but are now regularly used by most practitioners.

A Full Length Method of Tapping (EFT)

The full length method of EFT I am about to describe is based on Gary Craig's 'basic recipe' of EFT which I learned when I first trained to be an EFT Practitioner. (Whilst for many years Gary Craig provided a basic beginner's manual from his website, as of the printing of this book Gary Craig has retired. Please refer to the references in the back of this book for additional resources including websites and centres for learning more about EFT and other MTT therapies or training courses and workshops.)

Note: Whilst I am including a few extra points in the instructions of the full length method which I regularly use (the *top of the head*, *fist thump on the chest* and *under the breast* points) to avoid any confusion for those new to tapping I will not be including any other optional tapping points which I may use in sessions with my clients.

The full length EFT tapping instructions are as follows. Note: The first 6 steps are identical to those detailed in the **Seven Quick Steps to Tapping**.

Step 1 – Decide What You Want to Improve or Change

Tapping can help just about anything. Decide what you want to change or improve. You may have many things but pick just one for now.

Step 2 – Make a Tapping 'Set-up' Phrase for It

Insert what you want to work on in the underscored part of the following sentence (the classic EFT *Set-up Phrase*):

"Even though I have this problem or issue, I deeply and completely love and accept myself".

Example: "Even though I'm nervous about speaking tomorrow, I deeply and completely love and accept myself".

Step 3 – Make a 'Reminder Phrase' for It

Use all or a portion of the words that you have inserted in the underscored area of your tapping phrase as a *Reminder Phrase*. For example: "I'm nervous about speaking tomorrow", "I'm nervous" or "nervous about speaking". The *Reminder Phrase* helps your mind-body stay focused on what you want to change whilst you tap on your body.

Step 4 – Measure How You Feel (0-10)

Ask yourself how you feel about this problem and rate the intensity of the feeling from 0 to 10, ten being the worst. For example, you may feel sad, angry or any other emotion; rate this. In the case of physical pain measure how bad the pain is right now with zero meaning you don't feel any pain at all (the pain is gone or non-existent) and ten being the worst it could ever be. If you have some other physical restrictions or limitations measure them in whatever way you can, i.e., how far you can turn your neck.

The Set-up

Step 5 – Tap on the 'Karate Chop Point' whilst Saying Your Phrase Three Times

Tap continuously on the *Karate Chop Point* (please refer to the Karate Chop Point picture earlier in this chapter) of one of your hands using the fingers of your other hand whilst you say your complete *Set-up Phrase* three times (the 'Even though...I deeply and completely accept myself' phrase). The speed of the tapping doesn't actually matter, just tap continually. However I tap at about 100-120 beats per minute (the same as a baby's heart beat, about twice the speed of an adult. Which interestingly, I've been told matches the speed of the drum beats a Shaman or medicine man uses).

The Sequence

Step 6 – Tap on the Main Body Tapping Points whilst Saying Your Reminder Phrase

Now begin tapping on the tapping points on the body (please refer to the points as shown in the picture of The Main Body Tapping Points earlier in this chapter), one point at a time, starting with the first position on the top of your head and continue through all ten points whilst saying your *Reminder Phrase*. You will tap on each of the points approximately 6-7 times whilst repeating your *Reminder Phrase* at least once. This is normally done simultaneously however you can speak your phrase and then tap or vice versa if that is easier for you. It also doesn't matter which side of the body you tap on; you can tap on either side, both sides or alternate if you wish.

Once you have tapped whilst saying your *Set-up Phrase* (the 'even though' phrase about the issue you wish to address) and tapped on the other main points on the body whilst saying your *Reminder Phrase* you have completed what is referred to as a *round* of tapping.

Note: The pressure of your tapping should be gentle as some of the positions are quite delicate, especially around and under your eyes. Contact just needs to be made with each of the points. Tap gentle enough so that you do not bruise or hurt yourself. However be aware that it is normal for some points to be tender. It is also possible to tap without touching the body at all through intention (using just directed thought).

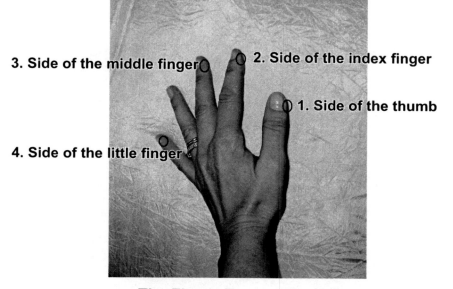

3. Side of the middle finger

2. Side of the index finger

1. Side of the thumb

4. Side of the little finger

The Finger Tapping Points

Step 7 – Tap on the Finger Tapping Points

Tap on the side of the thumb by the nail, the index finger, the middle finger, the small or little finger and then tap on the *Karate Chop Point* again. See the *Finger Tapping Points* shown above.

The Full Gamut

Step 8 – Whilst tapping on 'the Gamut Point' on your hand move your eyes in a particular pattern and perform a humming and counting procedure.

To perform the *Full Gamut* part of the tapping process, keep your head still whilst continually tapping on the *Gamut Point* on your hand. (Refer to *The Gamut Point* picture). Then whilst still tapping on the *Gamut Point*, close your eyes, open your eyes, look to the right, look to the left, look to the right then down to the floor to the right, look to the left then down to the floor to the left, look straight up (still keeping your head still, only moving your eyes), then roll your eyes in a complete circle clockwise, roll your eyes in a complete circle anti-clockwise then hum any song for 2-5 seconds (hum a few bars of your favourite song or *Happy Birthday* or *Mary Had a Little Lamb* will do), count to 5 or 10 and then hum a few more seconds of the song.

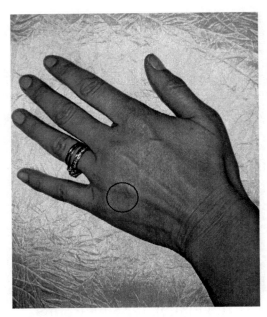

The Gamut Point

Step 9 – Repeat The Sequence (Steps 6 and 7)

Now tap again on the main points of the body, the finger points and the *Karate Chop Point* whilst saying your *Reminder Phrase*.

Step 10 – Measure How You Feel Now (0-10)

Now that you have completed your first **full round of tapping** measure any change in the intensity of how you feel by comparing this rating against your initial measurement.

Step 11 – Repeat The Sequence and The Full Gamut portions of the routine until you reach a rating of zero.

You can keep repeating *The Sequence* and *The Full Gamut* portions of the full tapping routine (starting at Step 6) using your same *Reminder Phrase* whilst your rating of how you feel decreases (drops). Once the rating (the intensity) reaches about two or three (or below) you can change the *Reminder Phrase* to indicate the change for example, if your *Reminder Phrase* had been "this pain" you can change it to "this remaining pain" or revise the *Reminder Phrase* entirely to match how you currently feel about the problem for example "this ache" or "this annoyance" or "this annoying pain".

Note: As indicated in the **Seven Quick Steps to Tapping** (the abbreviated method) you may simply repeat the tapping parts of the process, performing more *rounds* if the rating or measurement of how you feel is coming down. If it isn't reducing you may wish to start again from Step 2 and revise your tapping *Set-up Phrase* and *Reminder Phrase* to be more specific and precise. Also it is important that you state your phrases with conviction versus saying them casually. Sometimes it is helpful if you shout the phrases. Do not say them in a nonchalant, detached or numb fashion as you may limit your results if you don't say the phrase like you mean it.

Additional advice is offered in chapters 21 and 22, including a section entitled: **My Advice for Making Effective Tapping Phrases**.

Basic Tapping Worksheet

In the box below, please answer the questions and write them in the blank spaces provided. By doing this you will complete Steps 1 through 4 of the **Seven Quick Steps to Tapping** or the full length routine. Please note, you may wish to write in pencil so you can reuse this worksheet, or write your answers on a separate piece of paper.

Steps 1&2: What do I want to improve or change in my life? Write down a single issue or problem you wish to work on in the blank provided below. This will create your basic *Set-up Phrase* and your *Reminder Phrase* to be used when tapping. Remember to be very specific and be sure to use any appropriate *iceberg words* in your phrase if related to this particular issue.

"Even though_____

(The problem or issue I'd like to change.)

I deeply and completely love and accept myself".

Note: Remember you can adjust the ending to fit your personal beliefs and feelings however this ending has excellent results just as it is – even if it's uncomfortable for you to say it. For additional suggestions on creating your phrases see Chapters 21 and 22 of *It's Your Choice: Uncover Your Brilliance.*

Step 3&4: How do I feel about this? Think about how you feel about what you wrote above. This may be expressed as an emotion i.e., anger, frustration, confusion, sadness, or a physical sensation i.e., pain, stiffness, tingling, or maybe something else like feeling trapped, alone, worthless, etc. Be as specific and accurate as you can be. It's okay to list more than one feeling for each issue.

Emotion/Feeling (Physical or Emotional)   Rate Intensity (0–10) (SUDs)

a._____

b._____

c._____

_____

Step 5: Tap on the Karate Chop Point or rub the Sore Spot whilst saying your Set-up Phrase three times ("Even though...")

Step 6: Then tap on the Main Body Tapping Points whilst saying your Reminder Phrase

Step 7: Measure your results. Adjust your phrases if necessary and repeat Steps 5 through 7 until you reach a measurement of zero or when you feel it's time to stop for the day. Record any changes in the measurement so you know what level you reached for when you start working on this issue again.

Multi-Aspect Tapping Information Worksheet

1. What do I want to improve, change or eliminate in my life? List your problem, symptom, belief or issue in the blank provided below. Use any *iceberg words* you may have identified in your statement if they relate to this issue. Ask yourself "What do I want to accomplish?" and put that in the blank below.

I want to: _____

What may have caused or contributed to this thing you want to alter?

2. List the individual events or factors which you think may have contributed or are related. Being specific, list <u>any and all</u> events or memories which are somehow associated to your issue in the space provided below. Be sure to list all the events you are aware of (including the first time, worst time, the most difficult or frightening part, the last time etc.) no matter how tenuous – if you think it might be related it probably is. Additionally list any thoughts or beliefs you may have about yourself or others as they apply to this issue.

3. Then record how you feel about each. This may be expressed as an emotion i.e., anger, frustration, confusion, sadness, or a physical sensation i.e., pain, stiffness, tingling, or maybe something else like feeling trapped, alone, worthless, etc. Be as specific and as accurate as you can be and write it under the 'Feeling' heading. (You can list multiple feelings for each item.)

4. Take a measurement for each. Measure the intensity or severity of how you feel about each of your entries.

Event/Factor	Feeling	Rating (0–10)(SUDs)	Priority
a.			
b.			
c.			

Continue your list on an additional piece of paper if necessary.

5. Prioritise your entries in order of importance or intensity. Indicate under the 'Priority' heading the order of your contributing events or factors. Rank them by importance rather than chronologically. This may be obvious and easily identified, clearly indicated in your ratings already. The reason for doing this, is that the more significant the factor or event is to you and your mind often the greater and quicker results you can receive when you begin your tapping there. However, if some of these events or factors are too intense for you to work on right now, you may wish to tap on the other events or factors first or find a professional to assist you.

6. Now create a tapping Set-up Phrase ("Even though…") **and Reminder Phrase for each and begin tapping.** You may wish to use the **Basic Tapping Worksheet** now for each event or factor you listed above under item 4.

Notes about using the Worksheets

Whilst you may find some or total relief tapping on a general issue and can use the **Basic Tapping Worksheet** for this, it is often necessary to isolate particular events which may have created or support an issue or belief you wish to change. In this case you may find the **Multi-Aspect Tapping Information Worksheet** very helpful. This more thorough worksheet can help prompt you to identify multiple and contributory factors of an issue. You can use both worksheets together if you wish (starting with the **Multi-Aspect Tapping Information Worksheet** moving on to the **Basic Tapping Worksheet** for each factor or event.

When using either of the worksheets you may wish to write in pencil so you can reuse them as many times as you'd like or use a separate piece of paper for notes. Complete instructions and pictures of the tapping points to be used in conjunction with the worksheets can be found earlier in this chapter, with more advanced variations explored in Chapters 21 and 22.

Chapter 21
Some of My Tapping Steps In-Depth

Whilst tapping can be performed at a very basic introductory level by anyone and achieve undeniable results, it can sometimes take true detective work and a talented coach or therapist to break through your particular patterns and mindset. Tapping or EFT may look like an extremely easy and a quick therapy to use, but it can take years of practise and training to become truly good and efficient with it in all cases.

In this chapter and the next I will be offering you some of the wisdom I have gained over the years. This entire section may be beyond what you require. Please feel free to skip over it, if you wish, as well as Chapter 22. However, if you are a fellow therapist or coach, or you just want to learn more so you can assist yourself, I'd advise you to dip into the following pages as and when you need or want to do so.

Step 1 In-Depth – Decide What You Want to Improve or Change

As stated in the last chapter, to begin with you need to decide what you want to improve or change in your life, or what you want to get over. Basically this represents goals for you. Make a list of these things. Sometimes it's very obvious what you'd like to change, especially if you have any serious health issues, have experienced some sort of trauma or loss, or struggle with phobias or depression. When working on a more subtle issue, it can be useful to ask yourself what you would change about your life if you could and what events in your life do you wish had never happened to you? Another way to start is to ask yourself if you have any regrets?

Coming up with an issue to work on is not usually difficult for my clients. The difficulty comes when deciding where to start, especially when there seems to be many issues or it appears complicated and intertwined. My advice is to start with the most pressing or difficult issue or part of an issue first if it's safe and advisable for you to do so. Releasing the more extreme events, memories or problems often provide you the greatest payoff and relief. (See my explanation about prioritising or ranking your emotions and contributing factors to any issue detailed in my **Multi-Aspect Tapping Information Worksheet** at the end of the last chapter.) So, if it's safe and you feel able to, start with the worst things, the most challenging or annoying thing, the thing you really want to change the most, **first**.

If you have a list of issues or problems you want to work on, first list them by priority and put any items that are associated or connected together.

You might want to change how you feel about your mother or father who abused you. It could be that you want to eliminate your fear of bees or water, or maybe you suffer with exam nerves or are sad about losing a grandmother. It could be anything. Write it down. Whatever it is, whether it is physical or emotional, you can work at tapping it away. I say "work at tapping it away" because some things are quite involved and may require persistence and thoroughness to get rid of, whilst others just fall away with ease. It's not to do with the severity of the issue that makes some things more stubborn to release than others. It can be the many *aspects* or links and repetitive occurrences involved. In fact, often very serious traumatic events are more simple to clear than non-threatening on-going patterning.

Once you have an idea of what you want to work on, proceed to Step 2.

Step 2 In-Depth – Make a Tapping Phrase for It

Although you can tap using almost any phrase, in order to get the best results when addressing an issue or goal, I want you to follow a few guidelines. The tapping sentences I like to use include two basic components. The first half of the phrase or sentence discusses or identifies what you want to change or improve whilst the second part of the phrase is used to move you closer to your desired outcome or intention.

The classic EFT phrase (as discussed earlier) goes something like this:

"Even though I have this problem or issue, I deeply and completely love and accept myself".

Normally you simply replace the underlined portion ("I have this problem or issue") with the actual issue that you wish to address. You will see that my strategies deviate from this original phrase frequently however this is an excellent place to start whilst you gain experience with tapping. There is absolutely nothing wrong with using this original format just as it is. I fall back on this classic phrase often when I feel it will be the most effective or if it isn't clear to me where to go with an alternative ending.

My Advice for Making Effective Tapping Phrases

♦ Always be as specific as possible.

♦ Use your own words and style of speaking including your *tip of the iceberg words (iceberg verbs* or potential *iceberg adjectives* etc.) when appropriate. Note: Often *iceberg words* indicate the priority of *aspects* or related factors of your issue (see chapters 20 and 21 for information of *aspects* in regards to tapping and Chapter 19 where I summarise how to use *The Iceberg Process* and explain aspects in relationship to your *icebergs.* Additionally, you'll find a good example of the many possible aspects of someone with the often complex phobia of the fear of flying in Suggestion 5 in Chapter 22).

♦ Include expletives if it helps you express more accurately how you feel, including swear words or sarcasm, if that is how you would regularly speak about it.

♦ Make individual tapping statements for each event or element rather than lumping them all together or being too general.

♦ Don't make a pretty or nice statement because that's what you think you should say – make an accurate statement.

♦ Be genuine and honest with your phrases and with yourself. Lying to yourself, your therapist or coach does no one any good. It just wastes time and avoids results.

♦ **Only say things that you believe or totally agree with.** This is an Annie Cap thing or guideline. I want you to get used to being honest with yourself about how you feel. So many times we have had to hide our feelings that it's easy for things to get distorted even within ourselves. Don't make false or 'rose-coloured glass tapping statements' as in my experience correct or accurately described statements are much more effective. It's possible that totally false statements will have little effect if any, but I have not tested this. (Note: I tend to push or navigate my clients based on my intuition and experience prodding them along to speed the process. So I have an honesty rule for them to only say what they believe and not to agree with me just because. I ask them to maintain constant feedback as to how they are feeling and if we are track (if they agree with what is taking place)).

♦ Also although you can use an affirmation as a tapping phrase don't confuse a well-framed tapping phrase with an affirmation statement. Tapping S*et-up Phrases* are substantially different and frequently address negative issues you wish to change which is often a 'no no' in an affirmation.)

♦ Don't worry about saying bad things about other people including parents in your statements. This is not about placing blame. Tapping is about changing your thoughts, beliefs and feelings only. Firstly, they'll never hear you anyway and secondly the purpose is only to help you change and improve how you feel. To do that, it is important to start where ever you are today. Often I reassure my clients that it's just an honest place to begin and that the intensity or what they're feeling right now should shift within minutes when they'll have a more clear perspective.

◆ Say the *Set-up Phrase* you have devised to address your problem out loud to test it for accuracy and check that it is as specific as you can make it before you begin your tapping round. If you are performing your tapping words in your head for privacy issues, then recite your statement to yourself in your head to perform this check first.

◆ You can (and should) change the statement during your tapping if you feel compelled to do so, even mid-routine. You can change the words whenever you want to. It is not necessary to stay with the same wording whilst you run through the sequence of tapping. If once you've started tapping you want to say something else, take this as a sign that you are already shifting something. Acknowledge your urge and follow where it is leading you. As you begin to feel differently, you will naturally want to change your wording.

◆ If you make an error when saying your *Set-up Phrase* or *Reminder* statements or when writing them down, use the erred wording. With my many hours of working one-on-one with my clients, I've always found that their error, or mine for that matter, ended up being the accurate right thing to say to shift the problem after all. I believe the error is our subconscious mind again giving us a bit of assistance through our language and the error probably represents what you are truly feeling or thinking at a deeper knowing level.

◆ Grammar does not matter in tapping. The phrases do not have to make logical sense or be grammatically correct.

◆ And again please be honest with yourself.

Here are a few examples using my advice for making an effective *Set-up Phrase* (more suggestions or options can be found in Chapter 22):

"Even though I feel my mother ruined my life and part of me thinks I actually detest her, I hope someday I can forgive her but right now I don't think she deserves to be forgiven."

"Even though I always feel left out of the fun when we visit my in-laws and I really don't like going, I deeply and completely wish I never have to go visit them again."

"Even though Jim hit me and I don't feel good enough about myself to think I could get anyone else, I wish and hope someday I'll have the courage to leave him."

Step 3 In-Depth – Make a Reminder Phrase for It

As in the **Seven Quick Steps to Tapping** you can simply use the words that you have inserted in the underscored area of your *Set-up Phrase* for your *Reminder Phrase*. Remember its primary purpose is to keep your mind-body focused on what it is that you want to change or relieve.

Some people and therapists prefer to just use the words "This problem" or "This feeling" as their *Reminder Phrase*. This simplified approach can be an effective technique however I prefer to be more specific. I either use an abbre-viation of the issue stated in the *Set-up Phrase* as suggested or if I use "This problem" or "This feeling" I alter it to give it more definition and impact. I may say something like "This ridiculously annoying problem" or "This embarrass-ing fear of dogs problem" linking in with the feelings the client associates with the problem. Even when I'm dealing with pain, whilst some people get results saying "This pain" as a *Reminder Phrase*, I'm convinced I get quicker or better results with "This stinging, burning, flipping hell pain", saying exactly what the client thinks about it being sure to say it with gusto and conviction than saying "This pain" alone!

Additionally, I often change my *Reminder Phrase* on every point when I tap. Most therapists and coaches using EFT and MTT who have worked with very involved issues with their clients tend to have progressed to this style of tapping. I find it improves my results and speeds the process. However, it is not normally necessary to change the *Reminder Phrase* and you (and some therapists) may prefer to stay focused on only one aspect at a time ensuring that you clear it completely. There are times when jumping around, switch-ing aspects and tacks though is preferred. I've found sometimes it's neces-sary to jump aspects or even switch to what appears to be a very separate issue entirely in order to clear the original issue. I use this style of changing the reminder phrases almost exclusively now but I'm very careful to check the progress against the original measurements so I don't lose track and direction.

If you want to try this fluid style of tapping, changing each phrase on each point, normally the process is the same. You identify a starting *Reminder Phrase* but as you tap on each new point (after the first) you just let it flow and say whatever comes to your mind about this topic or use the various things you already know or have identified about the issue or problem you are work-ing on. It's not necessary to write out the alternative phrases before you start, however it may be helpful and you may decide to document them or record yourself. Say whatever you feel as you are tapping on each point. It's quite surprising sometimes what comes out of your mouth (mind) and very insightful. More importantly, it is very curative. An example of continually changing the *Reminder Phrase* for someone finding it difficult to quit smoking is presented in **Suggestion 17** of **25 Suggestions for Tapping** in Chapter 22.

Step 4 In-Depth– Measure How You Feel (0-10)-SUDs Level

As described in the **Seven Quick Steps to Tapping** this step is about taking a measurement of how you feel before you start in order to accurately track your results. This measurement is called a **SUDs** level in EFT which stands for *Subjective Units of Discomfort*. Often when you are measuring how you feel you will be attempting to measure a feeling (either emotional or physi-cal); therefore it is considered to be subjective and not objective. Feelings are personal. No one, other than you, can rate the intensity of your own sensations and emotions. However, I and other experienced therapists may be able to guess or intuit your **SUDs** level but it is up to you to determine how you rate it, how you are measuring it as well and what it's based on.

How to Take a SUDs Level Rating

When using the **SUDs** measurement you can ask yourself, ***"How do I feel about this situation and what would this feeling be if I measured it from zero to ten?"*** or ***"How bad is this pain...zero to ten?"*** Let me give you an example.

If you feel sad you lost your job and maybe very embarrassed, as well, take a guess at how high the sadness and embarrassment are, measuring each individually. Note: Some therapists or guides may instruct you to only measure one thing (often your worst or strongest feeling) but when my clients express two emotions, or even more, I go ahead and ask them to give a rating for each of them. So, in this example I'd ask my client to tell me how high or strong their 'sadness feeling' is and how high their embarrassment is from zero to ten. Maybe the sadness is a subjective seven and the embarrassment about getting fired is a nine. <u>Now we have two opportunities of reviewing how we're doing as we tap and probably more importantly we have two different angles to solve the problem.</u> If you have multiple items to measure, be sure to write down all of them and the initial individual rating for each. Another way is to just measure the worst or strongest feeling but you'll be missing an important component that you may need to release later anyway, so you might as well do it now. Don't miss out.

Is it Really Important to Take a Rating?

Lots of people ask if taking a rating is really important, "Yes, it is" in my opinion. Taking a **SUDs** level or measurement is a very important step in tapping as it sets a benchmark allowing you to recognise and acknowledge your progress or lack of progress.

You can measure your discomfort on this imaginary **SUDs** scale from zero (non-existent, no feeling) to ten (the highest or worst it's ever been or the worst you could imagine it to could ever be). Or you can use any other form of measurement that you would like but do it! I highly recommend it. Take the time and make the effort to measure and write your measurement down with a note of what you are measuring (the feeling etc.) along side your *Set-up Phrase*.

Do I Always Have to Take a Measurement?

When you are doing tapping (using EFT) on yourself and it's only for you, of course you don't have to take a measurement each time you tap or at all if you decide not to. As an experienced therapist I wouldn't think of tapping with my clients without taking SUDs measurements, however when I tap on myself I may not. I can sense any changes internally and I feel and know my results anyway.

There will always be times though when you just want to tap quickly to reinforce something or change how you're feeling right then and there. You don't need to take a measurement every time, just observe how you feel. As long as you're clearly benefiting from the tapping; you'll sense the shifts in other ways any way.

However if you are working on a stubborn or big issue, I would always suggest you register your *SUDs* levels. This is very helpful when you are actively or initially investigating an issue, especially a tough one that you are working to clear. The circumstances are quite different from just tapping secretly at your desk to calm yourself as you prepare for your meeting with your difficult boss.

There is another important reason why I normally recommend taking and keeping track of your measurements which I will discuss in the next section.

The Apex Effect

Whilst the *SUDs* level (your measurement) helps you see your results, it also helps you not deny them. It may seem strange but it is a common occurrence in tapping that clients don't always believe the results even though and probably because they've experienced significant change, especially when the change is dramatic. It happens often enough that there's a name for it, it's called ***The Apex Effect***.

Sometimes the quickness and the high degree of relief obtained from tapping is so startling that some people (many actually) literally can't believe it. They just can't get their head around the immense change they've just experienced, so rather than believe it they think it couldn't have happened at all and didn't!

I've encountered ***The Apex Effect*** occurring with some of my more skeptical clients but also, just as often, with very agreeable open-minded people. In all these cases, if I hadn't written the measurement information (the *SUDs* rating) down alongside of the original *Set-up Phrase* and the emotion we were measuring, it would have been impossible for them to have believed the dramatic results. Luckily I could show them the evidence, the original ratings in the form of my notes which they watched me write down in front of them and only after I had gained their agreement that they were accurate. Without the written record there would have been no way to convince them. Some therapists record their sessions for this exact reason.

When ***The Apex Effect*** kicks in, it often does so in a big way. Huge actually! Those experiencing it may even deny ever having the problem or boldly minimise the severity of it. Saying "No way, it wasn't really that bad" or "I couldn't have said that – it really doesn't bother me that much", now that the tapping has so gracefully relieved their problem. Seeing this occur is shocking but my take on it is that because the relief and change was so complete, it also changed the underlying beliefs and adjusted the feelings that created or maintained the problem in the first place. Even the perspective and various memories surrounding the problem may have been neutralised all in one lovely swoop.

So please write down how you feel and how strongly you feel it **before** you tap. I recommend noting down the *Set-up Phrase* too because what you would choose to say about your issue also changes when problems are released. I've had clients refute their own *Set-up Phrases* or *Reminder Phrases* just as frequently as the massive drop in their *SUDs* levels when **The Apex Effect** occurs.

What if You Don't Feel Anything?

Often new tapping therapists get hung up on finding the emotion linked to their client's issue and keep pressing them "How do you feel about that?" Frankly, it can be that you don't knowingly recognise any emotional link or be able to feel anything about your issue at all. You may be numb about the whole incident, totally detached or dissociated but that doesn't mean you can't tap and benefit from it.

You can try asking yourself some other questions to find something to measure, like "Where in my body do I feel this problem?", "What does this problem remind me of?", or "If my problem could talk what would it say?" and "What do I belief about myself because of this issue?"

If you can't find something to measure or it's just too trying or annoying, don't do it. Don't worry about it and just start tapping. As you sense a change within you, you will be compelled to alter your wording or feel lighter. You may even recognise that you are feeling more optimistic and just know that it's doing something, therefore *it's working.*

Using Size Comparisons, Colours, Percentages

With children and adults using the *SUDs* level doesn't always make sense. I regularly ask kids (and clients whose problems stem from when they were very little) to show me how big their emotion (like fear, sadness or loneliness) or symptom is using their arms or fingers. Or get them to tell me if their fear is as big as an ocean or a lake, or the size of a puddle or if it's tiny like a rain drop.

I often use child-like adjectives in my comparisons for kids like "Is it teenie weenie like a piece of sand, a ladybird (ladybug) or a pea or is it really really really big like the sky or as tall as your dad?"

Colours are an extremely valid and descriptive measurement for all ages. Asking what colour a feeling, problem or memory is can be a great measuring tool. It's just as appropriate and accurate as a numerical measurement. Maybe something feels muddy brown or black when you start out but as you tap it progresses to being yellow like the sunshine, or aqua blue like a calm tropical sea. I encourage you to be creative with how you measure.

Objective Measuring

Although commonly you'll be measuring something personal and therefore subjective, like an emotional feeling or a physical feeling, there will be times that you will be measuring something more objective and tangible, even something visible.

This is often the case when assessing physical restrictions or reactions. You may decide to measure how close you can get to touching your toes when bending over before your pain stops you or how deeply you can breathe (this is an EFT strategy in itself, called **The Constricted Breathing Technique**), how many stairs you can climb or how far you can turn your head or raise your arms. Additionally some bodily reactions are visible or they either happen or they don't. For example: trembling of hands, cheeks going red or sweating. You decide how and what you are measuring.

You've Measured, Now What?

Tap and after each *round* of tapping (see **Seven Quick Steps to Tapping** or **A Full Length Method of Tapping**) take a new measurement or your *SUDs* level (or objective measurement) and compare this against your original rating. Based on your results, the following information will help you know what to do next.

What if Your Rating Goes Up, Down or Stays the Same?

Your *SUDs* level measurement may have gone down, stayed the same or sometimes it will have gone up. All are normal.

Do not be concerned if your rating went up, you may have brought something out and up into your awareness. I always see it as helpful and promising when the rating has increased. Whilst people that are new to tapping may get worried or be fearful, thinking they've done something wrong, tapping isn't going to be able to help them or even thinking that the tapping is making their problem worse. Nonsense, there's nothing to worry about; this indicates you are on the right track.

If this happens (your rating goes up) observe the change in intensity and record it. Then decide if you want to change your statement to make it more specific and accurate taking into account the increased intensity. Notice if you remembered thinking of anything new or different when you were tapping or if you remembered or focused on some additional details. Also notice if there's been any change in how you feel about it. These are all good signs.

If your rating went down, you can either continue tapping with the same phrase for more tapping *rounds* or modify it if it's no longer accurate, appropriate or specific enough to how you are feeling now and then do another *round* of tapping.

If your rating stayed the same, I would check the accuracy of your statement. Ask yourself if it is honest, precise, emotive and expressive. Then if it is okay as it is, I would tap again whilst ensuring I say the statement with emphasis, firmly and more loudly. It's a common problem that people say their statements very casually and calmly even though what they are saying may justify screaming in anger or is about something very serious and certainly not commonplace. Don't be too blasé or nonchalant when tapping. It seems sometimes that the mind ignores your efforts if you do this.

If your rating continues not to change or move you may wish to try rubbing the **Sore Spot** (see Step 5 In-Depth below for details) whilst saying your phrases versus tapping the *Karate Chop Point* on your hand. Or use the full tapping sequence including the eye movements and humming and counting portion called the *Full Gamut*.

Whilst many therapists around the world only use a basic or abbreviated tapping sequence like that found in the **Seven Quick Steps to Tapping**, I default back to the complete routine if I don't get any movement on the ratings after a couple of *rounds* of tapping. (Additionally, I may use other blockage clearance methods like 'collarbone breathing' which I call 'chicken breathing' or other 'Brain Gym' type exercises commonly used by therapists working with people with dyslexia.)

Step 5 In-Depth – Tap on the Karate Chop Point Whilst Saying Your Phrase Three Times

There are a variety of ways you can begin your tapping sequences. Starting on the *Karate Chop Point* is only one possibility. Another point to start tapping on which is equivalent or perhaps slightly even better is rubbing on the **Sore Spot** on your chest.

The **Sore Spot** is not a specific point but is a tender place on your chest. It can be found by prodding around the area which is above your breasts but below your collarbone and outward towards your shoulder approaching your armpit. Usually if you poke around with your fingers gently in this area, on either side, you will find an area or point (*a spot*) that is more sensitive or painful than the others; this is the **Sore Spot**. If you elect to use the **Sore Spot** instead of the *Karate Chop Point*, you will rub it with your fingers in a circle (instead of tapping on it) whilst repeating your *Set-up Phrase*. I normally rub clockwise however you can go either direction.

The reason we start, in most cases, by tapping or applying pressure to the *Karate Chop Point* or the *Sore Spot* is that it corrects the direction or polarity of your energy system (if it needs to be). In EFT this is referred to as **Psychological Reversal** or **PR** and it occurs in many chronic conditions including depression and anxiety.

If you are not *psychologically reversed* in EFT and MTT energy terms you may not need to tap on either of these points at all to get results **but if you are it is a prerequisite to change**. Many therapists skip this step in order to save time if they feel (sense) or know their client is not *reversed*. But I rarely skip it even if they are not typically *reversed*. I almost always use one of these two points when tapping and sometimes it's all I use. For some clients just tapping on the *Karate Chop Point* or rubbing the *Sore Spot* can clear their issue without any further tapping! Therefore I have found it invaluable and extremely effective in its own right.

Whilst there are ways to determine if someone is *PR* or *reversed* they will not be described in this book. Suffice it to say that if you skip this step and do not get results and then add it back in without changing anything else in your routine or phrases you were obviously *reversed*. It is generally supported in the tapping community that if you are *reversed* (or you are being effected severely by an energy toxin) you will get little or no results from your tapping if you do not begin by tapping on the *Karate Chop Point* or *Sore Spot* first.

The times when I decide to only tap on the *Karate Chop Point* or rub the *Sore Spot* whilst my clients repeat their *Set-up Phrase* or *Reminder Phrase* I seem to know that I don't need to tap on any other point. I sense the phrase morphing or changing instantaneously as we tap or rub. As soon as we begin and start saying the phrase we may have spent some time carefully designing, the client already wants to say something else or I hear something different in my head. In this case just making this initial contact on the *Karate Chop Point* or *Sore Spot* and focusing on the issue causes the feelings, memories and beliefs to immediately change for the better.

Tapping on the *Karate Chop Point* or rubbing the *Sore Spot* is also helpful when refining your phrases as it can help you think more clearly. It can instigate a more balanced perspective even before you tap on any other points. I often tap on my client's *Karate Chop Point* or have them do it when we start discussing their issue and are clarifying their goals for our session/s together, especially if they are nervous or highly emotive. This not only helps them to formulate or distill what they want to say (allowing them to have better cognition)and what they need to work on. It has a great calming effect and sometimes is the only way they can speak about their issues. There have been many times when I would not have been able to decipher why the client had come to me if I hadn't adopted this strategy early on.

Chapter 22
25 Suggestions for Tapping

There is so much you can do with this flexible technique. This chapter includes twenty-five of the many variations I use when I tap with my clients in person or on the telephone. This information is a compilation of some of the more useful tapping techniques I use, however it is not comprehensive. That said, it offers the potential to advance your tapping and breakthroughs far beyond what you could accomplish with beginning levels of tapping. Yet, there's so much more to learn if you choose; I'm always learning. Again, you may elect to skip this chapter if you want to or don't need it.

My Suggestions for Improved Tapping

If you are getting good results with the classic standard EFT phrase "Even though I have this problem or issue or x happened to me I deeply and completely accept myself" you probably should continue doing just as you are but if not or if you are working on a complex issue, the suggestions in this chapter may help you gain some momentum.

Suggestion 1: Alter the ending words "I deeply and completely love and accept myself" of the standard EFT phrase if it is not truthful for you.

Most of my clients have difficulty saying they love and accept themselves when they first come to me. Many have found it impossible to even say or refuse to say it. Although I believe Gary Craig's intention of using this ending is excellent and is meant to trigger the mind to find out why we may not love and accept themselves (getting right down to some of the core issues) and to begin to repair the cause, I think it can work against some people causing them to resist tapping. For this reason I remove this initial barrier from the start and ask them to change the ending, if they're really uncomfortable with it, to "…

someday I hope I will be able to love and accept myself" or "…I'd like to accept myself but right now I can't". Alternatively "I can never accept what I've done" or "I can't even imagine loving and accepting myself" may be more appropriate endings. Emotionally, it can be just a step too far to force someone to start with this ending when they don't love and accept themselves at all.

The position, I usually take as I've said, when I'm helping someone is to ensure that the words they use when tapping are totally accurate for them. I tell them many times that they shouldn't just say what I say if they don't agree with it or if it is not the way they would normally speak. Remember I've discovered the words they choose have an influence on their mind, and an origin. So it is in my opinion, vital that they say what they really feel, in most cases (there are some exceptions as you will see). Although forcing someone to say "I deeply and completely love and accept myself" can trigger strong emotional and physical reactions, like tears of sadness, shaking or regret, as well as great healing, I've found it more effective to gradually move toward this ending of their statement. Then it is considered a major landmark of our progress when they can say they love and accept themselves and mean it.

Suggestion 2: Clarify your *Set-up Phrase* by asking 'because' to gain additional information and clarity.

To clarify the meaning or foundation of a belief you are trying to shift (change) add 'because' just after the first part of the standard phrase format and answer this question with the first thing that comes to your mind. The following are some examples of what I mean.

"Even though I believe I'm not good enough *because my mother through me out when I was fourteen*, I deeply and completely…"

"Even though I feel ashamed *because I was abused by my uncle*, I deeply and completely…"

"Even though I doubt my ability to get a job *because I stutter at interviews*, I deeply and completely…"

Suggestion 3: Try using totally different endings to your *Set-up Phrase* (for the same issue).

This is the art of being a good *tapper, tapping practitioner* or *tapping coach*. In order to really clear an issue, as I described in Chapter 17, **Breaking Those Tough Patterns, Moving to Acceptance and Forgiveness**, you may need to go through a whole series of transitions or '*reframes*' (alternative ways of thinking about something). You can benefit from working on your issue by varying the ending. These examples will give you an idea of what I'm talking about.

If you were to start with "Even though I failed my English exam and believe I'm not good enough, I deeply and completely love and accept myself", helpful ending variations or *reframes* could be:

"…I want to love and accept myself someday soon."

"…I deserve to allow myself to get over it."

"...that was in the past and I'll be more prepared the next time."

"...I plan to get some help from the tutor before I try it again."

"...I'm human and I can forgive myself."

"...I can feel okay about this once the shock wears off."

"...everyone could have failed that exam; they gave us so little time to revise (study)."

"...in the grand scheme of things it really doesn't matter anyway as I now have a good job."

"...I have other things that prove I'm good enough."

"...I passed my French exam easily so maybe I am good enough and I just find English boring."

"...I'm going to decide that it's okay."

"...I can permit myself to lighten up and treat myself with kindness."

"...I want to let it go and move on."

"...I choose to release my self-abuse soon, perhaps even today".

"...I've decided to stop chastising myself for it and putting myself down right now and believe I'm worthwhile just the way I am!"

"Even though I failed my English exam. It certainly doesn't mean I'm not good enough. It's right and healthy to deeply and completely love and accept myself now".

Suggestion 4: Change the end of the phrase around to something that you hope you can achieve or how you want to feel soon.

"Even though I'm upset about my father's comment about...I look forward to repairing our relationship soon."

"Even though I hate broccoli I keep reading it's good for me so I hope I can learn to tolerate it even if it doesn't become my favourite vegetable."

"Although I feel uncomfortable on boats right now, I'm learning to tap and I'm hopeful this different technique can help me get over it."

Suggestion 5: Add more detail in the first part of your tapping phrases to address some of the different *aspects* contributing to your problem. Note: You may find it necessary to make individual statements for each element (*aspect*, known factor or reason) for your issue.

"Even though I'm afraid of bees because it hurt when I was stung when I was eleven, I'll soon be able to relax and feel safe when I'm outside in the garden"

"Even though I'm scared of expressing myself because people might laugh or I may stammer again..."

More Important Information about Aspects

Remember in EFT *aspects* are the reasons and factors that have contributed or are contributing to your issue (and they're often represented in your *iceberg words*). Aspects refer to the both occurrences and specifics about an occurrence. An aspect can be considered the first time you became aware you had this problem, the last time, every time you experienced it, the most emotional time (embarrassing, scary) etc. or unique characteristics or features of the issue or occurrence, memory or event. Also *aspects* are the many emotions you felt about something. They may be a smell, the colours you saw, the size of something, the type of car, the physical feelings you had, the various emotions, the sounds, the setting, what you heard, etc.

All of these *aspects* act to support and maintain the problem, and helped to create your problem originally. They also may be triggers for you now. Working with *aspects* is a huge and important factor in clearing anxiety issues and phobias as an individual *aspect* may be capable of causing your mind to recreate the same feelings you felt before. Perhaps making you feel sick, weak, frightened or embarrassed or angry just like when you experienced your traumatic event/s of the past.

Example of the Aspects of a Phobia

To make *aspects* very clear to you, I'm going to offer you some possible *aspects* of the fear of flying below. Once you have the list of *aspects* related to your own personal problem, let me remind you to prioritise the order of your tapping so you work on the most significant items first (again, only if it's safe to do so). As you may find the whole problem will collapse after tapping on a single important aspect or just a few key aspects saving you massive amounts of time.

- You've heard landings and take-offs are dangerous.
- It frightens you that you can't get out of your seat when you want to.
- You don't like the feeling of the seat belts ever since your car accident.
- You hate being so close to other people because when you were sixteen you experienced a crush at a music festival.
- Your first flight you ever took, you were alone and your uncle forgot to collect you at the airport.
- The sound of the engines reminds you of a chainsaw and your dad teased you with a loud chainsaw when you were 13.
- You feel trapped when in a plane.
- You are afraid of catching diseases or picking up a virus.
- Turbulence makes it feel like the plane will fall out of the sky.
- You picture yourself crashing into the sea whenever you take off.
- You can't hear very well in noisy environments and it's disorienting reminding you of...
- You hate the feeling you get in the pit of your stomach when the plane rolls. It feels like the time you got scared on a ferryboat.
- You worry that if lightning hits the plane that you will explode in mid-air.
- You feel out of control.
- You don't like to use the public toilets (restrooms).

As you can see from my examples, often one phobia may be caused by other phobias or by non-related, past, negatively interpreted experiences. You may need to tap on the other memories to clear your particular problem like in this case of someone with the fear of flying. Complex phobias like the fear of flying, emetaphobia (fear of being sick or vomiting) or agoraphobia usually involve many connected memories and often 'sub-phobias' and by successfully clearing requires clearing all the others or inadvertently frees one from the others.

Suggestion 6: Try using "perhaps", "maybe", "probably", and/or "allow" or "permit" in your Set-up or *Reminder Phrases*. Or the words "I'm open to the possibility that…"

Using these words can make a super impact as they have the ability to open your mind to new options. We're encouraging your mind to consider making a new neural connection on the spot. Note: When I use my 'perhaps' or 'maybe' techniques I measure the likelihood that my client believes the statement to be possible or what percentage (0% to 100%) they believe the phrase to be accurate. This then becomes our *SUDs* measurement. You'll see what I mean when you see the example phrases that follow.

"Even though I'm afraid of bees because I got stung when I was seven… **perhaps** they are more interested in the flowers and I'll be fine today at the garden party."

"Even though I'm afraid of bees because…**maybe** the odds are I'll never be stung again.

"Even though I'm afraid of bees because…**perhaps** I can **allow** myself to believe I'll be fine today with my cousins."

"Even though I'm afraid of bees because…I'm going to **permit** myself to ignore them so I can have fun at the garden party."

"Even though I'm afraid of bees because…**I'm open to the possibility** that I can get over this and won't even notice the bees today at the garden party."

Suggestion 7: Replace "even though" with something else like "although" or "because" or drop it entirely and say the *Set-up Phrase* as a statement.

Tapping is very flexible, I've found the phrase does not have to follow a particular pattern although there can be advantages to various patterns including the basic standard format, especially while you are learning.

Suggestion 8: Drop the "I deeply and completely accept myself " ending or an alternative ending of the *Set-up Phrase* and simply say the first half of it focusing on your issue or goal alone. Whilst I find it advantageous to have two parts to my *Set-up Phrases*, the first stating or identifying the current problem and the second part articulating the goal, it is not necessary to keep to this format.

Suggestion 9: You can be general in your *Set-up Phrase* if you do not have specifics or don't know why you have your problem or if this makes you feel more comfortable or confident to start. Normally in tapping the more specific you are the better results. However, sometimes you can't remember the specific details, or they are not very clear to you or the importance is not obvious. In these cases it may be best to be general or to use a phrase like "Even though I have this fear taking a bath and I don't know why…"

Suggestion 10: Prioritise your tapping because you can reduce the amount of time it takes to clear a problem, as mentioned already a few times, I recommend tapping first on the most significant, most difficult or impactful issue or aspect about something or about an event (*the worst thing, the worst part or the worst aspect*) or the most challenging memory you have about your problem. **Special Note:** Don't do this if it feels unsafe for you, in any way. In which case, I'd advise you to work with a professional who can provide a more comfortable setting and utilise more advanced techniques making the work less intense and potentially much easier. An expert will be able to guide you more gently through the transitions or use the Tearless Trauma technique which you can find on-line.

In tapping we try to isolate the causes and associations of something through your history and emotions. If you can tackle the worst stuff first, then you may find you don't have to 'tap on' many of the other elements or exposures to similar feelings or events. If they were similar enough or the association is because of the same emotions your felt, the connection in the mind collapses (it's like the neural network itself is altered or broken) and the problem 'cellular memory' is released or neutralised with these pivotal prioritised tapping sequences.

Suggestion 11: Tap on all events and aspects that you think contributed to your problem if you can't collapse or release it with what you thought were the most significant elements. Even though there are frequently primary aspects that keep an issue or problem in place (and that ultimately release it), including phobic-like anxiety or inappropriate beliefs or patterns, you sometimes must tap on all the *aspects* and associated occurrences to clear it.

In the case of a problem which was caused, created or reinforced by five specific separate events or emotions, sometimes you can release it by only tapping one aspect which is acting as a lynch pin and releases the entire problem (or a couple) as discussed in Suggestion 11 but you may need to tap on all five events. (Generally this happens if they exhibit varying emotions in my experience or offer some other uniqueness).

Suggestion 12: Tap on events that you know about or heard about, even if you don't have a personal memory of them. They could have been involved, even if you don't have any easily accessible memory or feeling about them. They may totally shift or release an issue for you. Examples:

"Even though I fell off my aunt's lap when I was two and maybe that's why I am afraid when my feet don't touch the ground…I deeply and completely …"

"Even though I can't remember it, I was told I was very scared when my dad went away when I was three and supposedly I cried for weeks…"

"Although my mom left me in the store by accident when I was only little, long before I could even walk, I deeply and completely..."

"Even though my mum was in painful labour for thirty-eight hours when she had me and perhaps that has something to do with my claustrophobia today, I deeply..."

Suggestion 13: If you find it hard to talk about why you feel a certain way, it may be based on something that happened before you could speak – tap *on* it. I have helped many people clear long-term phobias by tapping about their first two years of life and before.

"Even though maybe this problem goes back to when I was a tiny baby, I deeply and completely..."*

"Even though I was a sick little baby and was in and out of (the) hospital, I choose to find comfort now."*

* Remember to be as specific as you can in your creation of your *Set-up Phrase*. Include as much detail as you know about the situation.

Suggestion 14: '**Go fishing'** when you don't know about the cause of your issue or problem. This can stimulate a recollection or clear serious problems even without an understanding of the source.

I purposefully tap even when the cause of an issue eludes my client. I call this *'going fishing'*. There are many times when you may not have a clue why you have a certain problem. The reasons may not be clear at all as to why, so I developed a workable solution for my practice.

What I do is assume (because I believe this is true) that the mind of my client really knows the cause although they are not currently or may have never been aware of it. They can't recall it, have forgotten or suppressed it for some reason. I also assume that their mind won't show it to them if they really aren't ready to see it or know about it and I feel safe *'fishing'* for it. This has never been NOT been the case when I've used EFT or MTT (although I have heard that it is a common occurrence with EMDR, Eye Movement Desensitisation Reprocessing sessions used by some clinical psycho-analysts and traditional counselors. EMDR involves moving the eyes continually to the left and to the right throughout the therapy session and I've been told by therapists practicing it that it can force a memory to the surface).

When tapping on a problem we are always trying to get at the cause of the problem to provide permanent relief. We are attempting to work on the roots or foundation of the issue, but if you don't know what those are it can appear more challenging to change your current situation. Try one or all of the following tactics:

"Even though I'm afraid of bees and I don't know why I deeply and completely want to get over it."

"Even though I fear confrontation and I'd like to know why, I choose to believe there's a way to get over it, my own unique way!"

"Even though I'm scared of vomiting and I don't remember even ever vomiting, maybe it was from something that happened when I was a little baby and relates to my severe gluten intolerance, I deeply and ...."

"Even though I can't articulate why I feel as I do but I think it has to do with my discomfort in cars which started when I was ten, I deeply and completely...."

"Although I don't remember anything that would cause me to be afraid of the dark and I'd really like to understand this, I can feel safe and deeply and completely love and accept myself anyway."

"Even though I have this odd and uncomfortable nervousness and I don't know why, maybe it's because (pause and then say whatever comes to your mind and repeat "or because" and allow yourself to answer the query whilst you continually tap on either the *Karate Chop Point* or the main body points), I deeply and completely...".

Using this technique, many times my clients recall a past event (or many events) which they had forgotten or didn't think were important. Whilst tapping with phrases like these and even if they don't recall an event, their intensity rating (*SUDs*) usually reduces anyway. So the tapping achieved the effect we wanted anyway.

Suggestion 15: Accept it is not necessary to find the cause, or find out *why* to clear something with tapping.

Although we often look for the reasons *why* or the cause of an issue when tapping (and I 'go fishing' in the hopes of helping my clients find out *why*), it is not essential to find out the reasons and does not (and perhaps should not) need to be the focus of your work. Don't get caught up in finding the cause or placing blame or feeling guilty. Clearing the issue and improving how you feel (often by changing your perspective) are what is important versus isolating the exact cause of a particular problem (although it may be nice to know).

You can clear or neutralise a problem and its impact on you without knowing *the why*, if you allow yourself to do this. Again this is where wording and reframing is valuable. Here are some suggestions for you if you don't know why you have a problem and *'fishing'* didn't help.

"Even though I don't know why I'm afraid of bees, that's okay, I don't need to know why to get rid of it and can deeply and completely love and accept myself."

"Even though I can't articulate why I feel as I do and maybe something happened to me, I can release this terrible feeling anyway without understanding it and start to deeply and completely..."

"Even though I don't know why, I don't have to recall it to change it..."

"Even though this fear has been with me forever and I'd love to know what it's all about, I choose to feel safe either way from now on."

"Even though I don't know why I'm afraid of snakes and I think I need to know the cause, maybe it's not important for me getting better. I can get better anyway."

"Although I'd really like to know why I feel _____ or I _____ it's not required to my healing and I'm going to stop looking for it so I can concentrate on healing and accepting myself the way I am."

Suggestion 16: Don't concern yourself with memorising or even knowing what meridian relates to the individual tapping points.

It's not necessary to know why you tap on certain places or what organs or areas of the body they may influence. It's actually better not to know and to trust your intuition. I purposely avoid thinking about what the points might mean. It is only a distraction and perhaps a waste of my time to monitor this. I believe it may even limit the success of my tapping. I find if I'm thinking too much about the process, I'm not able to be in the moment picking up all the various clues and nuances available to me whilst watching and sensing my clients' reactions (both physical and emotional) and listening inside myself.

Suggestion 17: Try changing your *Reminder Phrase* on each or alternate tapping point.

Most advanced therapists and coaches using EFT or another form of MTT (energy psychology) tend to find improved results this way. Just say what you feel as you start tapping on each point, keeping your comments somewhat limited to the primary issue you are working through with this particular *Set-up Phrase.* (I say *somewhat,* because it is common to uncover other links or memories when tapping like this and although memories that surface may appear to relate to another problem you may have, they may also be contributing to this issue as well.) Example using this strategy of changing the *Reminder Phrase*:

Starting *Set-up Phrase:* "Even though I'm having difficulty giving up smoking, I deeply and completely love and accept myself."

Starting *Reminder Phrase*: "Difficulty giving up smoking"

Top of The Head: "Difficulty giving up smoking"
Eyebrow: "Maybe I don't really want to quit"
Side of the Eye: "But I really do want to quit"
Under the Eye: "I know it'll help my breathing"
Under the Nose: "But it's part of my fun"
On the Chin: "It seems like the only fun I have any more"
Collarbone: "That's really sad"
Optional Fist Thump on Chest: "Smoking isn't really fun or my only fun"
Under Breast: "Yes it is, for me"
Under the Arm: "But I must quit, they've told me that"

Top of The Head: "It seems impossible"
Eyebrow: "I've been doing it for so long"
Side of the Eye: "But I'm ready for a change"

Under the Eye: "I really hate spending my money this way"

Under the Nose: "I want to quit even if it's difficult"

On the Chin: "Maybe I can do it"

Collarbone: "No maybe I can't, I've failed in the past"

Fist Thump on Chest: "Yes I can do it. I just don't want to yet"

Under the Breast: "Maybe I do want to?"

Under the Arm: "Of course I want to."

Top of The Head: "I think I could do it if my boyfriend stopped too"

Eyebrow: "Sod it; I can do it for myself"

Side of the Eye: "I just need to find something to do with my time that feels like fun"

Under the Eye: "What excuse can I use to get a break from the kids?"

Under the Nose: "Smoking is my time and that's why I'll miss it, It's not just fun, it's my exit plan"

On the Chin: "I don't need an excuse; everyone else takes time for themselves in my family"

Collarbone: "Even though I don't know how and I may have a few bad days, I believe I can do it"

Fist Thump on Chest: "It may be difficult at first but I want to do it"

Under the Breast: "I hate the smell on my clothes"

Under the Arm: "I resent how much they cost anyway"

Top of the Head: "I'm more certain now that I must stop"

Eyebrow: "I could go to Spain with the money I'll save"

Side of the Eye: "It's not that much fun anyway"

Under the Eye: "I always wake with a sore throat"

Under the Nose: "I'm ready to quit, I think"

On the Chin: "It doesn't have to be difficult"

Collarbone: "I can do it if I distract myself with gum, which helped before"

Fist Thump on Chest: "I won't even need that"

Under the Breast: "I can do this with the patch and won't even bother with gum this time"

Under the Arm: "It'll be easy"

Suggestion 18: Try adding or using "I forgive" or "I respect myself" to the end of your *Set-up Phrase* or both. Because forgiveness is so important to us, some people add it to their classic ending and use it for everything ("…I deeply and completely love, accept and forgive myself"). Examples:

"Even though I'm still smoking, even though I promised I'd quit, I deeply and completely accept, **forgive and respect myself."**

"Even though I feel I caused the fight before my husband walked out on me, I deeply and completely want to **forgive myself."**

"Even though I smoke because I feel weak and lonely most of the time, I deeply and completely wish I could love, accept, **respect and forgive myself** for feeling this way."

Suggestion 19: For physical symptoms as well as emotional, ask yourself "If there were any events in my life that might be contributing to or causing this problem what would they be?" This will help draw out any historical or current issues that may be making your symptoms or making any pain worse.

Suggestion 20: Additionally, even when your condition has a physiological foundation or medical diagnosis (i.e., you've been told you have a lung weakness or a prolapsed disc by your doctor), ask yourself "What emotion might be linked to this problem?" or "What emotion might be contributing to this and making it worse?"".

Suggestion 21: Guess. If you don't know what has contributed to your problem, take a wild guess. Ask yourself "What might have caused this?" or "What might be making this worse?" You may come up with something that appears unrelated but is actually the answer for you to find relief. When I have asked clients to guess, it can be amazing what they suggest, seemingly out of the blue, but of course it isn't because at some level they know. I've heard people say, "Oh, I expect it's the miscarriage I had. Did I not tell you about that?" or "I think it might be linked to the fact that I hate myself because..."

Suggestion 22: Try adding "that's okay" of "it's okay" to your phrases. It's a lovely way to build self-acceptance or to open you to a new way of thinking about something.

"Even though I don't cook very well and I don't deeply and completely love and accept myself today, **that's okay,** I hope to soon."

"Even though I don't know how to get over this problem, **it's okay**, I can still deeply and completely love and accept myself."

"Even though I've had a divorce and for a long time didn't respect people who gave up on their marriages, I can choose to believe **that's okay**."

Suggestion 23: Try adding "just the way I am" or "any way" to the end of your *Set-up Phrase.*

"Even though I don't know if I'll get over this problem, I deeply and completely love and accept myself **just the way I am**."

"Even though I don't know how or when I'll get over this problem, I deeply and completely love and accept myself **anyway**."

"Even though I failed my exams when I was eleven, I can decide to accept myself **anyway**."

Suggestion 24: Although earlier I stated to be honest with your statements, it is also effective to knowingly and purposely say strongly the exact opposite or the negative form of what you want and to use generalisations or extreme words (all, never, everyone, always, no one). For example:

"Although I never really want to get over this problem and I guess I better get used to it, because that's just the way it's going to be forever...I can still accept myself."

"Even though I thought I wanted to feel better, I was wrong I don't really want to, I like my life this way, it's definitely better this way, it's really great, definitely. No need to change it. I don't know what I've been complaining about. Why would I want to change this wonderful situation anyway, how silly of me, I like it this way..."

This sarcastic approach often causes people to being to laugh. It can become quite hilarious actually and it lightens an otherwise tough moment. However, the main reason I like to use this strategy is because it can have an interesting solidifying or strengthening effect. It can actually build not only, the desire to change, but the belief that you can, should and deserve to through the unlikely statements and contrast. It helps to remove resistance and begin expecting a change even more. It can activate a shift. It can feel and sound a bit odd, when you do it, but it's worth trying if you are feeling stuck and unable to change something or just feel you need to lift an otherwise emotional session of tapping. I often use this approach when things are getting too heavy and when attempting to help someone reach forgiveness when they're stubbornly hanging onto something they know they should let go.

"Even though I know my mum had it really tough and I wouldn't have wanted to endure and experience what she did and I know that's why she was such a crap mum, I've decided I'm never ever, ever in my entire life, not even on my death bed, going to forgive her, she doesn't deserve it..."

This is a super way to move from logical understanding (acceptance) to forgiveness and I usually get a few chuckles as well.

Suggestion 25: Try tapping on the points in a variety of different methods. You can tap on two points at a time, marrying points together. For example you could tap on *the under the nose point* and *the chin point* at the same time, etc. Or you can tap on points on both sides of the body at the same time, thereby tapping two points at once for the whole tapping round (both *eyebrow points*, both *under eye points* etc.). You can also tap continually on just one point, for example *under the eye* or *under the nose* or *under the collarbone* whilst you say your phrases.

There are many more techniques and phrases I could suggest but really it comes with practise and time. In EFT and MTT it's referred to as an art, the art of delivery and you'll know when you are working with someone who is really good at instigating change in you.

My Greatest Advice is "Don't Give Up"!

The greatest advice I can give you regards to your personal growth and ability to change or heal is to never give up. Don't give up trying and never lose hope. You can change your experience through consciously choosing to change your perspective and feelings. Whilst I have included a lot of information and strategies in this book, it certainly does not contain all the methods I use in tapping or that other professionals are getting excellent results with, by any means. That would just be impossible and would never fit into one little book. This book is not intended as an exclusive tapping instruction book; the central themes are that of understanding yourself (by expanding your consciousness), acknowledging your responsibility and embracing your true power of choice so you can shine in all your greatness.

Should You Do It Alone?

Although the basic tapping procedure itself is easy to perform and can help sometimes in minutes, I'm sure you can see from the many suggestions I've made that it can take a lot of practise and skill to be effective (and efficient) in clearing a variety of issues.

People often ask me if they can do this work alone. Of course you can, if you feel confident and safe to do so. Self improvement is available to everyone. All that is needed is a willingness and determination to do it. I encourage you to use all the information and exercises I've provided throughout this book, do them and practise them regularly.

Additionally, there are millions of pages of free information on the Internet. There are free manuals, videos, audios, DVDs, e-books and reams of valuable guidance available at the touch of your keyboard including demonstrations on YouTube, discussion groups on Facebook and even Twitter followers that are interested and sharing valuable yet easily accessible techniques. There are also training courses, workshops, DVDs and books like this one available to suit your individual needs.

Note: I have not included all the methods I may use to clear something that may be blocking your progress with tapping. There are too many variables to be included here. Some of the more commonly used methods are: 'collarbone breathing' which I mentioned in the last chapter and which I lovingly call 'chicken breathing' because of what you look like when you do it, 'cross crawl', 'touch and breath' when you replace tapping with touching and deep breathing, continually tapping on one point, breaking or changing state (changing your physical or mental position including tapping whilst standing up), simply drinking water during tapping sessions and many more.

If you're comfortable progressing alone and have the dedication and time — it's all there for you. You may find it easier, more comforting and probably much quicker to work with a good Meridian Tapping Techniques or EFT practitioner or coach, CBT counsellor or even a friend who has the same interests. There are many possibilities and benefits, whether you work by yourself or with an experienced therapist. You can even find 'tapping buddies' who are interested in exchanging tapping for free.

Finding one of us (a professional tapper) is easy. The best bet is to get a referral. Ask around and see if any of your friends have worked with someone they would recommend. I feel it's important to look for someone who is used to dealing with what you need help with. Just because someone has a qualification or is on this or that register does not mean they are good at what you need or otherwise suited or right for you. Talk with them on the phone, Skype or read their website to help you decide. Also, if you currently have a therapist and you've had limited success, perhaps you should consider whether you have applied what has been asked of you or whether their style or services are what you need. Be sure to also consider the things I have included in Chapter 16, **What Stops You from Improving Your Life? Common Pitfalls, Reasons You Don't Succeed and Self-Sabotage**.

Many professionals working in Meridian Tapping Techniques can assist you on the telephone so where you live and they work is no longer a barrier to getting help. This is a wonderful improvement because it means you can find someone confident in working with the sort of issues you have, even if they are half way around the world. So there really are fewer and fewer excuses if you want to change.

To navigate to the right type of people, just be aware of the many acronyms or names of therapies that fall under the banner of Energy Psychology or Meridian Tapping Techniques. These include such therapies as EFT (Emotional Freedom Techniques), TFT (Thought Field Therapy), TAT (Tapas Acupressure Technique), NLP (Neuro-linguistic Programming), IET (Integrated Energy Techniques), Matrix Reimprinting and many more. All of these forms have one major thing in common – they all engage in applying pressure to the body's' energy system whilst focusing on your issue. Many of the therapists in MTT incorporate hypnosis and kinesiology (muscle testing) techniques and even Time Line Therapy.

Look for a professional who is using a form of tapping or energy psychology. I would recommend that you find someone that embodies what you want; someone who *walks the talk* and displays the characteristics of a healthy, balanced and content individual.

The best of both worlds would be to apply yourself to working at your own pace (using tapping and cognitive strategies as included in this book or others) and to be working with a professional. Do as much as you can or want on your own to uncover your issues or blocks and then use a coach to move you past the complex, big or difficult stuff you maybe couldn't do by yourself. Also, don't be afraid to ask your therapist or coach to refer you to another if they can't help you. Sometimes a mentor can get you only so far and then you need someone new with different skills or a fresh angle to take you to the next level. Be honest, persistent and look for those with the expertise you need.

"Remember to turn over every pebble on the beach to see what lies beneath and what opportunities will surface."

Signs Your Life Might be off Kilter

- If you keep seeing the same unwanted patterns repeating in your life
- If you are making tons of effort but aren't reaching your goals
- If you are focused on the past and not able to enjoy today
- If you complain or criticise constantly
- If you over-react to situations, statements or people
- If you have difficulty feeling emotions or feel them too intensely
- If you feel no one understands you or your position
- If you avoid conflict at all costs
- If you can't say no and over-commit yourself
- If you do a lot of things that you do not like
- If you don't recall what you like or can't remember when you last enjoyed yourself
- If you tend to generalise or exaggerate
- If you feel everyone is against you or no one likes you
- If you avoid particular emotions or use inappropriate emotions
- If you avoid situations or otherwise restrict your life
- If you anger easily or rage
- If you are apathetic about life or can't see anything positive
- If you are afraid all the time
- If your fears and worries are growing out of proportion and you have more bad days than good or experience panic attacks or palpitations
- If you feel you just can't cope or feel overwhelmed all the time
- If you have constant underlying worry or anxiety

Chapter 23
In Closing

Whilst there will be those of you who will choose to trivialise my findings and dismiss my theory that your consistent choice of words is your subconscious mind or your soul revealing to you (a) what you are focusing on, (b) what you believe, and (c) those things in your life that require your attention, resolution or change. Happily, I know some of you will have already greatly benefitted from my ideas and that thought alone makes me happy.

There's also another option, though. Rather than believing or disbelieving my concept, you could accept that my premise may be true or possible and investigate your own current language, thoughts, behaviour and beliefs. I'm sure if you do this, you will find and acknowledge that your past has unquestionably flavoured them. Once you gain this understanding, you can then choose what to do about it and better manage your future choices.

"We are thoughts. It is all about your mind. Everything you think, everything you are being comes from these thoughts and feelings. Everything comes from within and nothing real comes from outside yourself."

Being aware, minding your conscious mind and your subconscious and replacing any ineffective rules will allow you to change whatever you want. It then becomes *your choice* rather than an automatic preprogrammed response how you perceive and live your life. You can *choose* to see things in a new way. Even if you can't erase your past or quickly fix your situation, you can *choose* to view it differently and reduce any negative feelings around it. That is within your power; it's your prerogative and the way forward.

You can change your mindset and upgrade your *iceberg programmes* with dedication and practise. *It's your choice* to recognise what keeps appearing in your life and learn from it rather than ignoring it. Your emotional strength will build as you seek to understand and clear yourself. Increasing your confidence and providing greater stability, helping you regain power over your actions and experience.

We have immense abilities within us and talent beyond the mass understanding of today's physics, medicine, psychologies and neurosciences. There have been those who have suspended their human need for food, levitated through focused concentration and cured *terminal* illnesses using the power of the mind, through positive thought and prayer. Dumb founded, the medical and scientific communities without another answer often blame these happenings on equipment or human errors (they must have made a misdiagnosis), whilst the religious communities often call these miracles.

Are they miracles or are they examples of the power we all have at our disposal? The real miracle may be the untapped power of the mind and the multi-dimensional entity that we really are. Miracles in their own right, I believe, also happen however I know our mind is participating in miraculous activity constantly and can and does make the unexplainable happen all around us. How our mind actually works, its' true capacity and functionality still baffles and eludes our experts. It's simply beyond today's human scientific grasp.

If we clear the destructive and distracting thoughts from our minds, I know we can do much more than we ever thought possible. I heard recently that Saint Augustine described the unexplainable accurately when he said **"Miracles are not contrary to nature but only contrary to what we know about nature."**

Don't limit yourself by others' standards, expectations or even the so called laws of nature; exercise your mind by practising more productive thoughts and choosing a heightened perspective and intention for yourself. *It's your choice* then to see things in an inspiring and balanced way. It's my hope that you will gain an appreciation and understanding of your influence on your reality so you can be presented with your own personal miracles as you actively seek happiness and begin to find it!

In brilliant expectation and gratitude, Annie Cap

Reminder Tips

♦ Choose to observe your words, thoughts (your *iceberg words, verbs and phrases*) and feelings and change them to be more supportive of yourself and in line with how you want to feel.

♦ Choose to uncover the subconscious programmes (*the Iceberg programmes*) and patterns that are working within you.

♦ Choose to stop putting yourself down and cease being your own worst enemy.

♦ Choose to treat yourself with care and kindness knowing and acknowledging that you are doing the best you can right now.

♦ Choose to understand and change any negative beliefs and issues you are holding onto.

- Choose to create new effective patterns for your life.
- Choose to use affirmations.
- Choose to tap (on your own or with a professional).
- Choose to see the best in yourself and others.
- Choose to be gentle on yourself whilst still taking personal responsibility for your actions.
- Choose to be honest with yourself.
- Choose to forgive yourself.
- Choose not to hold grudges and forgive others.
- Choose to not give up on yourself.
- Choose to learn to say "No" when it's appropriate for you.
- Choose to listen to your gut feelings and your intuition.
- Choose to do things that make you happy.
- Choose to keep moving forward. Don't stagnate and keep looking for answers.
- Choose to take action.
- Choose to expect good things to happen all around you.
- Choose to participate actively and consciously in your moment to moment choices.
- Choose to be responsible for your life **and choose to be grateful!**

Epilogue

Whilst writing this book, I realised that I'd used many phrases about driving and metaphors about cars. Initially as I became aware of my own *iceberg driving words* (and *iceberg verbs*) I suspected they originated from my relatively recent car accident when my car had been hit whilst I was driving down my own lane. I made a note to remind myself to *tap on* that accident but when I did, I was flooded with the realisation that I'd been involved in many accidents, either as the driver or as a passenger.

I recalled that in my twenties I'd been rear ended bad enough to write off (total) my car by someone who'd been talking on their mobile. Then I saw myself as a little girl of maybe four, falling out of the car and my mum's arm reaching out and grabbing my leg, saving me whilst she steered the car around a sharp bend avoiding oncoming traffic (I'd inadvertently opened the car door myself by leaning on the 1960's-style door handle). This memory probably explains why I like to always lock my car door now as an adult.

As I continued to tap I recalled further *related driving* memories. I'd forgotten I'd been concussed when my eldest brother's car had been run off the road as we came down the ski mountain. My mum's car scarily slipped off the icy road into a ditch when I was thirteen. Then in my mind, I saw the hole created in my driver's door only an inch away from my leg as I was hit by a man not paying attention to the signal light.

Still tapping, I remembered my eldest brother had almost died from a head on collision when I was three or four. He'd been in a coma for weeks after the fierce impact which amongst other things had pushed the entire engine of the car on top of his legs. Then I thought about how frightened I was by the stories of my dad being hit by a train before I was born. He only survived because he'd been thrown clear because he hadn't worn his seat belt. When I was first learning to drive, another brother 'rolled' his car totaling it. I then recollected his more serious crash on ice which made him decide to give up lorry driving. Thinking there couldn't be any more, another memory surfaced as I tapped. I saw my second eldest brother's grotesquely cut leg in my mind, after a minor crash riding his huge motorcycle in front of our house. I must have been less than five (maybe I'd fallen out of the car only a week before or after it happened). I remembered he'd been on leave from his tour in Vietnam and I'd been so happy to see him. Then I remembered how this same brother had severely crushed both his legs (oddly just as my eldest brother) competing in an amateur car race causing him to almost lose the use of them only eight or ten years ago. Just when I thought I'd exhausted all the scary or painful *car memories* but still tapping to make sure, I finally remembered my nephew was now paralysed from a car accident too!

It's no wonder I was using *driving words* and am a bit of a nervous passenger when people drive fast. I'd not only had my own car accidents when I was behind the steering wheel, I'd been a passenger, either literally, mentally or emotionally, to all the many accidents of my family. Although, my worry (and focus) had been presented in my language all this time, it'd been essentially ignored by me. I'd missed every sign of *my own icebergs and it's my theory!* I'd mistaken my *driving words* as a positive pattern, a *positive iceberg*. I'd thought they were a remnant from my telecom days when being 'a driver' or 'being driven' meant you could manage, lead and inspire others or were highly productive and self-motivated. It was *a good thing* – I'd thought! But my subconscious wasn't thinking about that form of *drive*. It had been concentrating and preoccupied with all these accidents and now I was ready to resolve them.

"You are thoughts and words; you become them."

Your thoughts and words represent a continuing narration of your saga. They are both a record of the past and a future description of your upcoming chapters according to my findings. Therefore if your life is not as you prefer, take note of how you are always subconsciously being directed to your beliefs or what needs to be reviewed (or even your positive reinforcing beliefs and memories). Use the hints you are being offered. Listen to not just what you say but what you speak about, how you feel and what you spend your time at and all your life choices.

Remember it's about your words, thoughts, beliefs, actions and **feelings**. Just as I have noticed my own repetition of car related words ('driven', 'hit', 'driver's seat', 'shift gears') you can find out what holds your attention. Look into what patterns are being offered to you for review. If they're useful, hurrah, keep them. If not, find a way to fix, erase or replace them. As you reach this higher vantage of awareness, *by choice,* this process can be easier than you previously thought and experienced.

Choose to be observant. A bigger brighter world awaits those who *choose to choose* what they focus on. Let me remind you that your language should consistently describe and support your greatest dreams rather than reflect your greatest fears, lack or unhappy past to ensure a shining brilliant future.

"Embrace your strength in your choice...it's always your choice...be confident with your choice and accepting of opportunity."

I thank you for reading my book and I encourage you to confidently strive for happiness, health and true abundance – a feeling of fulfillment and gratitude. Expect to see positive changes within you and within your world very soon.

References and Recommended Reading

Bruce Lipton, Ph.D., *The Biology of Belief, www.brucelipton.com*

Louise L. Hay, *You Can Heal Your Life*, Hay House, Inc., Published in the UK by Eden Grove Editions

William Arntz, Betsy Chasse and Mark Vincente, *What the Bleep Do We Know*, Published by Health Communications, Inc.

Joe Vitale, *The Missing Secret*, Audio CD by Nightingale Conant

Walter Isaacson, *Einstein: His life and Universe*, Published Simon and Schuster, UK Ltd.

Dr Wayne D. Dyer, *Your Erroneous Zones*, Published by HarperTorch

Rhonda Byrne, *The Secret*, Published Atria Books, Beyond Words Publishing, Inc.

Caroline Myss, PhD, *Why People Don't Heal and How They Can*, Published by Random House, Inc.

Dr Candace Pace, *Molecules of Emotions*, Published by Pocket Books, Simon and Schuster, UK Ltd.

Dr Masaru Emoto, *The Hidden Messages in* Water, Published Atria Books, Beyond Words Publishing, Inc.

Daniel Levinson, *Seasons of a Man's Life*, Published by Ballatine Books, Inc.

Dr Thomas A Harris, *I'm Ok-You're Ok*, Published by Avon Books, Harper and Row Publishers

M. Scott Peck, *The Road Less Traveled*, Published in the US by Simon and Schuster

Richard Bandler, *Using Your Brain: For a Change*, Published by Real People Press

David R. Hawkins, M.D., Ph.D., *Power Vs. Force: The Hidden Determinants of Human Behaviour*, Published by Hay House UK, Ltd.

Aaron T. Beck, *Cognitive Therapy and the Emotional Disorders,* Published by Penguin Books Ltd.

Lynn McTaggart, *The Field*, Published by HarperCollins Publishing

Stephen Wolinsky with Margaret O. Ryan, *Trances People Live: Healing Approaches in Quantum Psychology*, Published by The Bramble Company

Dr David Servan-Schreiber, *Healing Without Freud or Prozac*, Published by Rodale International Ltd.

Melody Beattie, *Co-Dependent No More*, Published by Hazelden Foundation

John Bradshaw, *Healing the Shame That Binds You*, Published by Health Communications, Inc.

Shakti Gawain, *The Four Levels of Healing*, US Publications Natarja Publishing, Published in the UK by Eden Grove Editions

Dr Ross Tratter N.D., D.O. with Dr Adrian Jones N.D., *Better Health Through Natural Healing*, Published by McGraw-Hill, Hinkler Books Pty Ltd.

Dawson Church, The Genie in Your Genes, Published by Cygnus Books, Energy Psychology Press an imprint of Elite Books

Gregg Braden, The Divine Matrix, Published by Hay House UK, Ltd.

Karl Dawson, *Matrix Reimprinting using EFT: Rewrite Your Past, Transform Your Future*, Distributed by Hay House UK, Ltd.

Bruce Lipton, Ph.D., M.D., Eric Pearl, D.C., Marilyn Schlitz, Ph.D., Arielle Essex, D.O., James L. Oschmann, Ph.D., Lynn McTaggart, Peter Fraser, Rollin McCraty, Ph.D., *The Living Matrix: New Insight into our Bodies, Minds and Health (DVD: A Film of the New Science of Healing)*

Alan Chapman kindly provided Maslow's Hierarchy of Needs diagram after gaining permission on my behalf from the Maslow estate. Alan's website is www.businessballs. com.

Useful Internet References including Informative EFT Websites

www.anniecap.com Website of Annie Cap, author and creator of *The Iceberg Process*

www.heartmath.com Institute of HeartMath

www.eftuniverse.com Website hosted by Dawson Church replacing Gary Craig's www.emofree.com website now off-line due to his retirement June 2010. This site contains the archives of case studies from Gary Craig's website and continues to have forums for discussion.

www.eftmastersworldwide.com and www.eftmasters.co.uk Websites sharing helpful information from the original EFT masters (note the master level certification was eliminated some years ago therefore there are only a few people who can rightfully use this title however many others who are operating at this high level as it is based on experience.).

www.efttrainingcourses.net Website of EFT Master Karl Dawson, creator of Matrix Reimprinting

www.theeftcentre.com Website of EFT Masters Sue Beer and Emma Roberts creators of IET (Integrated Energy Techniques) where the author trained initially

www.tatlife.com Website of Tapas Fleming, creator of Tapas Acupressure Technique (TAT)

www.attractingabundance.com Website of EFT Master Carol Look

www.emotional-health.co.uk Website of EFT Master Gwyneth Moss

www.masteringeft.com Website of EFT Master Dr Patricia Carrington, Ph.D.

www.judybyrne.co.uk Website of EFT Master Judy Byrne

www.eftdownunder.com Website of Dr David Lake and Steve Wells creators of PET (Provocative Energy Techniques) and SET (Simple Energy Techniques)

www.theefthub.com Website offering audio downloads

www.tryitoneverything.com, **www.thetappingsolution.com** and **www. eftzone.com**

www.noetic.org Institute *of* Noetic *Sciences*

www.hamburgeruniverse.com Website of Miceal Ledwith

www.theinstituteofmomentum.com Website of Peter Lee

Note Regarding My List of Referenced Websites

Please note as there are many reputable and highly experienced practitioners of EFT I am unable to list them all. This by no means is a reflection on their value or benefits; it's purely an issue of space and time. I have provided some of the websites that I personal have found helpful over the years. Additionally most of the authors in my recommended reading list will have websites you may wish to review.

Index

A

Abundance 2, 4, 8, 10, 36, 73, 137, 172, 218, 221

Acceptance.... 30, 60, 68, 100, 111, 133, 139, 140, 141, 147, 150, 151, 157, 198, 207, 208

Acupressure 22, 163, 171, 210, 221

Abused 24-27, 29, 30, 36, 53, 58, 126, 133, 167, 168, 186, 198, 207, 208

Adoption 133

Adrenalin 88, 127, 133

Affirmation 21, 22, 52-60, 69, 72, 88, 97, 124, 155, 161, 165, 187, 215

Aggression...33, 113

Agoraphobic 27, 201

Alcoholic 35, 85, 167

Anger 22, 42, 58, 66-68, 87, 88, 125, 169, 182, 183, 193, 211

Anti-depressants.................................143

Anti-inflammartory 64

Anxiety.........................4, 20, 24, 25, 27, 31, 43, 56, 89, 117, 139, 143, 148, 156, 169, 194, 200, 202, 211, 229

Apathy 66, 137

Apex Effect, The 191, 192

Appreciation...........................17, 47, 65, 214

Aspects...........3, 5, 105, 132, 140, 166, 168, 169, 172, 186, 187, 189, 199, 200, 202

Aspects of a phobia (fear of flying)...........200

Assertiveness 68

Attracting 8-10, 15, 16, 71, 221

Attraction, the Law of... 1, 2, 7-12, 15, 52, 56, 95, 96, 104, 160, 165

Attitudes..... 22, 39, 51, 74, 77, 90, 93, 95-98, 112, 125, 129, 137, 160, 165, 172

Auto-immune 4, 85

Awareness..1, 2, 3, 4, 16, 22, 43, 53, 54, 59, 65, 72, 74, 77-79, 84, 92, 94, 101, 103, 104, 106, 107, 113, 115-117, 126, 139, 150, 155, 161, 169, 193, 208

B

B6 143

B12 143

Bandler, Richard...........................45, 46, 219

Basic needs 132

Basic Recipe, The 177

Basic Tapping Worksheet 182

Belief..1, 3, 8, 12, 15, 16, 19, 20, 21, 23, 27, 30, 34, 37

Belief system ... 1-3, 8, 12, 16, 19, 20, 21, 23, 27, 30, 34, 37

Blocking 15, 16, 97, 156, 161, 209

Body Tapping Points, see Main Body Tapping Points

Breath, Breathing 115, 153, 167, 168, 193, 194, 205, 209

Buddha 55

C

Cataract...85

CBT, see Cognitive Behavioral Therapy

Changing states..209

Chronic illness 3, 20, 27, 87, 171, 229

Chronic Fatigue Syndrome, see ME

Cod Liver Oil, See Omega 3

Cognitive Behavioral Therapy (CBT)............. ....1, 21, 22, 25, 54, 56, 209

Cognitive shift.................................140, 256

Collarbone breathing (aka chicken breathing) 194, 209

Conscious, consciously 1-5, 8, 15, 20, 30, 36, 54, 61, 65, 67, 72, 77-79, 88-91, 95, 99, 100, 103, 106, 123, 129, 130, 132, 139, 145, 153-157, 161, 165, 209, 213, 215

Consciousness 9, 62, 69, 77, 78, 115, 130, 139, 157, 209

Constipation.......................................29, 31

Counter intention 15, 16, 156

Counter-statement............ 21, 22, 54-59, 161

Conflict....................2, 15, 33, 34, 43, 62, 68, 74, 84, 96, 111, 112, 124, 125, 139, 141, 149, 150, 161, 211

Consistency........4, 16, 37, 53, 105, 156, 161

Constricted breathing 193

Core beliefs ... 16, 23, 81, 109, 111, 141, 163, 168

Core issues..................... 16, 20, 23, 111, 197

Cortisol 67, 88

Craig, Gary 74, 116, 173, 177, 197, 221

Crystals, water...69

Cutters 31, 85

D

Dopamine 143

Dawson, Karl 157, 158, 219

Depression....3, 16, 27, 49, 76 143, 144, 169, 171, 185, 194

Dissociation 145

Dyer, Wayne Dr 126, 219

E

Ears 88, 131

EFT, see Emotional Freedom Techniques

Einstein, Albert....................................77, 219

Electro-magnetic...160

Emotional Freedom Techniques 1, 20, 21, 31, 45, 68, 74, 86, 87, 114, 116, 144, 146, 156, 161, 168, 171-173, 177, 185, 186, 188-190, 193, 194, 197-199, 203, 205, 208, 209, 210

Emoto, Masaru Dr 69, 71, 219

Empower ...23, 66, 80, 90, 95, 102, 112, 140, 147, 161

Energy 76, 86-89, 111, 116, 124, 128, 133, 140, 142, 144, 145, 157, 159-161, 171, 172, 194, 195, 205, 210, 219, 221

Energy coccon..154

Energy medicine...171

Energy Psychology, EP 1, 45, 87, 89, 156-159, 161, 171, 205, 210, 219

Energy toxins............................142, 144, 145

Environment.......46, 54, 61, 62, 76, 81, 114, 116, 117, 124, 129, 138, 142, 143, 200

EP, See Energy Psychology

Epigenetics 92

Erickson, Milton 45

Expectation.............. 8, 19, 27, 40-42, 47, 93, 95-98, 107, 110, 111, 114, 115, 124, 128, 129, 159, 161, 162, 165, 214

Eye 4, 28, 47, 81, 84, 117, 143, 146, 168, 175, 176, 178, 179, 194, 203, 205, 208

Eye movement.................................194, 203

F

Faint...31, 85, 90

Father....16, 21, 25, 32, 36, 54, 74, 78, 77, 108

Fear of 141

Fear of bees 186

Fear of being sick (vomiting) 201

Fear of dogs 189

Fear of change 40, 125, 145

Fear of failure 21, 40, 141, 166

Fear of flying 40, 187, 200, 201

Fear of loss...125

Fear of success 40, 141

Fear of water 186

Finger Tapping Points................................179

Food intolerances................................32, 144

Ford, Henry...93, 95

Forgiveness.......66, 68, 139, 140, 147, 148, 150, 151, 167, 198, 206, 208

Frequency.....................8, 15, 16, 22, 65, 93

Fright, Frightening...21, 23, 26, 30, 64, 85, 87

Frustration 66, 182, 183

Full Gamut, The 179, 180, 194

G

Gamut Point, The .... see Full Gamut, the

Gamut, The Full.......................179, 180, 194

Genetics 91

Genes.................................91, 92, 172, 219

Goal....................1, 8, 16, 21, 40, 52, 102, 106, 133, 142, 155, 161, 165, 166, 170, 172, 185, 186, 195, 201, 211

Gratitude 17, 65, 151, 167, 214, 218

Grief....... 21, 31, 66, 69, 77, 87, 88, 133, 171

Grinder, John 45

Gut.........................29, 32, 54, 128, 144, 215

Gut feeling 32, 128, 144, 215

H

Happiness...............................1, 10, 14, 17, 49, 51, 62, 74, 87, 94, 96, 102, 103, 105, 127, 132, 141, 151, 214, 218

Harris, Thomas Dr 50, 74, 219

Hawkins, David Dr 66, 219

Hay, Louise..88, 219

Heart..........27-29, 65, 71, 85, 87, 88, 138, 174, 178

Heathmath 65, 88, 160, 221

Hopeliness.............. 21-24, 79, 124, 137, 162

Hormones..88, 144

Hypnosis.............1, 45, 46, 90, 113, 157, 210

Hypnotherapy 171

I

IBS see Irritable Bowel Syndrome..............29

Iceberg adjectives.............................162, 187

Iceberg beliefs 160, 162

Iceberg memories............................162, 164

Iceberg phrases...162

Iceberg, The Iceberg Process (TIPs) 4, 35, 87, 159, 160, 165, 187, 221

Iceberg programmes 3, 35, 159, 213, 214

Iceberg put-downs 162

Iceberg words.......3, 160, 165, 169, 182, 200, 214

Iceberg verbs............................162, 187, 217

IET, Integrated Energy Therapy................210

Illness 4, 16, 29, 23, 24, 27, 34, 45, 54, 63, 77, 83, 84, 86-91, 125, 143, 144, 171, 172, 214

Imbalance...........................87, 143, 144, 172

Incest 29, 83

Inherit... 74, 111-113

Intensity .. 46, 65, 67, 68, 145, 149, 157, 172, 174, 175, 177, 180, 182, 183, 187, 189, 193, 204

Intention 8, 15, 16, 19, 62, 71, 89, 90, 96, 98, 104, 1333, 146, 156, 159, 161, 175, 178, 186, 197, 214

Intention, rejecting 15, 16, 156, 161

Internal conflict 1, 15, 43, 62

Internal critic 49, 52, 54, 155, 169

Irrational.............................56, 102, 127

Irritable Bowel Syndrome (IBS) 29

J

Joy.... 2, 12, 64, 66, 74, 87, 88, 95, 103, 105, 125, 127, 130-134, 137, 164, 211

K

Karate Chop Point, the 174, 178-180, 182, 194, 195, 204

Kidney..88

Kinesiology 1, 45, 66, 145, 171, 210

Kinaesthetic..46, 47

Knives...85

L

Law of Attraction, the... 1, 2, 7-12, 12, 15, 52, 56, 95, 96, 104, 160, 165

Ledwith, Miceal...221

Limiting beliefs..............16, 41, 124, 141, 153

Lipton, Bruce 91, 172, 219, 220, 221

Liver 65, 88, 208, 221

LOA, See Law of Attraction, The

Lovable.. 15, 23, 27, 49, 51, 55, 57, 106, 221

Lungs 68, 88

Lupus...85, 86

M

Main Body Tapping Points, The......175, 176, 178, 182

Magnesium...143

Maslow, Abraham 73, 126, 220

Maslow's Heirarchy of Needs 73

Matrix Reimprinting 87, 157, 210, 219, 221

ME, ME/CFS...................................36, 27

Meridian..... 1, 20, 45, 87, 144-146, 168, 171, 173, 205, 209, 210

Meridian Tapping Techniques (MTT) 1, 20, 45, 144-146, 168, 171, 173, 205, 209, 210

Metaphor 85, 116, 155, 217

Mother 4, 11, 16, 36, 41, 54, 57, 74-77, 85, 86, 98, 102, 109, 110, 111-113, 118, 119, 128, 131, 167, 171, 186, 188, 198

Molecules 15, 63, 64, 219

Morphic Field...159

Multi-aspect Tapping Information Worksheet 183

MTT see Meridian Tapping Techniques

Myalgic Encephalopathy, see ME

Myss, Caroline............................83, 84, 219

N

Names 7, 163, 164, 210

Negative self-talk..55

Neural network 53, 154-156, 161, 202

Neuro-linguistic Programming, NLP 45, 90, 210

Neuro-peptides..............................63, 67, 68

Neuro-proteins...160

Neutralise....41, 107, 171, 172, 191, 202, 204

NLP, see Neuro-linguistic Programming

Nocebo 91, 92

O

Optimism 66, 137, 165

Objective 3, 15, 98, 124, 189, 192, 193

P

Pace, Candace Dr 83, 172, 219

Pain 20, 24, 31, 33, 35, 36, 41, 54, 55, 64, 67, 68, 85, 86, 88, 90, 111, 114, 127, 130, 135, 150, 156, 162, 168, 171, 172, 174, 177, 178, 180, 182, 183, 189, 190, 194, 203, 206, 207, 217

Panic....... 25, 27, 31, 40, 78, 87, 88, 90, 135, 144, 145, 153, 156, 211

Panic attack.....25, 31, 78, 89, 144, 145, 153, 211

Parents 21, 23, 26, 42, 50, 74-76, 87, 106, 109, 112, 113, 117, 131, 150, 166, 167, 187

Patterns 2, 14, 19, 25, 27, 28, 35, 40, 42, 43, 45, 59, 62, 65, 80, 81, 87, 90, 101, 103, 109, 114, 115, 133, 138-141, 147, 148, 155, 158, 159-161, 163, 164, 166, 185, 198, 201, 202, 211, 214, 215

Parts, the Parts Technique ...90, 91, 149, 157

Peck, Scott 50

Perls, Fritz 45

Personality Disorder 144

Persistence....................53, 58, 112, 145, 186

Perspective...... 2, 5, 73, 113, 151, 156, 191, 195, 204, 209, 214, 229

Phobia............4, 20, 25, 27, 114, 117, 144, 156, 169, 171, 185, 187, 200, 201, 203, 229

Physics 62, 79, 214

Placebo..91, 92

PMS..144

PMT..144

PMDD...144

Placebo..91, 92

Pleasing 141, 142

Polarity..194

Power 1, 2, 4, 5, 7, 14, 15, 21, 23, 35, 45, 49, 59, 62, 63, 66, 78, 80, 90, 92, 95, 96, 98, 99, 101, 102, 112, 114, 129, 132, 137-140, 147, 156, 161, 164, 209, 213, 219

PR, see Psychological Reversal

Protection 73, 157

Psychological Reversal (PR) 194

Psychology............1, 45, 87, 89, 90, 156-159, 161, 171, 205, 210, 219

Q

Quantum Physics 62, 79, 93, 219

R

Radio 36, 65, 74, 117, 134

Rapid Reiki Regression 157

Reiki...113, 124, 157

Relationships.... 4, 10, 25, 26, 31, 42, 52, 73, 85, 87, 95, 110, 112, 132, 137, 142, 162

Releasement 149, 151

Reminder Phrase.....173, 275, 177, 178, 180, 181-183, 188, 189, 192, 195, 201, 205

Repetition 28, 218

Resistance..........22, 128, 139, 140, 148, 208

Responsibility 5, 7, 23, 62, 63, 73, 81, 87, 93-95, 97-101, 103, 138, 140, 141, 147, 148, 150, 151, 153, 205, 215

Restrictions...............124, 126, 138-140, 174, 178, 193

S

Sadness.............67, 69, 168, 182, 183, 190, 192, 198

Satir, Virginia 45

Secret, The 7-9, 14, 165, 219

Self-confidence...4, 50

Self-esteem............21, 32, 50, 76, 103, 112, 164, 171

Self-harm...31, 85

Self-sabotage 84, 140, 210

Sequence, The 178, 180, 188

Serotonin 64, 67, 143

Set-up, The...............178, 188, 189, 191, 201

Sexual...26, 29

Shame................16, 26, 27, 29, 30, 41, 51, 64-67, 111, 147, 149, 150, 156, 162, 198, 219

Sheldrake, Rupert.....................................159

Shock.............22, 24, 27, 29, 33, 46, 87, 88, 101, 114, 139, 149, 167-169, 191, 199

Signal...65, 217

Signature 160

Smoking....................................189, 205, 206

Sore Spot, The 182, 194, 195

Sorrow 65, 87, 88

Speed of Light 160

Spleen 88

St John's Wort 143

Stomach ... 29, 32, 40, 54, 88, 144, 168, 200

Stress......4, 7, 8, 20, 27, 45, 50, 51, 67, 83-85, 88, 110, 111, 114, 117, 143, 167, 169, 171

Stress hormones 88

Subconscious or Subconscious mind......3, 4, 5, 8, 15, 29, 30, 42, 45, 46, 54, 56, 61, 78, 85, 90-92, 96, 110, 111, 132, 137, 149, 151, 153, 154, 156, 157, 158, 166, 169, 188, 213, 218

Submodalities......................................45, 46

SUDs 182, 183, 189-193, 201, 204

Subjective Level of Discomfort, See SUDs

Supplements.....................................87, 143

Symbolism..86, 116

T

Tachycardia 27, 28, 85

Tapping.............. 1, 20-26, 30, 33, 40, 45, 52, 57, 60, 68, 85, 87, 89, 97, 107, 113, 114, 124, 130, 137, 140, 142-146, 151, 156-158, 161, 163, 161-169, 170, 171, 210

Tapping Points, see Karate Chop Pointm, Main Body Tapping Points, Gamut Point or Finger Tapping Points

TAT, Tapas Acupressure Technique....163, 210, 221

TFT, see Thought Field Therapy

Teresa, Mother...102

Throat 168, 206

Thought Field Therapy, TFT.......1, 4, 5, 87, 144, 210

Timeline Therapy 157

TIPs, see Iceberg Process, The ....

Touch and Breath 209

Toxins, energy 142, 144, 145

Trance 114, 129, 157

Transactional Analysis......................1, 50, 74

U

Universal..4, 7

Unworthy 27, 42, 50, 110, 114

V

Values15, 34, 77, 111, 117, 119, 121, 122, 154

Vibration.........8, 14-17, 19, 61, 62, 65, 69, 93, 96, 151, 159

Victim....27, 29, 30, 84, 94, 98, 101, 103, 147

Visualisation 46, 65, 157

Vitamins..143

W

Water........3, 43, 69, 71, 112, 142, 164, 186, 209, 219

Weight 26, 35, 55, 151, 171

Well-being...................52, 91, 137, 144, 160

What the Bleep....................................79, 219

Williamson, Marianne 151

Willingness 66, 87, 138, 209

Worksheets......................................182, 183

Worry.......................................10, 11, 14, 31, 36, 56, 60, 64, 81, 87, 88, 125, 131, 135, 148, 150, 166, 168, 187, 192, 193, 200, 211, 218

X

X-ray 36

Y

Z

Zinc...143

About the Author

Annie Cap is the seventh child of seven brothers and sister. Coming from a large family has a lot to do with her understanding of people and their motivations. She spent her childhood growing up in Oregon and Washington in the northwest of the United States. As an adult she moved to Seattle and lived there until moving overseas in the 1990's. She now has dual citizenship and resides full-time in the South of England with her husband Simon and their rescue cat Tino.

Formerly a successful telecommunications professional for almost 20 years, her career took her all over the USA and eventually to London and Europe. Annie has held national and regional management roles for global companies whilst in the USA and technical support positions in leading edge technologies. Whilst working in England for an international smartcard company, headquartered in Germany, she was responsible for sales to key accounts. Annie has a strong business, technical and sales background as well as a passion for helping others and creating solutions. She left her telecommunications career ten years ago to pursue a full time career in therapy and coaching wanting to motivate individuals.

Annie now spends her professional time assisting people recover from illness and coaching business professionals, entrepreneurs and performers. After thousands of hours, she found that regardless of the issues or symptoms being presented her unique strategies were working for almost everyone. These help to remove limiting personal beliefs, reconcile the past and encourage active involvement in achieving dreams and improving health. By increasing people's awareness, Annie has helped many recover from chronic illnesses; including ME, depression and disabling phobias and anxiety. She maintains that any one's life can be improved if there's a willingness to lift perspective.

Annie loves international travel, adores nature and is artistic, sporty and sociable. Some of her most memorable moments include: scuba diving with giant manta rays in Australia, her wedding day, getting close to white-tip sharks whilst diving with her husband in Egypt and swimming with dolphins in Florida. She loves to snow ski the powder, practise yoga, meditate, garden, paint and take photographs as well as entertain and engage with her close friends. She felt honoured to have had a one-woman exhibition of her paintings and currently exhibits in a few galleries and restaurants near her home in England.

www.anniecap.com

Lightning Source UK Ltd.
Milton Keynes UK
16 November 2010

162948UK00001B/56/P